TO BE
DISPOSED
BY
AUTHORITY

The Rail Problem

The
Rail Problem

R. W. S. PRYKE & J. S. DODGSON

Martin Robertson

First published in 1975 by Martin Robertson and Company Ltd., 17 Quick Street, London N1 8HL.

ISBN 0 85520 093 6

Typeset by Trade Linotype Ltd., Birmingham.
Reproduced, printed by photolithography and bound at The Pitman Press, Bath.

Contents

List of Tables

Preface

With BR's deficit approaching £500 million per annum a book on the rail problem needs no justification. What however is necessary is to explain how we obtained the information on which it is based. A considerable amount of factual material was gleaned from published sources and in particular from official publications, the annual reports of the Railways Board and other nationalised industries, and from railway journals and the trade press. But our main source of information was 70 interviews and meetings, 170 telephone conversations and the 56 letters and documents that we received.

In all we made contact with 203 people many of whom provided us with facts and figures on a number of occasions. Of these individuals 43 were in British Rail (with whose employees we had 33 interviews and meetings), 16 were in the electricity industry, 8 worked for the National Freight Corporation, 7 for BSC, 5 for the Coal Board, 5 for Passenger Transport Executives, 4 for London Transport, 2 for the Post Office, and 1 each for British Airways and the National Bus Company. We also obtained information from 4 individuals in the private sector of road transport and the Road Haulage Association.

Besides those concerns within the public sector that have already been mentioned we were also helped by a large number of rail users and customer industries. We were provided with facts and figures about cement and other building materials by 15 persons employed by Associated Portland Cement, the Cement Makers Federation, Foster Yeomans, English China Clays, the Sand and Gravel Association etc. We were assisted by 11 who work in Shell-BP, Esso and other oil companies. Information was received from 7 concerns that deal with Freightliners including the London Brick Company, BR Shipping, the Port of London Authority, the British Transport Docks Board at Southampton and the Felixstowe Dock and Railway Company. Six individuals in ICI and other chemical companies gave us help. Information on other BR traffics was obtained from 14 persons in Fords, the Society of Motor Manufacturers and Traders, the Newspaper Publishers Association, the Mirror Group, Littlewoods, the British Independent Steel Producers Association, the Milk Marketing Board, etc.

Nine individuals and bodies that provide British Rail with equipment were contacted, e.g. Plasser, Matissa, Litton Industries, Pyes, the Joint Committee on Privately-owned Railway Wagons. Information was obtained from 5 trade union contacts in the NUR, the TSSA, the Union of Post Office Workers and the International Federation of Transport Workers. We were helped by 19 people in Government Departments and official bodies including the DoE, DTI, the Railway Inspectorate, the Transport and Road Research Laboratory, the Medical Research Council's Air Pollution Unit, the CSO, NEDO, the GLC and the Civil Aviation Authority. We were helped by six individuals from the German Federal Railway, the Netherlands Railways, the Swiss Federal Railways and SNCF. Last but not least we were assisted by 16 rail and other experts including Mr Paul Baecker, Mr Gerrard Fiennes, Mr C. D. Foster, Mr Richard Hope, Dr Stewart Joy, Mr B. Mellitt, Mr Keith Richardson, Dr Clifford Sharp and Mr Richard Wragg. Much valuable information was also obtained from answers to questions put down in Parliament by Mr Ian Mikardo.

To all these individuals and organisations we are extremely grateful. In particular we would like to express our gratitude to the British Railways Board for its very generous help, and within the Board to thank Mr T. R. Barron and Mr J. G. Urquhart. We should also like to thank Mr A. W. Tait and Mr Ken Westoby who formerly worked for BR. It should however be stressed that neither the British Railways Board nor the other individuals and organisations that are mentioned in this Preface are in any way responsible for the opinions that we have expressed or for any factual errors that we have made. They are our responsibility and ours alone.

This study would scarcely have been possible without the grant which we received from the Nuffield Foundation, and we are pleased to acknowledge the financial assistance that we obtained. We are also grateful for the efficient way in which Mrs Dorothy Lewis and Mrs R. McElvogue handled the typing and retyping of the manuscript.

CHAPTER 1

The Failure of
the 1968 Transport Act

Britain's railways became a pressing national problem during the second half of the fifties. In 1955 they were still just in balance on operating account, and a large programme of investment was launched in the hope that their finances could be retrieved through modernisation and renewal. By 1960 British Rail had a working loss of £68 million, and the Government had reluctantly recognised that a new strategy and management were necessary.[1] Sir Brian Robertson, who as Chairman of the British Transport Commission had presided over the railways' financial debacle, was replaced by Dr Beeching. Then, under the 1962 Transport Act, the Commission, which had hitherto controlled a wide range of transport activity, was broken up, and the railways, together with the railway hotels and shipping services, were placed under a separate British Railways Board.

In the spring of 1963 the Reshaping Report appeared, and the Board embarked on a programme designed not only to close unprofitable branch lines, but also to reform railway working and secure new business. As a result there was a dramatic improvement in the utilisation of rolling-stock and of labour. There was a change to more efficient methods of freight working and new traffic was secured. Despite this very considerable record of achievement, Dr Beeching and the new Board failed to make the railways break even. The operating loss, which reached £104 million in 1962, fell, partly due to economic recovery, to £67 million in 1964, but thereafter started to rise again.

1

THE 1968 ACT

Dr Beeching regarded the Reshaping Report as only a first
instalment, and early in 1965 the Board published a second
programme of rationalisation. This proposed that traffic should
be concentrated on select routes, and implied that, with the
exception of some suburban lines and isolated stretches of heavily
used freight track, the rest of the system should be either closed
or reduced to single track. Such medicine was far too strong and
unpalatable for the Labour Government, which was committed on
ideological grounds to a large railway system, and the Government and the Board agreed early in 1967 that a basic network of
some 11,000 route miles should be retained out of the existing
13,200 miles. However, Barbara Castle, the Minister of Transport,
wanted to eliminate open-ended subsidies and impose some
financial discipline on the Railways Board. The solution adopted
was to identify those passenger services that were losing money
and to cover their estimated deficits through a subsidy. It was
hoped and expected that the Board would then be able to break
even provided its capital charges were scaled down, and if it were
relieved of responsibility for the highly unprofitable freight
sundries service.

That this should be possible was the conclusion of a Joint
Steering Group which undertook much of the detailed planning.
In mid 1967, the Railways Board prepared an estimate for the
Group which suggested that, provided freight sundries were
hived off, they and their ancillary activities would by 1974 have
eliminated their working deficit. The Steering Group was somewhat sceptical about the realism of this forecast, and concluded
that the financial position might well be around £15 million worse
than the Board anticipated. On the other hand, the Group proposed that the railways should eliminate their surplus track
capacity, and concluded, on the basis of estimates by British Rail
(BR), that this would lead to an additional saving of £15 million.
The subsidy for unremunerative but socially necessary passenger
services was put at £50 million, but it was estimated that by 1974
interest payments would have risen to £80 million. Hence it
appeared that British Rail was likely to incur a net loss of £30

million, although it was thought that the figure might range from as little as £5 million to as much as £55 million.[2]

The fact that the railways had no real chance of meeting their capital charges, even with a subsidy, indicated that a financial reconstruction was necessary, and this and the other changes were put into effect by the 1968 Transport Act. As a result, interest was reduced by £26 million and depreciation by £25 million. The Steering Group did not allow for Freightliners being hived off (along with freight sundries) to the new National Freight Corporation, but even when this is taken into account the financial reconstruction should have enabled BR to earn a small profit provided that it managed to cut its working loss in line with its estimates, and did not over-invest.

The Government regarded these financial arrangements as a full, fair and final settlement of the railways' claim for assistance, but within BR the attitude was very different. According to Dr Stewart Joy, who as a consultant to the Ministry was closely involved in the work of the Joint Steering Group (JSG):

> From the outset the railway members seemed to attach less importance to the JSG's deliberations and supporting research than did the Ministry of Transport. In part this was the expected reaction of a group of tired managers, feeling misunderstood, groggy with enquiry, and beyond embarrassment about the mounting and apparently uncontrollable deficit.

However, Joy believes that there was a more fundamental explanation.

> Beeching [he writes] had failed to shake the belief of BR management that the Nation wanted to have a comprehensive railway service, regardless of its cost. From this came the notion that the railway managers were the only fit judges of the required scope and quality of service. . . . In effect, in 1967, the Board was again saying, 'this is the railway the Nation wants, but our annual deficits show that they do not seem prepared to pay for it; if we can somehow put the deficit on a regular and more automatic basis, all will be well.' In brief, and this was the most common attitude of the BR representatives on the JSG, they thought its purpose was to 'whitewash the deficit'.[3]

This may seem a harsh judgement, but it is confirmed by what others who were involved in the work of the Steering Group say about the attitude which BR adopted. Moreover, the Transport

Act had scarcely taken effect before BR's Chairman, Sir Henry Johnson, was suggesting that government subsidies should also be made towards the cost of unremunerative but socially desirable freight services.[4]

The moral which the Board appears to have drawn from the Transport Act was not, as the Government had intended, that BR must do its utmost to cut its costs and trim its investment, but that, if the need arose, more assistance would be forthcoming. Despite the Government's protestations, this was implicit in the new financial arrangements, because the new grants were dependent not on the unrequited benefits the loss-making services conferred but on the size of their deficits. Since the loss on many of the subsidised services was enormous, this suggested that the social benefits that railways provide must also be huge. Certainly, if they were large enough to warrant the retention of the branch-line services, they would be more than sufficient to justify the upkeep of the main-line system should it too become unprofitable.

THE FAILURE OF THE ACT

The Transport Act of 1968 has failed in its objective: British Rail is once again heavily in deficit, despite the financial reconstruction and the receipt of a large subsidy. In 1969, the railways and their ancillary activities had a net profit of around £20 million, after taking into account the £76 million which they received from the Government. However, by 1971 they were once again in deficit, and in 1973 they sustained a net loss approaching £50 million, despite £94 million of subsidies.

To see what has gone wrong, the Steering Group's estimates can, after a certain amount of interpolation and adjustment, be contrasted with performance. If the Railways Board's estimates of mid 1967 had been correct, BR and Freightliners would in 1973 have earned more than sufficient to have covered their operating costs. Instead, as can be seen from Table 1.1, there was a working deficit of about £75 million at end 1966 prices, which was significantly larger than the loss of about £60 million that would have been incurred in 1966 if the railways' accounts had been on their 1969–74 basis. That the financial performance was so much

TABLE 1.1: *Comparison of British Rail's Actual and Estimated Revenue and Expenditure (£ million)*

	Actual in 1966 at current purchasing power	Actual in 1973 at 1966 purchasing power	BR's implicit forecast for 1973 at 1966 purchasing power
Revenue:			
Passenger	180	193	185
Parcels and mails	58	49	56
Freight	216	122	159
High-capacity containers[a]	1	17	21
Miscellaneous	9	8	8
Total revenue	464	389	430
Working expenditure on original basis	542	..	441
Working expenditure allowing for fall in depreciation brought about by 1968 Transport Act	522	462	421
Working loss or surplus	−58	−73	+ 9

[a]Mainly Freightliners, which have been treated as if they still formed part of **BR** in 1973.

Note: In this and other Tables, figures may not add up to totals due to rounding; .. means that the figure is not available.

worse than had been anticipated was due in almost equal measure to a shortfall in revenue and to the fact that costs were greater than had been expected.

The Board's forecasts implied that, between 1966 and 1973, the railways' income would decline from £464 million to around £430 million. In the event, after allowing for inflation, BR and Freightliners earned only about £390 million, and there was in consequence a shortfall of £40 million. This was more than explained by the large gap between the revenue that was forecast for freight and Freightliners, and what was actually earned. Income from parcels and mails was also lower than had been expected, but passenger revenue was rather greater than had been anticipated.

On the expenditure side, the railways' costs, after allowing both for inflation and accounting changes, have fallen from approximately £520 million in 1966 to about £460 million in 1973, largely due to the transfer of National Carriers to the National Freight Corporation. If the Railways Board's estimates had been correct, expenditure would have only been about £420 million in 1973. This is some £40 million less than the actual figure for 1973, despite traffic levels substantially lower than had been anticipated.

A variety of explanations and excuses have been offered by the Board. In particular it blames the state of the economy. In its Annual Report for 1973, which was a boom year, it attributes the deterioration in its finances to the 'recession in the economy'; while the Board's Controller of Corporate Finance, Mr Derek Fowler, argues that, 'Failure to sustain the marginal profits achieved in 1969 and 1970 is wholly accounted for by external economic factors. Both the gross national product and industrial production have been substantially below the levels assumed by the Joint Steering Group.'[5] This ignores the fact that BR was a party to the Steering Group, but is it true that economic circumstances have been less favourable than expected?

The Group assumed, in effect, that over the period 1967–73 national output would increase by $19\frac{1}{2}\%$ and industrial production by $21\frac{1}{2}\%$. In practice, the former rose by $17\frac{1}{2}\%$ and the latter by $19\frac{3}{4}\%$, so that they fell only slightly short of the level postulated. On the other hand, consumers' expenditure which, it was implied, would rise by 14%, grew by just under 20%. Of particular significance for BR were the forecasts for coal and steel. It was suggested that coal consumption and exports would amount to about 139 million tons. In the event there was a shortfall of 5 million tons, but this should have had only a trifling impact on BR's financial performance. The Board itself estimated that if consumption and exports were 15 million tons lower than was expected, its net revenue would be reduced by about £4 million. Hence, a shortfall of 5 million tons would mean that its operating profit would only be around £1·3 million less than was forecast. Steel production in 1973 was significantly less than had been expected: 26 million tons as against 31 million. However, from the Board's estimate of its receipts from steel traffic, it appears that this shortfall would account for a *revenue* loss of only about £4 million. Allowing for the fact that consumers' expenditure has grown much faster than was expected, it must be concluded that the railways' financial difficulties cannot be blamed on the economy's failure to perform in the way that was expected.

Another reason which the railways give for their financial difficulties is that they have been subjected to exceptionally strict price control. Between 1967 and 1973, the general price level, as measured by the price of all final goods and services sold on the home market, increased by 52%. Meanwhile, passenger fares rose by 64%. It is impossible to tell how much BR increased its freight rates over this period, but it has itself estimated that there was a rise of 26% between 1969 and 1972. This was almost exactly the same as the increase in the prices of all goods and services during that period. Although freight charges increased by less than the general rise in prices during 1973, it seems likely that, overall, BR increased its prices at about the average rate between 1967 and 1973. It was not until 1974, after the 1968 Act had already failed, that price restraint and external economic events had a really damaging effect on BR's finances.

British Rail's failure to reach its financial objective cannot therefore be attributed to price restraint, unless what the railways are complaining about is that they have been prevented from putting up their charges by more than the general amount. This they needed to do in order to have any hope of breaking even, because their unit costs were rising exceptionally fast, due to their over-optimism about the amount of traffic they would receive and their lack of success in reducing their costs as much as they had planned. Staff costs constitute about three-quarters of BR's total working expenses, and it is here that we must seek the major explanation for the railways' financial collapse.

Although the figures have never been disclosed, the financial forecasts which British Rail prepared for the Steering Group look as if they were based on the assumption that the wage and salary bill would be cut from £388 million in 1966 to around £275 million in 1974, implying that, with a 3% annual increase in real earnings, British Rail was expecting to reduce its labour force from 350,000 in 1966 to not more than 200,000 in 1974. At the end of 1969 a new estimate of future manpower requirements prepared by BR's work-study staff showed that, if the existing productivity levels were maintained, British Rail would be able to reduce its labour force to 216,000 by the end of 1974, but that if efficiency were tightened up the work force could be slimmed down to 201,000. However, by the end of 1973, BR still had 228,000 workers and its employment is now dropping very slowly.

The railways' failure to reach their target is scarcely surprising in view of the fact that they gave up the attempt at a relatively early stage. During the autumn of 1970, BR forecast that rail employment would be down from 214,000 in 1970 to 200,000 in 1975. This must exclude the workshops, and, from British Rail Engineering's estimate for the period 1971–76, it appears that their requirements would have been forecast at about 30,000. If so, BR's forecasts implied that its employment in 1975 would be around 30,000 higher than its work-study staff had estimated that it would require in 1974.

THE CORPORATE PLANS

Despite the pessimistic view which was taken about the possibility of reducing the rail labour force, it was forecast in the First Corporate Plan, presented to the Minister in December 1970, that the railways would show only a tiny net loss in 1975. The deterioration in profitability was so small because BR was now taking a considerably more optimistic view of its revenue prospects than it had at the time of the Joint Steering Group. It had then been expected that the railways would earn around £415 million in

1974, or at least this is what it appears the forecast would have been if the loss of Freightliners had been foreseen. The Corporate Plan's figure for 1975 was, after allowing for inflation, equivalent to about £470 million. Hence, British Rail was now forecasting that its earnings would be around £50 million greater, although its real receipts during 1969 were slightly smaller, than its Steering Group prediction.

Both the Board's own economists, and the officials who examined the Plan in the Department of the Environment, took a much less rosy view. According to a working party which later reviewed rail policy:

> The Department took the view that the prospect was much worse than the Plan indicated. . . . Certainly, it was clear from the Plan that, up to 1975, the railways could not earn enough to finance the replacement and renewal investment on which the cost and revenue forecasts were premised. Over the period of the Plan there was a cash flow deficit of about £200 million.

It was proposed in the Plan that over £100 million per annum should be invested in the railways between 1971 and 1975, which was somewhat more than they had invested in previous years. Those responsible for the 1968 Transport Act had hoped and expected that the Board would cut its capital expenditure according to its financial cloth. However, the Board had, ever since the days of the Joint Steering Group, believed that it should invest £100 million a year, and it was not going to be deterred by the fact that it would have to borrow large sums from the Government on which it could not hope to pay the interest.

The Second Corporate Plan was, like the First, an optimistic document, despite the fact that there had already been a marked deterioration in the railways' financial position. It was forecast that the volume of freight would increase from 206 million tons in 1970, and 196 million in 1971, to 219 million in 1976, although it was thought that thereafter there would be some decline. A large increase in Inter-City traffic was foreseen with passenger miles up by an estimated 22% between 1971 and 1976, and by a further 32% between 1976 and 1981. The Department of the Environment was highly sceptical about the realism of the Board's revenue estimates. Its officials said later that:

> In the Appraisal Report, the Department concluded that there was considerable risk that the overall rate of growth foreseen

in traffic and revenue on Inter-City passenger services would
not be achieved. They took the view that the freight traffic
forecasts were at the upper end of the range of possibilities and
that it was much more likely that the actual result would be
10%, or about 20 million tons, lower than forecast by 1977 . . .
So the prospect was an even bigger cash gap than the £200
million forecast over the period . . . The Plan forecast deficits
on corporate revenue account up to 1974, break even in 1975
and a surplus of £44 million in 1977 (at estimated 1977 money
values) . . . The Appraisal Report concluded, 'The rail business
is, in our view, certain to be in deficit in 1977 after attributing
to it an appropriate share of interest. It is unlikely that even
after the contribution of the ancillaries, the Corporate Revenue
Account would be in surplus . . . Indeed, the Plan seems to
imply that the late 1970s are a highwater mark in the Board's
business. Beyond 1977 the Plan holds out no hope to us of a
net improvement in surplus. Indeed, it would seem that heavy
investment in renewals would be required around 1980 if freight
traffic is to be retained even at a declining level, and this would
be likely to worsen the financial situation . . . we feel bound to
take the view that, taken as a whole, the investment planned in
the commercial railway cannot be justified on normal risk-
taking criteria.'

THE ECONOMISTS' RESPONSE

That the railways' financial prospects were extremely gloomy
was also clear to the Board's own economists, who made the
point most forcefully in a paper prepared when the First Corporate Plan was being drawn up. They forecast that by 1975 the
railways' profit, after subsidy but before capital charges, would
have fallen to half the level it had been in 1970, and that by the
early 1980s it would have been replaced by a rapidly mounting
deficit. Moreover, as early as 1975 the Board's cash inflow, which
included not only the rail surplus, but also the gross profit from
subsidiary activities and other receipts, would be down to £88
million.

This would be quite inadequate to finance interest payments
and investment. As a result, the Board would have to borrow £87
million from the Exchequer, and by the mid 1980s the figure
would have risen to a staggering £400 million per annum. The
economists concluded that a railway of roughly the present shape

and size, which would require over £60 million of capital expenditure per year, was

> not capable of supporting a level of investment sufficient to maintain itself . . . One must conclude that unless some of the basic assumptions can be proved to be at fault, then either a faster manpower reduction than postulated must be made, or other than a purely financial justification for the railway system found, or the whole exercise must be repeated at smaller system sizes until an equilibrium position can be reached.

Some of the basic assumptions on which this analysis rested were far too optimistic. The rail surplus, after subsidy but before interest and depreciation, which was estimated at £50 million in 1975, was already down to £35 million by 1973. Nevertheless, the Board was provided by its economists with advance warning of its rapidly deteriorating financial prospects, and it would be wrong to excuse the Board on the ground that it has been the victim of events and developments which could not have been foreseen. It should have been clear from the moment that British Rail gave up hoping to make large savings in manpower that it was heading for disaster.

Having discussed the railways' financial prospects, the Board's economists, under Dr Stewart Joy, examined the third option they had identified, the slimming down of the route system to a viable size. By December 1970, a study had been made which suggested there was a profitable core network of 3800 miles consisting of the London area commuter network and the principal Inter-City routes. These included the East Coast main line as far as Edinburgh; the West Coast route, including the line to North Wales and the spurs to Blackpool, Heysham and Barrow; the Midland main line; London–South Wales; and part of the route to the West of England. Parcels business, which could not be divided between networks, was included *en bloc*. All freight except Freightliners had to be ignored because the necessary information could not be obtained from the railways' Finance Department who were unsympathetic to the whole exercise. This meant that some profitable freight was excluded, so that the core system was smaller than it might have been.

The results of the exercise are shown in Table 1.2. It was estimated that in 1975 the core system would have a revenue of nearly £290 million (at end 1969 prices), which was rather over

TABLE 1.2: *Estimate by British Rail Economists of the Profitability in 1975 of the Core System, etc.* (£ million, end 1969 prices)

	Core system					Remainder of the system				Total BR
	Inter-City	London	Freight-liner	Parcels	Total	Social passenger	Inter-City	Freight	Total	
Working expenditure:										
Train services	34	42	5	19	100	23	17	122	162	262
Terminals and miscellaneous	8	21	–	32	61	12	6	20	38	99
Systems	24	38	–	1	63	21	say 10	say 26	57	120
Administration	10	12	1	4	27	6	7	19	32	59
Total working expenditure	76	113	6	56	251	62	40	187	289	540
Revenue:										
Earnings	98	124	8	58	288	25	31	196	252	540
Grant	–	–	–	–	–	41	–	–	41	41
Total revenue	98	124	8	58	288	66	31	196	293	581
Working profit	22	11	2	2	37	4	–9	9	4	41
Interest	9	11	–	2	22	4	5	14	23	45
Net Profit	13	–	2	–	15	–	–14	–5	–19	–4

half the forecast for the whole of British Rail. Total working expenses were put at around £250 million, and the core network had a working surplus of £37 million, and a profit of £15 million after meeting its share of the Board's interest. On the other hand, the remaining Inter-City services appeared to have a working deficit of around £10 million, and freight traffic was, taken as a whole, in a financially unhealthy condition.

These estimates assumed that given sufficient determination, administrative costs could be reduced to the levels which were implied by a detailed breakdown of railway expenditure, known as the Cost Centre Exercise, which had recently been carried out. It was argued that 'the main barrier to reduction of the Board's rail activities to a more profitable level is not the interdependence of traffics, but an inhibition about the Board's ability to reduce its overheads in step with a reduction in physical operations.' However, it was pointed out that initially revenues would fall faster than costs and that contraction would be a difficult under-taking. The real weakness of the economists' estimates was that they were derived from or consistent with the First Corporate Plan, which is turning out to be widely over-optimistic about traffic, but did not assume the fullest possible progress in cutting costs.

THE NETWORK STUDIES

As a result of this study, the Railways Board decided that its Finance Department, which was strongly critical, should carry out a full investigation of whether a smaller rail system would be profitable. A number of networks, whose main characteristics are shown in Table 1.3, were then examined in detail.

The cost and revenue estimates for each of these systems can be roughly calculated from the physical data which is given in Table 1.3, and from the Board's forecasts for its total expenditure, and its passenger, freight and parcels revenue, in 1976. The expenditure of each of the networks was estimated on the assumption that their share of BR's operating costs would be the same as their share of its employment. Networks 1 and 2 were, in addition to the earnings of the London and South-Eastern services, credited with 85% of the revenue from the Inter-City

services, because they include 2100 miles of Inter-City route, and
BR is known to have estimated that it could earn 85% of their
revenue from a system of only this size. Network 3 was assigned
93% of Inter-City revenue, which is the figure suggested by BR's
estimates of the passenger mileage on commercial trains. Network 4 was credited not only with all of the Inter-City revenue,
but also with the great bulk of BR's earnings from stopping
trains.

TABLE 1.3: *Networks Studied by British Rail*

Network[a]	Route (track) mileage	Composition	Freight tonnage (million)
1	3 800 (8 900)	London and South-East commuter network (1 500 route miles); Inter-City passenger (2 100); Freightliner and parcels requiring no significant extra mileage.	11
2	4 000 (9 700)	Network 1 plus trainload and wagonload freight services requiring spurs of not more than two miles.	37
3	6 500 (14 700)	Network 2 plus route required for most of the trainload and wagonload traffic provided for in the Second Corporate Plan. Extra passenger and Freightliner services made practicable by the extra route.	190
4	8 900 (19 600)	Network 3 plus about 125 provincial grant-aided services; consequential extensions to commercial passenger and freight services.	205
Second Corporate Plan system	11 000 (21 100)	The present network, less about 75 of the 200 provincial grant-aided services.	219

[a]Networks 5 and 6, which are not shown, were similar to 4.

It appears from the Beeching Report that 100 stations generate around 70% of what BR earns from Rail Express and other traffic such as newspapers, and it is known that stopping services produce very little. It was consequently assumed that Networks 1 and 2, which contain 120 Inter-City stations, account for the great bulk of this revenue. The final step was to work out what each of the systems might receive from freight, the main problem being to decide how much wagonload freight each network

Commercial passenger miles (million)	Employees (rail only)	Total revenue (£ million)	Expenditure excluding interest and depreciation (£ million)	Gross profit (£ million)
. .	110 000	335	310	+25
. .	130 000	357	367	−10
8 700	170 000	526	479	+47
9 400	200 000	590	564	+26
9 400	210 000	610	592	+18

would have been assigned, since its rate per ton is high. It was known that Network 4 was assigned 37 million out of the total of 44 million tons, and it was assumed that Network 3 would have been credited with 30 million tons, but that the smaller networks would receive none.

The result of these calculations is shown in the final columns of Table 1.3. Network 3, which includes 60% of the route, appears to be the most profitable system with a gross surplus of something like £50 million. That Network 4 should appear to be less profitable need cause no surprise: it is considerably more extensive and would, according to BR, require considerably more staff, but it would only carry an extra 15 million tons of freight, and a relatively small amount of additional passenger traffic. What does seem strange is that Networks 1 and 2 should turn out to be so much inferior to Network 3. This was because BR estimated that as many as 110,000 workers would be required to run the commuter trains of London and the South-East, to provide the principal Inter-City services and to carry the 11 million tons of freight which the smallest system would receive. It was thought that a further 20,000 would be needed to cope with the additional 26 million tons of freight that would be handled on Network 2. Network 3, on the other hand, was credited with nearly 180 million tons more freight than the smallest system, as well as slightly more passenger traffic, but the labour force was only 60,000 greater.

This strongly suggests that the smaller networks were weighed down with an unnecessarily large number of administrative workers, and that the Finance Department suffered from what Joy had diagnosed as 'an inhibition about the Board's ability to reduce its overheads in step with a reduction in physical operations'. It is interesting to observe that he estimated that his core system would require only 100,000 workers, whereas the Department thought that Network 1, which was very similar, would require an additional 10,000 staff. Whether the labour force of the third network was itself inflated by the inclusion of unnecessary administrative staff is not clear, but it seems quite probable, as the exaggeration of overhead costs seems to have been a general feature of BR's estimates.

Although BR's network studies appear to be biased against the smaller systems, they do seem to have suggested that a substantial reduction in the size of the system was desirable from a financial point of view. In so far as the railways' financial estimates can be reconstructed, it appears that a network containing around 60% of the existing route was the best option, because it would come nearest to paying its way. This seems, at first sight, to be at variance with the Department of the Environment's subsequent statement that

> The results of the studies did not produce a conclusive case for or against any of the networks. Margins of error were considerable. And the differences in net cash flow between the large and small networks were more a reflection of differences in grant payments than anything else. The comparative ranking of the networks measured in terms of use of resources, was not necessarily the same as that based on financial return to BR . . . It was common ground between BR and the Department [of the Environment] that the results were inconclusive and that further and more refined studies would be necessary. On the basis of a somewhat more favourable financial return for BR shown by Network 4, the Chairman suggested that further study should be concentrated in this area. Although the Department felt that the smaller networks could not be ruled out for all time, they recognised the need to limit the scope of the immediate work. They therefore advised the Minister that the Chairman's proposal could be accepted . . .

This is a choice piece of bureaucratic prose in which the civil servants have managed to obscure the facts and confuse the issue. However, a careful reading of the passage indicates that Network 4 only appeared the most financially attractive system because it had been credited in BR's estimates with the large subsidy for the provincial grant-aided services. This is a wholly fallacious approach. A railway system of any shape or size can be made to seem desirable if it is automatically provided with a sufficiently large subsidy. What was more relevant was whether a smaller railway system would be self-supporting, and how much financial support the larger networks would require. It was simply begging the question to include the existing government grants in the profitability calculations.

It is evident, from what the Department said, that when these grants were excluded the Board's studies showed that a network smaller than 4 came nearest to paying its way. There is therefore no conflict between our finding that Network 3 had a considerable gross surplus, and the official gloss. The Department agreed to rule out the smaller networks and to make a more detailed examination of the larger networks. This was probably a sensible decision as the smaller systems would almost certainly have been politically unacceptable, and might well have involved social costs that would have more than offset the financial benefit. However, it is evident, with the wisdom of hindsight, that the Department was gradually being manoeuvred along the line that BR wished it to follow, and was coming to accept that no alteration in the size of the system would have any impact on its financial position.

THE SECOND STAGE STUDIES

The Department of the Environment and BR now agreed that four fresh networks should be investigated. The smallest of these, known as 7B, contained 75 provincial grant-aided services out of the 200 or so which then existed. These included most of the services in the provincial conurbations which, together with those in London and the South-East, were regarded as 'hard core'. It was thought by the Department that this system would, at 6700 route miles, need to be only 200 miles longer than Network 3. However, BR believed that 7B should comprise an extra 1700 miles, because BR assumed, to quote its own words, that 'Where passenger services would be withdrawn, about half the routes losing all passenger services would still be required for freight services of sufficient importance to warrant retention of the route.'

Until then BR had argued that, if grant aid was withdrawn from a substantial block of services, this would have a cascade effect, because the government subsidy includes a contribution towards track, signalling and other joint costs. As the grants more than meet the railways' escapable costs, it was expected that any significant reduction in the size of the subsidy would compel BR to withdraw a large number of commercial services, and shut a considerable proportion of the route they used. The Board now stated that this would not be necessary, which implied that the commercial services in question were so profitable that they would be able to bear the full expense of the facilities which they shared with the subsidised services. This seems highly unlikely as much of BR's freight did no more than cover its direct costs, and may not even have done that. Nor was BR assuming that it would be able to greatly reduce the costs of maintaining those lines which would be kept open for freight after grant-aided passenger services had been withdrawn. All of the route which was included in system 7B, but not in Network 3, was to be double track.

It seems clear that BR was planning, when grant aid was removed, to retain a large amount of unprofitable freight. This would inevitably have made system 7B appear less profitable than it should have been, and have suggested that the closure of a large block of grant-aided services would, even from a financial point of view, be of little or no benefit. Such was the conclusion drawn by the officials who reviewed the railways' system studies. They reported that there was

> no material difference between Networks 7A, B and C other than in the scale of grant-aided services which each contains. Nor is there likely to be any significant difference in their financial out-turn compared with the present Plan.

In another place there was a reference to

> the very small differences in the . . . networks . . . in terms of resources, traffic, revenue and costs. These are not, in our view, separate strategies but merely minor variations on a single strategy.

It seems incredible that the civil servants who examined the Board's studies should have accepted that a railway system from which a large number of unprofitable services had been excised would be no more profitable than one which contained them. Yet in their report they do not even express surprise that the Board should have come up with this startling result.

THE DEPARTMENT'S VERDICT

While the Railways Board was producing its system studies, the Department of the Environment was attempting to determine what costs rail users and the community would incur if closures took place. Its findings will be discussed later, but are scarcely relevant here because the Department was ultimately convinced by BR that closures were financially irrelevant. True, the officials concluded that 'The Department's studies and those of BR taken jointly do provide additional confirmation that the possibility of withdrawing a substantial number of grant-aided services should be further pursued.' But this recommendation lacked any force, and carried no conviction, because there could be little case for withdrawal if no real financial benefit was in prospect. No Minister was going to incur the odium of closing lines if his advisers told him that there would be no financial saving.

Although the civil servants wanted BR to continue investigating the possibilities of contraction in the passenger and freight fields, they ended their report by calling for a new approach to the railways' financial difficulties, namely cost reduction. They pointed out that by 1976 the Board's deficit, even after grant assistance,

> could be well in excess of £100 million. We can see no prospect, on present plans, of stabilising the deficit even at that high figure. There is no solution in another capital reconstruction. And a policy of revenue subsidies would involve ever increasing payments. What is needed is a major change in plans for the operation of the railways. There is no reason to assume that viability cannot be achieved . . . In our view, the search for a commercial solution should be continued . . . The Second Corporate Plan looked principally to the increase of remunerative traffic to solve the problem. But no solution along these lines now appears possible. The problem must be tackled, in our view, principally through cost reduction, and labour costs in particular.
>
> It is tempting to turn to labour-saving investment as the answer. This may have a part to play. But no one should overlook that rising interest and depreciation have been the downfall of the railways in the past and that this is a significant element in the financial deterioration implicit in the present Plan.

CUTTING COSTS

At long last, cost reduction and a lower level of capital expenditure were being seriously suggested. When the railways' financial problem first became evident in the autumn of 1970, during the preparation of the First Corporate Plan, the railways' economists had observed that a further reduction in manpower was one of the options facing the Board. However, Stewart Joy appears to have turned his attention to the problem of how large the system should be, although this could only be properly determined when all the possible ways of reducing costs and making the existing network as profitable as possible had been considered. In his paper on the core system, he simply adjusted his estimates of the current cost of the services which were included on the assumption that real wages would increase by 3% per annum, and that the labour force would decline by 1% each year as a result of productivity gains, which was what the First Corporate Plan seems to have implied.

Similarly, the Department, when commenting on the Board's Plans, appears to have assumed that nothing more could be done to cut costs. In its Appraisal Report on the Second Corporate Plan, it commented that 'the best efforts which can be made to contain operating costs will not quite succeed in doing so'. Officials seem to have been impressed by what they subsequently referred to as 'the very substantial improvements in productivity planned', but these would only occur if traffic increased in the way that was forecast, and the Department was rightly sceptical as to whether it would. The labour force under the Second Corporate Plan was estimated to decline by only 1½% per annum between 1970 and 1976. Moreover, it was expected that it would still total 210,000 at the end of the period, which was about 10,000 more than work-study officers had estimated would be necessary in 1974, and this despite the exclusion of a considerable number of workers whom the work-study staff had included.

Within BR, there were those who were pressing for faster progress in the reduction of manpower. In an internal memorandum, presented in the summer of 1972, one of the members of the Railways Board said that there was reason to believe that the railways could be made viable, and suggested that another look should be taken at the planning assumptions behind the network studies. He argued that BR needed to buy its way out of 'inherited restrictive practices', and that the transition to an economic level of manpower would not cause insuperable problems. 'There are fears', he wrote, 'of massive unemployment; but past rationalisation has displaced more men than will be thrown up in any future reorganisation. Experience indicates

that these will be absorbed by a changing economy as they have
been in the past.'

He conceded that there would be difficulties with the unions,
and that, as the network studies had shown, the cost in redundancy payments could be substantial, but suggested that BR might
be able to obtain financial assistance from the Common Market.

Once it is clear that surplus men can be displaced and the
financial burden of their displacement removed from the railway accounts, the future prospects may look very different. . . .
It is . . . wasted effort to invest in the automation of a real job
when a ghost job remains in existence alongside. Any meaningful discussion on improved productivity on BR through
technology should therefore start with a critical re-examination
by management of the problem of hidden redundancy. What
are the functions of the second man in the locomotive and the
guard for example?

BR's INTERIM RAIL STRATEGY

Unfortunately the suggestion that BR should do more to raise
its productivity, which was now being made inside the Department and the Board, was not taken up. After the system studies,
the railways presented to the Department, in January 1973, what
they called their Interim Rail Strategy. According to the outline
which was published in June of that year, BR was planning to
reduce its labour force from 230,000, at the end of 1972, to about
190,000 in 1981.[6] At first sight this does not seem too unsatisfactory. It represents a reduction of about 2% per annum, and
the Board was expecting that there would be some increase in
traffic. The traffic estimates in the Interim Strategy imply an
overall increase of nearly 1% per annum between 1971 and 1981,
which would mean a 3% rate of growth in labour productivity
over the same period.

However, as we shall see, the traffic forecast was over-optimistic,
and a comparison of the Strategy's employment figures for 1981
with the work-study estimate of 201,000 for 1974 suggests that a
considerably faster rise in productivity should be possible. Moreover, the work-study estimate assumed substantially more freight
than the Interim Strategy, and the retention of all, or nearly all,

the grant-aided services. The Strategy, on the other hand, allowed for the closure of 73 provincial services, and, unlike the work-study estimate, did not include corporate and common-service staff. If adjustments are made for differences in coverage, the gap of 11,000 between the work-study and the Interim Strategy estimates of employment almost disappears, and freight traffic would more than account for the rest. In other words, the gains in productivity which BR is planning to make by 1981 are less than those which its work-study staff estimated that it should have made by 1974, despite the very considerable programme of investment which the Board is hoping to carry out.

As part of its Interim Rail Strategy the Board proposed to invest £1787 million, at 1972 prices, over the period 1973–81, an annual rate about double that of recent years. When it presented the system studies, BR appears to have told the Department that it only needed to invest about £1200 million between 1973 and 1981. What occasioned the rise was the leak of a Departmental 'Review of Rail Policy' in the *Sunday Times* on 8 October 1972, and the outcry when it became known that extensive rail closures had been under consideration. As a result, the railways began to press for a higher level of investment, which they now thought they had a chance of being granted.

The combination of large-scale investment and a rate of productivity growth insufficient to meet the anticipated rise in real earnings meant that BR was heading for an enormous deficit. The published version of the Interim Strategy did not provide any estimate, and the Board confined itself to the statement that additional financial support would be required, and that the method by which it should be provided ought to be 'flexible and robust'. This was tantamount to saying that it wanted a large and open-ended subsidy. In fact, the Board estimated that, under the existing financial rules, the railways and ancillary businesses would incur a net loss of £70 million per annum over the period 1973–81. However, because investment was much greater than depreciation, the cash-flow shortfall was over twice as large, and averaged £145 million a year. The Government would have to finance this, as well as providing BR with the subsidy for its grant-aided passenger lines which had already been taken into account. What this subvention was estimated at we do not know, but as BR received £68 million in 1972, and the amount was increasing year by year, the Board must have been assuming that it would receive a very large sum. Indeed, when all forms of support, including infrastructure grants, are allowed for, it is difficult to believe that the railways were hoping to be provided with anything less than £250 million per annum.

In the published version of the Interim Strategy BR did not try to make out a reasoned case for such massive public assistance. It simply stated that 'any significantly smaller network would require greater financial support than the present-day railway', although this was a very misleading summary of what the system studies had shown. The Board went on to assert that 'the right transport policy will require the railways of the future to play a significantly wider role, with their considerable social and environmental potential being fully exploited'. No attempt was made, either in the published or the secret version of the Interim Strategy, to quantify these social benefits, and see whether they justified the cost. However, it was evident that so far as freight was concerned, there would be no additional benefit because it was forecast that traffic would decline from 195 million tons in 1971 to 191 million tons in 1981.

The Board tried to forestall this criticism by stating that it had assumed that the existing competitive situation beween road and rail would continue. This was why it described its plans as an Interim Rail Strategy, and contrasted this with a programme based on the concept of 'the truly necessary railway which places greater emphasis on social and environmental factors'. However, this was a very unconvincing argument, because no hint was given of the contents or cost of this programme, for the very good reason that BR had not given any serious consideration to the matter.

THE 1974 ACT

Despite the high cost and unconvincing nature of the Interim Strategy, it was largely accepted by the Government, and it was announced towards the end of 1973 that, excluding the Channel Tunnel rail link, rail investment would increase to £225 million in 1977–78, at 1973 prices. It is impossible to do more than speculate about how the Government was won over to a policy of large-scale capital expenditure and massive financial support. However, it had no doubt been greatly impressed by the outcry at the *Sunday Times* leak, and probably believed that it would gain some much needed popularity by helping the railways. A large programme of rail investment also fitted in with the Government's general policy of national regeneration through enormous public and semi-public projects and programmes such as Maplin, the Tunnel, Concorde and the British Steel Corporation's development strategy. Finally, mention must be made of British Rail's Chairman, Mr Richard Marsh, who by all accounts played a major part in persuading the then Minister of Transport, Mr John Peyton, that BR deserved support.

How much assistance the railways would require, and how this was to be provided, had not been revealed before the Conservatives lost power, but they had a Bill prepared. It was taken over by the Labour Government, and, with the addition of a clause providing for financial help towards the construction of private sidings, passed into law as the 1974 Railways Act. This replaced the specific Exchequer grants, that were the principal feature of the 1968 Transport Act, by a general subsidy for rail passenger services. The Act also extinguished part of the Board's capital debt. It was decided that henceforth expenditure on the replacement of track, previously treated as a capital item, was to be regarded as an operating cost. Thus, it was necessary to write off that part of the debt burden that represented investment in track, which will reduce the Board's interest payments by about £40 million per annum.

The Act enables £1500 million of subsidies to be paid to BR from the Exchequer. When the Bill appeared in June 1974 it was expected that this would only be sufficient to meet the railways' financial needs for about five years, because the railways' financial situation was deteriorating rapidly, and provision was made for large expenditures of a capital nature. The new Labour Ministers were unhappy about the size of the investment programme, but felt that they had to be as generous to the railways as their predecessors because of their Party's intimate association with the rail unions and the strength of the environmental interest.

Even before the Railways Act had come into force, it was apparent that new legislation and additional financial support would be required within a year or two. At the end of 1974, the Minister of Transport announced that it was estimated that the Exchequer contribution towards the cost of the rail passenger services would come to £341 million in 1975 (and the total subsidy will be still higher because BR will continue to receive grants from the Passenger Transport Executives under Section 20 of the 1968 Transport Act). As the bill will be greater during subsequent years, the provision of £1500 million made in the Railways Act will not last anything like five years. Moreover, despite the generous way in which BR is being treated in the apportionment of track and signalling expenses between passenger and freight, it will probably incur a deficit on its freight operations, which it is still supposed to run at a profit. Before long, the Government will therefore have to decide whether it wishes to start subsidising rail freight traffic, or whether it is going to make a fundamental reappraisal of rail policy.

We are convinced that such a reappraisal is necessary, and the purpose of this book is to formulate a new strategy for the railways. In order to do this, it is necessary to begin at the beginning, and try to discover how much traffic BR can hope to obtain. We shall then try to estimate how much investment and what level of employment will be necessary to carry the available traffic.

It is therefore our intention to try to forecast the future and to decide how BR should respond. This may seem a presumptuous undertaking and in an increasingly uncertain world many of our estimates will no doubt turn out to be wrong. Nevertheless it seemed right to try to chart an alternative course for British Rail because however thick the fog the railways will have to be steered in some direction and they will surely sink if they remain stuck on the rock of inaction. Thus we have boldly set forth what we think and what action should be taken. It has been suggested that our estimates should have been presented in the form of ranges. This would have appeared more academic but would have put the reader to the trouble of constantly calculating the mid point to discover what we really think. However the reader should not attach undue weight to our figures. They are to be regarded as back-of-an-envelope calculations which hopefully give some idea of the orders of magnitude involved.

CHAPTER 2

The Prospects
for Passenger Traffic

Passenger traffic deserves pride of place in any consideration of British Rail's future revenue because, although freight and parcels accounted for over half of railway revenue up to 1970, the position has since been reversed. In addition, growth prospects are brightest for passenger traffic. Rail passenger services can be divided into four broad categories. Firstly, there are Inter-City express services, operating over about 4000 miles of BR's network and producing 44% of passenger revenue (excluding revenue from subsidies) in 1973. They received almost no financial support from the Government under the 1968 Transport Act, in contrast with the other passenger services, most of which were subsidised. Secondly, there are the London and South-East services which accounted for 45% of fare revenue in 1973. The London and South-East network includes most commuter and express services in the Southern Region, together with commuter services in an area extending for about 40 miles around North London. Thirdly, there are commuter services in the other main conurbations. Responsibility for these rests, under Section 20 of the 1968 Act, with the Passenger Transport Executives (PTEs), who must bear the losses incurred, although these were supported by a 70% Central Government grant in 1974. The PTEs decide on the levels of service and fares, but BR remains responsible for the actual operation of these lines. Finally, the remaining subsidised services include local services not in the conurbations, stopping services on main lines, cross-country and secondary services, and rural branch services.

Traffic and revenue from the different groups of services over the period 1963 to 1973 are shown in Table 2.1. The revenue figures have been deflated by the overall price index for all final goods and services sold on the home market to yield revenue at general 1972 purchasing power. We will continue to adopt this convention in the remainder of the book and, unless stated to the contrary, prices and revenues will be given at 1972 purchasing power.[1]

INTER-CITY PASSENGER SERVICES

Table 2.1 shows that over the period from 1963 to 1973 Inter-City revenue at 1972 purchasing power rose from £99 million to £119 million. However, we estimate that, but for the effects of industrial action, revenue would have reached nearly £125 million in 1973. Over the seven-year period from 1964 to 1970 passenger

TABLE 2.1: *British Rail Passenger Traffic and Revenue*

Year	Traffic (million passenger miles)				Revenue (£ million, 1972 purchasing power)			
	Inter-City	London & SE	PTE & other	Total	Inter-City	London & SE	PTE & other	Total
1963	. .	. .		19 230	98·9	163·3		262·2
1964	6 070	13 800		19 870	99·5	161·7		261·2
1965	6 090	12 620		18 710	101·3	157·1		258·4
1966	6 170	12 280		18 450	99·9	156·4		256·3
1967	6 430	11 660		18 090	100·3	148·9		249·2
1968	6 660	7 700	3 480	17 840	102·4	103	40	244·9
1969	7 160	7 860	3 380	18 400	114·7	107	36	257·6
1970	7 730	7 980	3 180	18 890	121·0	113	34	267·1
1971	7 670	8 400	2 650	18 720	125·5	123	33	281·2
1972	7 370	8 170	2 560	18 100	120·5	119	34·5	274·0
1973	7 650	10 850		18 500	118·8	121	32	271·6
1981a	9 000	8 550	2 800	20 350	162	144	34	340

a 1981 figures, in italic throughout, are authors' estimates.

mileage rose while real fares per mile fell below their 1964 level. 1971 and 1972 saw a downturn in passenger mileage, associated with a fairly rapid increase in real fares. Government-imposed delays to fare increases in 1973 then led to a reduction in real fares, and, as a result, traffic rose again and, but for the impact of industrial action, would have regained its 1970 peak.

BR's Interim Rail Strategy indicated that Inter-City passenger mileage was expected to grow from 7400 million passenger miles in 1972 to 11,400 million miles in 1981, while revenue was expected to increase from £120·5 million in 1972 to £240 million at 1972 purchasing power in 1981. These figures include Channel Tunnel traffic. BR's autumn 1973 Inter-City projection, excluding Channel Tunnel traffic, was 11,000 million passenger miles in 1981, generating £203 million of revenue; this projection had not been substantially altered by autumn 1974. Thus BR is expecting that passenger mileage will increase at something like the rates of growth between 1966 and 1970. This is in spite of expected real fare increases of 11% between 1972 and 1981, in contrast with the slight fall in fare levels between 1966 and 1970.

BR's projections depend to a large extent on service improvements which will divert traffic from air and road, and will also generate entirely new journeys. To appraise these projections we first consider the past impact of rail-service improvements on traffic. We then review anticipated service improvements up to 1981, and attempt to gauge whether such improvements will be sufficient to justify BR's Inter-City forecasts. Finally, we consider the likely competition from other modes up to 1981.

The impact of service improvements

The period from 1960 onwards was one of rapid improvement in the quality of BR's Inter-City services. The number of station-to-station runs over 60 mph rose from 90 in 1960–61 to 1630 in 1970–71, while the number of runs over 70 mph rose from zero to 340. It is clear that service improvements do have a very clear impact on traffic flows, with large reductions in journey times leading to major traffic increases. This has occurred on all types of service which have been improved, whether by electrification or by the acceleration of diesel services. Frequency also has an important impact on traffic. Secondly, BR believes that a substantial proportion of this traffic growth is due to newly generated traffic. Thus, in the case of their London–Manchester service, it believes that 60% of its traffic gain on this route between

1964 and 1970 was generated traffic, compared with 25% which was diverted from air and 15% which was diverted from road. Thirdly, BR has discovered that a period of some three years generally elapses before the full effect of service improvements is achieved.

One approach to the forecast of future rail traffic would be the use of transportation models to predict future flows between particular points. However, in contrast with the intra-urban situation, little work has been done in Great Britain on modelling inter-urban traffic flows, partly because of the lack of inter-city traffic statistics apart from those for domestic air routes. Data on rail flows are collected by BR but rarely published, and the data which exist are often inconveniently aggregated into service groups which include flows between a number of towns.

Models which are used to predict flows of traffic between different pairs of zones are generally of the gravity type, which seek to explain traffic between two zones as a function of the sizes of the zones and the cost of travel between them. For example, the amount of traffic between two towns might be positively related to the populations of the towns, and inversely related to the distance between them. In this way, using data from two one-day traffic surveys in 1966, Evans developed a gravity model to explain traffic flows by car, coach, rail and air between London and different provincial towns as a function of the population of the provincial town and the journey time between that town and London.[2]

BR has itself adopted the gravity-model approach, but for rail flows only. As well as recognising the problems arising from lack of data, BR believes that this approach is justified on the grounds that inter-modal competition is not too important in Great Britain. For example, most long-distance car trips involve a relatively high number of car occupants, and the car is used to carry luggage and to provide a means of transport at the destination, so rail is not a viable alternative. This view is in part supported by evidence from a study of rail passengers carried out in 1969 on certain Inter-City routes.[3] Travellers were asked whether they had considered an alternative mode to rail for their journey, and, depending on the particular route, an average of 40–65% replied that they had not.

BR's gravity-model approach involves the estimation of inter-city rail flows between London and provincial towns on the basis of the socio-economic characteristics of the town (e.g. population), the quality of the rail service, and the quality of alternative modes. The model is calibrated on existing cross-section data by multiple regression techniques, and can then be used to predict the effects on flows of future changes in the independent variables, for example, rail journey speed.[4]

From this work BR has concluded that the key transport quality variables which appear to affect traffic flows are: the rail price, as measured by the average fare paid by all passengers on the line; the quality of the rail service; and the speed attainable on parallel road routes. Rail service quality is measured by perceived journey speed, which depends on waiting time as well as on journey time. Although passengers can time their arrival at a station to coincide with departure times, survey data indicate that travellers allow a longer waiting time if the rail service is infrequent, so that frequency is an important component of rail-service quality. The model indicates that as speed increases the rate of increase of traffic declines. In one version of the model it was found that a 1% increase in speed would increase traffic by 2% at 50 mph and by 0·6% at 150 mph. The overall rail-fare elasticity appears to be about unity, i.e. every 1% increase in price leads to a 1% reduction in traffic. First-class travel is price inelastic, for second-class full-fare traffic the elasticity is about one, while second-class reduced-fare traffic is very elastic. Rail traffic is, as might be expected, inversely related to road journey speed, though statistical problems prevent an accurate assessment of the cross-elasticity in the model.

These models appear to provide a reasonable representation of existing inter-city rail travel flows. The degree of explanation given by the model is fairly high, and individual variables are statistically significant. The signs and magnitudes of these variables appear sensible. There is, however, an objection to the use of this type of model to predict future traffic flows. The gravity model indicates how the flow of traffic varies at a particular point in time with variations in the quality of the transport service between each pair of towns and with differences in their socio-economic characteristics. It does not show how the traffic between a *given* pair of towns will change over time when the quality of the transport service alters. Estimates of generated traffic derived from such models, particularly in BR's case where new traffic is expected to be large in relation to existing traffic, must therefore be treated with some caution. Nevertheless, BR can point with some confidence to the fact that its previous forecasts have consistently underestimated traffic growth from service improvements.

The studies we have discussed consider service quality in terms of journey speed and frequency, but there are other components of rail quality which may affect travellers' choices but which are difficult to quantify. These may include such factors as on-train catering facilities, station design, the comfort of coaching-stock, and the impact of BR's marketing promotion.

Inter-City growth prospects and the effects of competition

We have derived our initial forecasts of 1981 Inter-City traffic by projecting 1972 traffic levels, route by route, in line with the service improvements planned, using the speed elasticities derived from BR's model. The 1972 traffic levels were first adjusted upwards to allow for the effects of industrial action by the Associated Society of Locomotive Engineers and Footplatemen (ASLEF) in that year. As well as considering the effects of increased speed, some rough allowance was also made for the impact of increased frequency of service. The effects of service improvements were assumed to be spread evenly over a three-year period commencing with the introduction of new services with the new timetable in May of each year. A more difficult question was whether there would be any trend rate of growth or decline in traffic in the absence of changes in service quality. Though there does not seem to be any measurable relationship between Inter-City rail travel and gross domestic product (GDP), there is some evidence that increases in income reduce rail travel, even though rail travel is consumed largely by the better-off members of society, so that a slow-down in the growth of income and in the increase of car-ownership levels might even lead to some increase in rail travel.[5] In view of the expected reduction in the real rate of growth of GDP over the period between 1973 and 1981, and in view of the increased real costs of motoring which we discuss below, our forecasts incorporate an assumption of a growth of ½% per annum in Inter-City traffic in the absence of service improvements. This increase was applied to traffic on each route, though experience indicates that any such natural growth of traffic will not in practice be spread evenly among the different routes.

Between 1972 and 1974 there were speed improvements on both the East and West Coast routes. Track work completed in 1973 on the East Coast line permitted acceleration of trains by removing the Peterborough speed restriction. On the West Coast line, services to Glasgow were accelerated with the completion of electrification in 1974. Speeds were also increased to towns in the North-West such as Preston, Blackpool, Barrow and Carlisle, and the introduction of more powerful electric locomotives led to an increase on the London–Birmingham–Manchester/Liverpool route.

BR's main speed improvements in the future will come with the introduction of two new types of train, the high-speed diesel train (HST) and the advanced passenger train (APT). The HST is a conventional train with two diesel motive-power units, one at either end of a set of BR's new, but conventional, Mark III coaches. This train will have a top speed of 125 mph and should be in full service by 1976. The APT is a revolutionary form of lightweight train, in which the coaches of the train will be able to tilt in order to travel much faster around bends than a conventional train. The initial APTs will be built with a capability of 155 mph but this is unlikely to be achieved in passenger service until the late 1980s. They will initially operate at the same top speeds as the HST, but will have a faster average speed because of their ability to corner faster. Two variants of the APT were originally planned, an electric version to operate on overhead electrified lines, and a gas turbine version to operate elsewhere. Serious problems have arisen with the gas turbine engine, and the electric version will be the first to appear.

The routes and dates for the introduction of the two types of train were outlined by BR in November 1972, but the HST will now be introduced two years later than originally intended, and the APT four years later than intended.[6] The HST will be introduced in 1976 on the London–Bristol–South Wales line, where it will increase speeds between London and Bristol and Cardiff by about 30%. Further HST sets should be introduced on the East Coast route in 1977 and 1978, on North-East–South-West services in 1979, on London–West of England services in 1980 and on the London–Nottingham–Sheffield line in 1981. The first production-version APTs will be introduced on the London–Glasgow route in 1981, and on other West Coast main-line services in the early 1980s.

On the basis of these service improvements and assuming unchanged real fare levels, our Inter-City traffic forecast for 1981 is 9500 million passenger miles. If real revenue per passenger mile remained at its 1972 level, this would imply 1981 Inter-City revenue of £156 million at 1972 purchasing power. The two main reasons for the difference between this estimate and BR's forecast of £203 million are that BR's forecasts assumed an underlying natural rate of growth of $1\frac{1}{2}\%$ per annum, and that BR was assuming that real fare levels will be raised by 11%. BR may well have to raise real fares on some services because of capacity problems. Our forecasts imply a 29% increase in passenger mileage between 1972 and 1981, whereas BR is planning to increase Inter-City train mileage by only 13%. This would imply unacceptable overcrowding on peak-hour trains on the main Inter-City routes. The users of such trains are those travellers with lower than average elasticity of demand, so that fare increases on such trains might lead to an increase in BR revenue. The extent of the increase is difficult to judge. If one-half of BR's Inter-City revenue were derived from peak-hour trains, and if the overall elasticity of demand of travellers on such trains were 0·6, then a 20% real fare increase on such services would increase revenue by about £5 million.

BR also adopts a further argument to justify real fare increases. It suggests that travellers react adversely to very large fare increases, but do not react noticeably to small fare increases. BR therefore proposes to increase real fares slowly over the period 1972 to 1981 and thereby hope that travellers will not perceive that real fares have risen. This argument is difficult to justify logically, and it is also difficult to refute, but we are sceptical whether BR could achieve an overall increase of 11% in real fare levels from 1972 to 1981 without having more than the marginal impact on traffic which BR has itself allowed for. Perhaps in view of the increase in the real costs of private motoring, a 5% increase in real fares, which would increase BR's revenue by about £7·5 million, would be feasible without major traffic loss.

Because the effects of real fare increases are so uncertain, we propose to add a conservative sum of £10 million to our original revenue forecast to allow for the possible impact of real fare increases on BR Inter-City revenue.

This new revenue forecast assumes that service quality on other modes is unchanged, so that before we reach our final revenue forecast for 1981, it is necessary to consider whether BR will face fiercer competition from other modes. Express rail services face competition from the airlines, from the private car and from the coach network. Some evidence on these modes' share of long-distance travel is available from information from the Long Distance Travel Panel, which provides data on trips of over 25 miles in length within the United Kingdom by means of a sample of travellers. In the period from mid 1968 to mid 1971, 79% of all trips sampled were by car, 10% by rail, and 11% by bus and coach, with air representing less than 1%. Rail accounted for 13% of work trips, 9% of holiday or pleasure trips, and 10% of trips for personal business.[7]

Over the period from 1965 to 1972 traffic on inland air services, which exclude services over water (i.e. to Belfast, the Channel and Scilly Isles, the Isle of Man and the Scottish islands) which are not directly competitive with rail services, rose by 25% from 2·4 million passengers in 1965 to 3·0 million in 1972. Over the same period traffic rose by 49% on the London–Edinburgh and by 22% on the London–Glasgow routes, but fell by 4% on the London–Leeds, by 17% on the London–Liverpool and by 27% on the London–Manchester routes. There appears to be a clear split between growth on the longer-distance routes, and decline on the short-distance routes.

Excluding traffic on rail services which do not parallel inland air routes, the airlines' share of the rail-plus-air market fell as relative air fares rose from 1965 up to 1968. After 1968, relative air fares fell, but the airlines' market share continued to fall (though more slowly) up to 1970, when it began again to rise through 1971 and 1972 as relative rail fares rose more rapidly. A second factor affecting air traffic was changes in rail quality on specific routes, particularly on the London to Manchester and Liverpool route following electrification. Air traffic between London and Manchester grew fairly rapidly before 1966. The reduced rail journey times as a result of electrification had a severe effect on this, and BR's share of the rail-plus-air market between these two cities rose from about 70% to about 85% between 1966 and 1971. After 1971 real relative rail fares began to rise, and as a result there is reason to believe that air traffic began to show some gains. Air travel is less important between London and Liverpool, but again rail made substantial inroads into air traffic immediately after electrification.

On the basis of the present passenger mileage by air, capture of all internal air travellers would increase BR's Inter-City revenue by some £15 million at 1972 prices. Thus complete diversion from air could represent only a small (18%) proportion of the Inter-City revenue gain which BR hopes for up to 1981. In any case, capture of all the air market is hardly likely. There is not a lot of traffic for BR to gain on the shorter routes because of the proportion of inter-line passengers, who are making an international journey by air, and are unlikely to switch to rail, partly because it is less convenient, and partly because they pay a cheap add-on fare for the domestic leg of their journey. In 1973 about 90% of all passengers on the London–Birmingham route, 60% between London and Manchester and 40% on the London–Newcastle route were inter-line passengers. Even if BR managed to capture all non inter-line passengers on the London to Manchester and Liverpool routes, this would increase its revenue by only £½ to £¾ million. On the longer and more important London to Scotland routes, air traffic densities would permit the introduction of wide-bodied jets which should reduce costs per seat mile. In addition, completion of the Heathrow tube in 1976 will reduce access time by air to London. Even introduction of the 125 mph APT on the London–Glasgow rail route in 1981 will only reduce the rail journey time to 4¼ hours, and it follows that BR will continue to face serious competition from air on its longer routes. Nevertheless, the large increase in fuel prices suffered by the airlines suggests that they will be unlikely to win any traffic back from the railways unless they adopt disastrously unprofitable pricing policies for domestic air services. British European Airways had not covered the variable, allocated and apportioned costs of its domestic services since 1968, and even before the energy crisis it is possible that the only profitable inland routes were those from London to Glasgow and Newcastle.

Express coach services are operated by the nationalised

National Bus Company (NBC) and the Scottish Transport Group (STG), and by independent operators. NBC revenue from express services was about £10 million in 1971, STG revenue about £2 million, and independents' revenue about £9 million. Although traffic on their express services has been falling in recent years, the NBC believe that, particularly in view of the completion of the main inter-city motorway network, they are now in a position to develop an expanded and much improved nationwide coach service. This will be achieved by better marketing and promotion, by better coaches, better quality stopping-places, more through services, and the abandonment of the present system of prior booking of tickets on long-distance services. Coach travellers appear to be largely leisure travellers in the lower income bracket, and so there is some scope for the coach companies to win some traffic of this type from BR. If the nationalised sector were to succeed in increasing its express revenue by 50% by 1981, and if 20% of this traffic gain was from BR, then Inter-City revenue would be reduced by the order of £2·5 million.

We have already noted that BR has discovered a negative relationship between rail traffic between towns and the average speed of road travel between these towns. In addition, BR's traffic has clearly suffered from the opening of particular motorway links, for example the M4 between London and Bristol. Nevertheless, BR believes that its traffic growth on a given route regains its previous growth within a few years of the opening of a parallel motorway. In addition, the main inter-city motorway network in Great Britain was already completed by 1973. More important, increases in fuel prices have increased the real cost of motoring. We estimate that, on the basis of figures published by *Commercial Motor*, total motoring costs at constant purchasing power rose by about 16% between the middle of 1972 and the end of 1974, while petrol costs rose by 50%. It therefore seems unnecessary to make any adjustment to our revenue forecast to allow for fiercer competition from the private car.

We are now in a position to set out our final Inter-City revenue forecast for 1981. Our initial forecast of £156 million should be revised upwards by £10 million to allow for our estimate of BR's scope for increasing real fares. While we do not believe any allowance need be made for changed competition from air or from the private car, a reduction of £2·5 million seems realistic in view of the greater competition BR should feel as a result of the vastly improved national coach network. Finally, our discussion in Chapter 7 suggests that there is some uncertainty about whether introduction of the HST on London–Sheffield, North-East–South-West, and London–West of England services can be justified. In order to make our investment and revenue figures consistent, it is therefore necessary to deduct a further £1·5 million from 1981 Inter-City revenue. This yields a final figure of £162 million, which would be earned from traffic of about 9000 million passenger miles.

LONDON AND SOUTH-EAST SERVICES

Rail is by far the most important method of transport for the journey to work in Central London. Of the daily 1·1 million peak-period arrivals in Central London in 1972, 39% travelled by British Rail, 35% by underground rail, 13% by bus, and 13% by car. BR carries a much higher proportion of longer-distance commuters; 83% of the peak-period arrivals from outside Greater London arrived by BR. Revenue from London and South-East services at 1972 purchasing power rose from £103 million in 1968 to £123 million in 1971, a 19% increase. Passenger mileage over the same period rose by 9% from 7700 million passenger miles in 1968 to 8400 million in 1971. It follows that BR was able to increase real fares per mile on these services by 10% between 1968 and 1971. BR's Interim Rail Strategy forecast that passenger mileage on London and South-East services would rise to 9900 million passenger miles by 1981, while revenue would increase to £146 million. This implies an 18% increase in traffic between 1971 and 1981, together with a 2% increase in fares. The large increase in traffic appears rather unlikely. Many London and South-East services face severe peak-hour capacity problems, and improvements in the pipeline are unlikely to increase train-miles worked in the area by more than 5% between 1973 and 1981. In these circumstances it seems unreasonable to assume that BR will be able to increase passenger mileage by nearly 20%, but traffic and revenue are likely to show some increase.

Although planning studies indicate that the number of job

opportunities in Central London is unlikely to rise, there is a long-term trend towards longer-distance commuting which will tend to increase the number of passenger miles. Increased petrol prices should divert some passengers to rail, while there will also be some diversion because of service improvements. The electrification of the Kings Cross suburban lines, due for completion in 1977–78, might increase total BR peak-hour arrivals in Central London by about 1½%. The other main electrification scheme, from St Pancras to Bedford, might be completed by 1981, though the resulting traffic generation would probably take two or three more years to mature. Service quality should also improve on the Southern Region as a result of signalling and track works which will increase capacity into Central London and reduce overcrowding and unpunctuality.

Revenue may also rise as a result of increased real fares. BR argues that the fares charged on most services in the South-East area are below the level which would be commercially justified, i.e. demand is inelastic. This seems likely in view of the importance of the rail sector and the heavy congestion on peak-hour roads in London. At present, the social costs of increasing fares exceed the benefits, however, because increased fares will encourage more people to use their cars and thereby impose congestion costs on existing road users. Hence, it is worth the Government's while to subsidise these services. However, our analysis of the social benefits of alternative methods of transport in Chapter 9 suggests that the use of urban road space would be made more efficient by the introduction of some form of road pricing or restraint scheme. Such a policy would lead to an increase in the cost of motoring and some former motorists would transfer to rail. Further, since the price of motoring would now more closely approximate to its marginal social costs, the argument for providing rail services in the South-East at prices below costs would be less strong, and some increase in rail fares could be justified.

A rough estimate must be made of 1981 revenue from London and South-East services. We assume that the service improvements planned, plus the effects of increased petrol prices, traffic restraint and the increase in average journey length caused by longer-distance commuting, will together increase passenger mileage by 10% between 1971 and 1981. Secondly, we assume that there will a 15% increase in real fares over the same period. On the (fairly arbitrary) assumption that the elasticity of demand for these services is 0·5, BR would earn £144 million from traffic of 8550 million passenger miles on its London and South-East services in 1981.

PASSENGER TRANSPORT EXECUTIVE AND OTHER SERVICES

Passenger Transport Executive (PTE) and other passenger revenue at 1972 purchasing power fell from £40 million in 1968 to £32 million in 1973. Passenger mileage fell from 3480 million passenger miles in 1968 to 2560 million in 1972. Route closures cannot explain this fall in traffic. Only 469 miles of passenger route were closed between 1968 and 1972. These lines would be very lightly used, and in any case the bulk of the closures took place between 1968 and 1970, when passenger mileage on this group of services was declining at a slower rate than it did between 1970 and 1972.

The PTE services accounted for 1400 million passenger miles and £17 million of revenue in 1971. The Interim Rail Strategy predicted a rise to 2000 million passenger miles and £26 million by 1981. These traffic increases would be due to the large-scale investment schemes, often involving new or reopened lines, being planned in many of the PTE areas. Delays in government approval for many of the schemes, together with further delays caused by shortages of materials and by industrial troubles mean that these forecasts are already over-optimistic. Moreover, in Chapter 7 we suggest the exercise of caution in further approvals. If our suggestions were accepted, passenger mileage on PTE services might increase to 1600 million passenger miles, generating £20 million of revenue, by 1981.

Traffic on the remaining passenger services generated 1300 million passenger miles and £15·5 million revenue in 1971. It seems reasonable to assume that traffic on these services will continue to decline. If traffic falls by 1% per annum, these services will generate about £14 million revenue by 1981. This assumes that no services are withdrawn.

In all, PTE and other passenger services may earn about £34 million in 1981 and carry around 2800 million passenger miles of traffic.

COMBINED PASSENGER FORECASTS

Our forecasts for different sectors of BR's passenger business can now be combined. We estimate that total passenger revenue in 1981 will be £340 million, compared with £274 million earned in 1972. Traffic is expected to rise from 18,100 million passenger miles in 1972 to 20,350 million miles in 1981. While all our forecasts must be subject to considerable uncertainty, we believe that they represent a realistic appraisal of the potential revenue gain which BR should be able to achieve from the different sectors of its passenger business.

These forecasts imply that total passenger traffic will return to a level which was last exceeded in 1961 and which is only 3% below the average level of passenger traffic in the 1950s. Of our forecast increase in revenue of £66 million, £20 million will be due to the effects of real fare increases, very roughly £5 to £10 million to recovery from the effects of industrial action in 1972, and about £40 million to growth of traffic. About 70% of the revenue gain due to traffic growth will occur on Inter-City services, and almost all the remainder on London and South-East services. This means that by 1981 Inter-City services will account for 48% of passenger revenue and London and South-East services for 42%, compared with 44% and 49% respectively in 1973.

CHAPTER 3

Parcels, Letters and Papers

In 1973, the railways earned over £70 million, at 1972 purchasing power, from carrying parcels, letters and newspapers. The revenue from the different traffics is shown in Table 3.2 on page 50. In 1972 British Rail earned nearly £10 million from carrying newspapers, £15 million from letters and £50 million from parcels. The bulk of the receipts from parcels came from the railways' own Express Parcels service (£33 million) but substantial sums were also derived from transporting parcels for the Post Office (£11 million) and National Carriers Limited (£6 million).

PUBLIC SECTOR PARCELS

British Rail's future earnings from parcels will depend, among other things, upon the overall growth or decline in parcels traffic. Apart from the three organisations which have already been mentioned—National Carriers, the Post Office and Rail Express Parcels—the other national parcels network within the public sector, British Road Services (BRS) Parcels, makes little or no direct use of the railways. Together, these organisations account for something like 85% of all parcels business, excluding own account work.

Over the past decade there has been, as Table 3.1 shows, a marked reduction in the volume of public sector parcels. In 1965, 530 million packages were carried, but by 1972 the figure had fallen to 420 million. One reason is that manufacturers have been establishing strategically placed warehouses, which they supply in bulk from their factories, and from which they distribute to the local market with their own delivery vehicles. There has also been

42

TABLE 3.1: *Volume of Parcels Traffic Handled in the Public Sector (million packages)*

	British Rail Express Parcels Service	Post Office	National Carriers	British Road Services Parcels	Total
1965	86·0	219·4	129·8	94·9	530·1
1966	81·0	206·8	111·9	91·3	491·0
1967	74·0	201·5	100·7	91·7	467·9
1968	75·0	196·5	96·9	87·5	455·9
1969	73·0	194·1	99·8	84·0	450·9
1970	72·0	193·5	100·0	77·8	443·3
1971	73·5	158·1a	100·0	77·5	409·1
1972	63·5a	186·0	95·0	74·5	419·0
1981	*62·5*		*323·5*		*386·0*

a Affected by industrial dispute.

a reduction in the number of outlets, and an increase in their size, due to the rise of the supermarket and the growth of the cash-and-carry type of distribution. As a result, the flows out of factories have tended to grow larger, and it has become increasingly possible for firms to supply their customers direct.

The advantage of a parcels service which operates over a large part of the country is that it deals with sufficient traffic for it to be able to establish a direct link, whether by road or rail, between one important town and another. However, this can only be achieved at the price of sorting the parcels at either end of their trunk haul, and of extra loading and unloading. Any parcels network therefore entails considerable expense, and will only be competitive where the volume of traffic is insufficient for firms to supply their customers direct. As this has become increasingly possible, the publicly owned parcels systems have lost business.

As their traffic has declined, their costs have tended to increase, because of the difficulty of reducing their depot staff in line with the fall in the number of parcels being handled. These workers account for a substantial part of the cost of running a parcels service. For instance, in 1969 the wages and salaries received by depot staff comprised 28% of the total cost of running BRS Parcels, and formed 47% of its aggregate wage and salary bill. Due to the combination of falling traffic and the high proportion of depot staff, productivity has been stagnant or declining. In

1972, the number of packages handled by each BRS worker was 6% lower than it had been in 1965. Falling productivity and rising wages led in turn to a swift increase in prices. Over the period there was an increase of about 95% in its revenue per parcel. Figures for productivity are not available for the other parcels concerns, but they have been operating under similar circumstances, and have also been pushing up their prices at a rapid rate. Between 1965 and 1972, the Post Office's revenue per parcel rose about 80%, and that of the Rail Express Parcels Service increased around 65%. Meanwhile the prices of all goods and services rose by just under 50%.

It is evident that there has been a vicious circle, where falling traffic has led to higher costs and a rapid rise in prices, which has, in turn, resulted in a further loss of traffic. There is no reason to believe that the reduction in the traffic handled by the national parcels networks has come to an end. It is, however, difficult to believe that it will go on falling as rapidly as it has since 1965 ($-3\cdot3\%$ per annum), especially as the rate of decline has been rather slower during the last two or three years. If a freehand trend line is drawn through the observations, it appears that by 1981 total traffic will be down to 386 million parcels, which implies that it will fall by just under 1% per annum.

RAIL EXPRESS PARCELS

Ignoring 1971 and 1972, which were badly affected by industrial disputes, the Rail Express Parcels Service has had a remarkably stable share of all public sector traffic. Both in 1965 and in 1970 it carried 16·2% of the total. If it maintains its share of the market it will, on the assumption that the public sector handles 386 million parcels, carry just over 60 million in 1981. This happens to be almost exactly the same number as it handled during 1972, which was a poor year for the Rail Express Parcels Service because of the railways' labour troubles.

Although our estimate is based on a number of questionable assumptions, it seems unlikely that the number will be any higher. BR's most important customers are the mail-order houses, who between them account for about a third of its revenue. The largest of these firms—Great Universal Stores—has during the past few years switched a considerable part of its traffic to its own distribution vehicles. Littlewoods, the second largest concern, is planning to use the railways less, and to deliver more by road. Although it intends to go on using Rail Express Parcels to a considerable extent, it wants to become less dependent on BR. It is concerned about the large increase in the rates charged by the public-sector carriers, it is unhappy because of the disruption which the railways' industrial disputes have caused, and it has found that rail delivery times can be improved upon. Where it uses its own vehicles, half of all parcels are delivered within a day, whereas only about a fifth of Rail Express parcels arrive so quickly. One reason is that the average length of the rail haul is so much longer, because mail-order depots are concentrated in northern industrial areas. This is a general feature of the mail-order industry. It is to be expected that when old depots, many of which are old textile mills, are replaced they will be spread more widely throughout the country, and the average haul will drop. If so, BR will gradually lose business.

It will be assumed that, at 1972 purchasing power, Rail Express will produce £30 million of revenue in 1981, which was about what it earned during 1972 and 1973. This guesstimate assumes that the volume of traffic and the level of charges will be more or less maintained at the 1972 level.

POST OFFICE AND NCL PARCELS

As we have seen, the railways not only provide their own parcels service, but also obtain a large amount of revenue from carrying parcels for the Post Office and National Carriers Limited (NCL). The next few years will almost certainly see a large fall. The general decline in the volume of public-sector parcels traffic is likely to lead to some reduction in the amount of business available for BR. But the main reason for anticipating that the Post Office and NCL will use the railways less is that they are both in the process of rationalisation, and are reshaping their trunk haulage systems.

At present about 90% of Post Office parcels travel by rail for some part of their journey, and the figure for NCL appears to be around 70%. Under the existing arrangements the Post Office feeds parcels from its 1200 outward sorting offices onto the railway network. It incurs a large loss on parcels and is starting, as part of its drive to cut costs, to mechanise sorting. Mechanisation is only worthwhile where there is a large throughput and traffic is therefore being concentrated at 27 dispatch offices. The movement of parcels within the areas they serve will be undertaken almost exclusively by road. In most districts neither the distances nor the flows of traffic will be large enough to make rail economic because of the extra loading and unloading which is usually involved.

Apart from three or four dispatch offices which have been designed for rail use, the Post Office considers that it will be both cheaper and faster by road where parcels are being hauled less than about 120 miles. As a result, British Rail will be out of the running for much of the traffic between one area and another, for even here many of the hauls will be less than 120 miles. Moreover the Post Office's investigations suggest that, where they are available, Freightliners provide the best service for long-distance traffic. In future, the direct use of rail by the parcel post will be restricted to those long-distance routes where there is no Freightliner service, and to those sorting depots which are tied to the railway system. As a result, it seems likely that, by 1981, British Rail's direct revenue from this source will be down to about £3½ million per annum.

National Carriers has already made substantial changes in its trunk haulage system which have led to a reduction in the use of rail. What, in the main, NCL pays for is the number of loaded-wagon movements which the railways make on its behalf. In 1968 these totalled about 1·1 million, but by 1972 they had been cut to something over 300,000. This was partly due to NCL's loss of traffic, and to the introduction of road trunking, though the principal reason was that National Carriers tightened up its efficiency, and reduced the number of depots from 180 in 1969 to 115 in 1973 by cutting out those which handled very little traffic. As a result, there has been a sharp increase in the average load per wagon. In an attempt to preserve its revenue, British Rail pushed up its real charge per loaded-wagon movement by over 40% between 1968 and 1972. It would be surprising if NCL did not respond to this enormous increase by reducing its dependence on the railways, and switching far more of its trunk haulage to road. This, indeed, is what its management appears to have in mind, especially as they are somewhat dissatisfied with the quality of service which the railways provide. Moreover, there is probably some further scope for improving efficiency and so cutting the number of wagon movements, although the big gains in this direction have already been made. It would not, therefore, be surprising if BR's revenue from National Carriers were to fall from £4½ million in 1973 to, say, £1½ million in 1981.

LETTERS

Having considered the railways' revenue from carrying parcels for themselves and for other organisations, we must next try to discover how much they are likely to earn from transporting letters and newspapers. During 1973–74 the number of letters posted was the same as it had been ten years previously. The stagnation in the volume of correspondence is hardly surprising in view of the massive increase in charges. Between 1963–64 and 1973–74 there was a rise of about 170% in the price of the inland letter post compared with a rise of only about 80% in the cost of all goods and services. The rise in tariffs was, in turn, largely explained by the fact that productivity (for the letter and parcels services together) was no higher at the end of the period than it had been at the beginning.

Although changes in the volume of correspondence have been partly the result of productivity and price movements, they have also been partly the cause. The letter service has two characteristics which, unless the volume of mail is growing, make it very difficult for the Post Office to raise productivity and hold prices relatively stable. First, the proportion of fixed costs is very high. Of the total staff hours which are devoted to letter and parcel post only some 35% relate to operations, such as sorting, where there is a fairly direct relationship between staff time and the volume of traffic. It takes a postman virtually the same time to deliver one item to a house as it does to deliver several, and a drop in the proportion of houses he visits does not lead to a corresponding reduction in the distance he walks. In the second place, there is relatively little scope for any further mechanisation of collection, delivery and counter service. Mail is already collected by vans, and postmen on delivery work already have as much transport as can be economically justified. Moreover, because they are costly to maintain and fill, stamp machines tend to be uneconomic. It is only in sorting that there is any great opportunity for mechanisation.

Machines have now been developed which identify those letters that can be handled by other machines; which sort letters into first and second class and arrange them so that their addresses are visible; and which permit operators to type the postal code onto the envelope in the form of chemical dots. These are identified by an automatic sorting machine, which puts each letter into the correct pigeon-hole ready for dispatch to the appropriate sorting office at the other end of its journey. When it is complete, the mechanisation of letter and parcel sorting will eliminate some 14,000 jobs. As some 150,000 workers are engaged on letter and parcel work, this is a relatively small saving. Moreover, it will largely be offset by higher capital charges, and not all the benefits will have been secured by 1981, because of the Post Office's delay in deciding how the sorting-office system for letters should be reshaped and because of the difficulties which, partly in consequence, it has had with the Union of Post Office Workers.

The Post Office should also be able to make some savings in manpower by pressing forward with the various productivity improvement schemes which it has in hand. The gain in efficiency that it should be possible to achieve is by no means negligible, but it will be insufficient to cover the increase in real wages. This, together with the existing deficit, means that letter tariffs are likely to go on increasing at a rapid rate, which will have an adverse effect on the volume of correspondence and on productivity. It therefore seems possible that a vicious circle will develop, and there will be fewer letters for BR to handle.

The mechanisation of letter sorting will also lead to a reduction in the use of rail. The Post Office is planning to reduce the number of sorting offices from 1600 to 80, because of the large amount of correspondence which each sorting installation can handle. Because of the relatively small size of the new concentration areas, it will not be worth using rail to collect or deliver mail within them. Moreover, many of the new sorting offices will be so near each other that the inter-area transfer of letters will inevitably take place by road. Only about a third of the mail which the railways carry is hauled more than a hundred miles and, because rail conveyance almost always involves extra handling, it would be very surprising if the cost by road were not already lower for much of this traffic. It is also hard to believe that, where distances are relatively short, rail has any advantages in terms of speed. Certainly the Post Office has long been dissatisfied with the quality of service which the railways provide. Where distances are long the Post Office will continue to depend on the railways, although some traffic may be transferred to Freightliners where they happen to provide a convenient service.

The Post Office had hoped to complete the mechanisation of sorting by 1981, but this now seems unlikely. Nevertheless, a significant amount of progress should have been made by then, and it will be assumed that this, together with some decline in the overall volume of correspondence, will lead to a reduction in BR's revenue from £15 million in 1972 to £10 million in 1981.

PAPERS

It also appears likely that there is going to be a considerable reduction in the railways' earnings from carrying newspapers. At present the *Express*, the *Mirror*, the *Mail*, and the *Telegraph* print in both London and Manchester. They supply that part of the country which lies south of Stoke, Derby and Scunthorpe by rail from London, and the region to the north by rail from Manchester. The other nationals distribute papers from London to the whole of England by rail, but supply Scotland by air. The use of road is confined to local distribution from the railhead, and to distribution within London and Manchester.

Under the contract which lasted up to the end of the 1974, the newspapers were committed to use rail. Now that the publishers are free to change their system of distribution, it is likely that considerable alterations will be made, and that by 1981 there will have been a large-scale switch to road transport. It is no longer true that rail provides a better and more reliable service than

road. During the railways' industrial troubles at the beginning of
1973, when there was a temporary switch to road distribution,
the newspapers did not find it necessary to print any earlier, and
the Mirror Group found that the alternative arrangements were
in general more efficient than rail. While the standard of service
by road has improved, the standard by rail has deteriorated, or at
least this was the conclusion of the consultants engaged by the
Newspaper Publishers Association.

There is therefore almost bound to be a significant reduction in
the railways' traffic and revenue. Moreover, it is possible that by
1981 the newspaper industry will have started to decentralise its
printing operations, and, if this happens, newspapers will be distributed by road from the local centres and BR will lose further
business. In 1972 BR earned £9 million by carrying newspapers,
but it would be unwise to assume that by 1981 it will receive more
than £5 million.

TABLE 3.2: *British Rail's Revenue from Parcels, Letters and
Papers (£ million, 1972 purchasing power)*

	1968	1972	1973	*1981*
British Rail Express Parcels Service	35·3	32·6	32·0	*30·0*
Post Office parcels	13·1	11·3	. .	*3·5*
National Carriers	11·9	5·8	4·4	*1·5*
Total parcels revenue	60·3	49·7	. .	*35·0*
Letters	14·7	15·0	. .	*10·0*
Newspapers	8·8	9·2	. .	*5·0*
Total revenue	83·8	73·9	71·2	*50·0*

CONCLUSIONS

This completes our survey of the railways' prospective revenue
from parcels, letters and papers. As can be seen from Table 3.2
BR's revenue has been falling and is likely to go on falling. In
1963 the railways earned something like £105 million, at 1972
purchasing power, but by 1968 the figure was around £84 million,
and it was down to £71 million in 1973. This decline was **largely,**

though not exclusively, due to the steady erosion of receipts from the wagon load parcels service that is now in the hands of National Carriers. Revenue from this source is likely to continue to fall, but as it is now quite small this is not the main reason why BR's earnings from parcels, letters and papers are likely to decline. The principal explanation is the reduction in revenue from the Post Office for carrying parcels as a result of the mechanisation of sorting, and the consequent alteration of its transport requirements. It seems likely that this will deprive BR of about £8 million of revenue over the period 1972–81. There will also probably be a decline in receipts from letters and news-papers. The loss in revenue from letters has been put at £5 million, while the reduction in newspaper traffic could be around £4 million, though both of these figures involve a considerable amount of guesswork. The only type of business where it seems probable that receipts will be more or less maintained is BR's own parcels service, Rail Express. However, it is unlikely that there will be any growth in traffic, although this is what BR seems to be hoping for.

CHAPTER 4

Iron and Steel

In 1973 British Rail earned £36 million, at 1972 purchasing power, from carrying iron and steel products and the raw materials which the industry uses. To discover what the figure is likely to be in 1981 it is necessary to estimate how much steel will be produced and what the pattern of production will be.

STEEL SUPPLY AND DEMAND

Examination of the period since 1955 shows that there is a relatively simple relationship between the growth of industrial production and the consumption of finished steel. In any five-year period, for the initial 12% by which industrial production grew, steel usage increased by 6%, i.e. by a factor of 0·5. For growth between 12% and 16% the factor rose to 1·0, and for growth between 16% and 20% it increased to 1·5.

There are two reasons for the gearing effect of higher production on steel consumption. Over time the development of stronger steels, better designs and new materials are reducing the weight of steel required for any given purpose. Thus if the economy stood still there would be a reduction in the tonnage consumed, and some growth is required merely to offset this tendency. Second, a fast rate of growth is likely to be accompanied by a high level of capital expenditure and investment goods are exceptionally steel-intensive.

During the past decade the national output, as represented by the gross domestic product (GDP) at constant prices, has been increasing at a trend rate of 2·75% per annum. However, the energy crisis and our current economic difficulties make it unlikely that growth will be as fast as this between 1973 and 1981. Unless those who make short-term economic predictions are hopelessly wrong the rate of expansion from about 1977 would have to be unbelievably rapid to produce such a high average figure. On the other hand, because output per worker tends to grow each year, some rate of advance is necessary to prevent unemployment increasing to levels which are, in the long term, politically unacceptable. Over the past decade the underlying growth in productivity, as represented by GDP per worker, appears to have been 2·9% per annum. The discrepancy between the increase in productivity and production is explained by the fact that there has been a small reduction in the size of the labour force. Estimates by the Department of Employment suggest that between 1973 and 1981 the work force will rise by 0·4% a year.[1] Married women would, however, be entirely responsible for this increase and if employment prospects are poor they might give up seeking jobs or never begin looking. Moreover it seems likely that output per worker will increase more slowly, partly because of the well-known relationship between the growth of production and productivity, and partly because of the low level of investment. However, past experience makes it seem unlikely that the under-lying rate of productivity growth will drop much below 2·5% per annum. It will therefore be assumed that the GDP will increase at this speed between the last nine months of 1974 and 1981 which, as the national income fell during 1974, implies a growth rate of only 2·25% over the period 1973–81. Nevertheless it is possible that unemployment will soar and even that there will be an economic collapse. Although it is intended as a pre-diction, a growth rate of 2·5% would then become a target at which the Government should aim in order to counteract high unemployment.

Granted this rate of increase GDP will increase by something under 20% between 1973 and 1981. Industrial production tends to outpace GDP when the latter is rising fast but to lag behind if the rate of growth is very slow. Consequently industrial produc-tion is expected to increase by only 18·7% over the period 1973–81. If the past relationship between production and the use of steel continues to hold good, but there is some reduction in the amount of crude steel per ton of finished steel because of continuous casting, steel consumption will rise from 22½ million

ingot tons during 1971–73 (and nearly 24 million during 1973) to about 25 million in 1981. This represents a rise of 10·7% between 1971–73 and 1981 (for a 25% rise in industrial production), and compares with an increase of 16% between 1961–63 and 1970–72, a previous nine-year period during which industrial production grew very slowly (by 29·5%).

The next step in estimating the steel industry's sales is to fix on the amount by which exports will exceed imports, for its total sales are, of course, equivalent to the home market plus net exports. Between 1960 and 1972, as can be seen from Table 4.1, net exports fluctuated between 2 million and 4 million ingot tons but fell away in 1973, and became negative during 1974 because the industry was unable to satisfy demand. Although the British Steel Corporation (BSC) is hoping to sell large amounts of steel abroad and should have plenty of capacity by 1981, it seems unlikely that net exports will recover to more than about 3 million tons. Now that tariffs are being eliminated as a result of Common Market entry, the continental steel-makers will be able to ship steel to us relatively cheaply from coastal works such as Dunkirk. But most of their principal consuming areas are inland, and transporting steel to *them* will involve BSC in considerable expense. The Corporation's past performance does not suggest that it will manage to overcome its competitive disadvantage. The British steel industry is woefully inefficient by international standards: BSC's labour productivity, as measured by crude steel per worker, only increased by 9% over the period 1968–73, and its unit fuel consumption was only reduced by 7%. Due to its failure to get its new plant working properly, and persistent labour disputes, the Corporation produced less steel during 1973, when demand exceeded supply, than its private predecessors had made in 1965. Nor does it appear from the Corporation's plans that there is likely to be any spectacular improvement in efficiency.

It will therefore be assumed that in 1981 the demand for British steel will total 28 million ingot tons, of which the home market will constitute 25 million and net exports 3 million. It is now necessary to discover what the pattern of production is likely to be, since the independent producers make very little use of BR. In 1973 they had an output of around 3 million tons of crude steel, including Brymbo which was sold by BSC during the course of the year. About 2 million tons of extra capacity has come into operation since then or is on the point of being commissioned. This suggests that the private sector will be able to produce at least 5 million tons by 1981. However it still has a certain amount of obsolete capacity, and produced 1¼ million tons of open-hearth steel during 1973. The industry is likely to experience considerable difficulties during the next few years and competition between BSC and the private producers is likely to intensify. It therefore seems likely that some old plant will be closed and not replaced. However it is difficult to believe that the private sector will be producing less than 4½ million tons by 1981.

With the demand for steel at 28 million ingot tons and the private sector producing 4½ million tons, the Steel Corporation will have an output of 23½ million tons in 1981. This is 1 million tons less than it produced in 1970 even if Brymbo is excluded, and is only slightly more than it made during 1973. Moreover it is far less than the Corporation hopes to produce. It began in February 1971 by saying that it wanted to produce 41½ million ingot tons in 1980.[2] This was rightly vetoed by a sceptical Government, but BSC received permission in February 1973 to press ahead with a ten-year expansion programme, costing £3000 million, that would enable it to produce up to 36½ million tons of steel during the first half of the 1980s; and the Corporation was originally hoping that this would be reached soon after 1980.[3] However neither of the major projects at Port Talbot and Redcar have been started. The Corporation let a year slip by and then, when Labour came to power, the Government started a review of BSC's plans for closure and rationalisation. This prevented the Corporation from going ahead with its expansion scheme at Port Talbot, which was the project that it had hoped to launch first, as this was intimately bound up with the cessation of crude steel production at Shotton. The Government has now decided that this will not take place before the end of the decade and it seems very doubtful whether, in view of the industry's deteriorating prospects, the Port Talbot or Redcar schemes will have been completed, or even started, by 1981.

However there is little doubt that BSC will by 1981 have sufficient capacity to produce well over 23½ million tons of crude steel. By then it will be able to obtain 18½ million tons of output from its five key works, namely Port Talbot, Llanwern, Appleby Frodingham, Lackenby and Ravenscraig. In addition up to 4¼ million tons of basic oxygen capacity is likely to be available at three of the Corporation's smaller works, Consett, Corby and Normanby Park. Shotton, which has a present capacity of approaching 1½ million tons, is also likely to continue producing steel unless lack of demand makes closure inevitable. But it seems unlikely that the steel-making facilities will have been modernised and expanded by 1981, if only because of the lengthy construction periods in steel and the time the Corporation takes to plan projects. In addition the Corporation should have over 5 million tons of electric arc capacity in 1981, provided that the Cleveland plant remains open. By 1981 BSC should therefore be able to produce about 30 million tons, or more if allowance is made for the fact that it should be possible to obtain more output than the Corporation's figures suggest.

There is therefore a gap of over 6 million ingot tons between the amount of steel that the Corporation is likely to be able to produce and the 23½ million tons which it seems likely that it will be able to sell at a profit. Perhaps the Corporation may make additional exports on which it does no more than cover its short-run marginal costs, or perhaps some of the smaller works will have to be shut. However the most likely outcome is that the Corporation will have the plant to produce 30 million tons but that it will not be fully utilised due to lack of demand, operating difficulties and labour disputes. This is certainly what past experience would suggest. In 1973, when the Corporation had a ready market, it only managed to produce 23½ million tons, although it had 26 million tons of capacity.

RAIL REQUIREMENTS

It is now possible, having investigated the industry's future shape and size, to see what its requirements for rail transport may be. It can be seen from Table 4.2 that during 1973 BR carried 35 million tons of materials and products. This was less than in 1970, when the figure had been nearly 40 million tons, and much lower than in 1964, or the early 1950s, when rail carryings had been around 45 million tons. The reduction in carryings of iron ore from 20 million tons in 1964 to 15 million tons in 1973 was mainly

TABLE 4.2: *Composition of British Rail's Iron and Steel Traffic (million tons)*

	average 1952–54	1964	1970	1973	1981
Raw materials:					
Iron ore	16·0	19·8	17·2	14·9	*14·5*
Limestone and lime	1·9a	3·3	2·5	1·9	*1·25*
Scrap	6·6	6·0	4·9	3·9	*1·75*
	24·5	29·1	24·6	20·7	*17·5*
Products:					
Crude, semi-finished and finished steel; iron castings	14·9	14·6	13·6	12·3	*11·0*
Pig iron	4·0	2·2	1·5	1·5	*1·25*
	18·9	16·8	15·1	13·8	*12·25*
Total raw materials and products	43·4	45·9	39·5b	34·9b	*30·0*
Revenue (£ million, 1972 purchasing power)	..	61·6	45·6	35·8	*28·5*
Revenue per ton (£, 1972 purchasing power)	..	1·34	1·15	1·02	*0·95*

a 1951

b British Railways Board *Annual Report* figure, which differs slightly from the sum of the separate commodities.

due to the switch from home to imported ore. Because this has a high ferrous content, whereas home ore is lean, there is less bulk for British Rail to carry. Moreover what home ore plants do take—and Scunthorpe and Corby will go on using a large amount—mainly arrives by private line, because the more distant and less economic workings that BR used to serve have been closed. The change from home to foreign ore is now more or less complete, and it seems unlikely that there will be any alteration in the balance between inland and coastal works. Had production been concentrated at big coastal works, as the Corporation originally intended, BR's traffic would have declined still further due to the partial or total closure of Shotton, Corby and Consett. It seems clear that all of these works will now be retained; and, although the movement of iron ore into Ebbw Vale will come to an end, this will be offset by the greater tonnage that will be received at those works which are being expanded. As a result BR is likely to carry about the same quantity of ore in 1981 as it did in 1973, viz. 14½ million tons.

Limestone is another important material which is used in the blast furnace for the production of iron. British Rail's deliveries of limestone fell from 3·3 million tons in 1964 to 1·9 million in 1973 and its share of the market slumped from 59% to 36%. It has been suggested that the big steelworks in which production is being concentrated are likely to be served by larger and more distant quarries which, unlike many of the small quarries of today, will be rail-connected. However there is no sign that the reduction in BR's share of deliveries is coming to an end and a further fall is to be expected. In the middle of 1974 the transport charge for the limestone that was received by rail was about 40% greater than the cost by road. It has therefore been assumed that by 1981 BR will only be carrying 1¼ million tons of limestone to steelworks, or about 25% of total deliveries.

The steel industry does not use blast furnaces to produce all the iron which it needs because it uses scrap instead. Part of this scrap arises in the works, but a large amount is also purchased. In 1964 BR carried 6 million tons of scrap but by 1973 the figure had declined to just under 4 million tons, because the railways' share of deliveries fell from 59% to 37%. In 1981 purchases are likely to be much the same as in 1973, but there will almost certainly have been a further sharp reduction in BR's traffic. The mini-mills that are being constructed in the private sector are largely dependent on local supplies of scrap which will arrive by road. What is perhaps even more important is that most scrap is at present carried as a back load in coal wagons. During the next few years there will be a great reduction in their number and a considerable switch to circuit working, which means that if scrap is to be carried wagons will, for the most part, have to be set aside for this purpose. So long as scrap continues to move in wagonload quantities, as 90% of it did in the early 1970s, the cost would be prohibitive. BR is trying to reorganise the movement of scrap in order to increase the proportion of trainload working. Although there is probably some scope for this, and some of BSC's works are only equipped to receive scrap by rail, it would be unwise to assume that the railways will be carrying more than 1¾ million tons of scrap in 1981.

Turning now to the products of the iron and steel industry, the railways carried nearly 12½ million tons of iron castings, and finished and semi-finished steel, during 1973. In 1964 the figure was 14½ million and if the tonnage goes on falling by the same amount, i.e. by about 250,000 tons per annum, it will be down to about 10·3 million by 1981; and if rail traffic declines at the rate that it did between 1970 and 1973 it will be even lower. Henceforth British Rail will receive no benefit, as it presumably has in the past, from the general growth of output. For if our estimates are right the growth in sales will be more or less confined to the private sector, which makes very little use of BR for the distribution of its products. On the other hand the railways will gain some extra traffic from BSC because of the way in which it is rationalising its activities, although the amount will be very much smaller than it would have been if the Corporation's original plans had been carried out. What is happening is that a number of plants, of which the most important are Ebbw Vale and West Hartlepool, are being or have already been restricted to finishing operations. By 1981 BR should be supplying them with about 2 million tons of semi-finished steel over and above the amount that it was already supplying on a planned basis during 1973. As a result of the severe operating difficulties which it encountered, large unplanned movements took place in 1973. If allowance is made for this abnormal traffic it appears that BR will only receive about 1½ million tons of additional work.

At one time it seemed possible that British Rail would carry more finished steel because of the enormous tonnage that would be produced on South Teesside, and at Port Talbot and Scunthorpe, and the need to dispatch steel in large quantities on a disciplined basis if chaos was to be avoided. However a high proportion of the output from these works was accounted for by bulk flows of semi-finished products to those plants which would no longer make their own steel; and it is now clear that the output of the principal steel-making centres will be considerably less than was originally planned. No doubt there will be some increase in trainload working, but a high proportion of the steel that the railways carry will continue to be wagonload traffic which is vulnerable to road competition. At present trainload working appears to account for only 16% of the finished and semi-finished steel that the Corporation moves by rail from one works to another and dispatches to customers. A further 28% of the tonnage is steel that is transferred in wagonloads between the Corporation's plants. BR is unlikely to lose this work, partly because quality of service is relatively unimportant, and partly because in mid 1974 the cost per ton mile for this type of traffic appeared to be about 50% greater by road than by rail.

However the remaining traffic, and it represents well over half the total, is vulnerable to competition from road haulage. It is mostly finished steel, where the lorry has the advantage that there is less damage, and where it is important if BSC is not to lose its customers that it should provide a prompt and reliable service. The cost per ton mile was 15–20% higher by road than by rail but an analysis of railway rates during 1970 showed that BR includes a heavy fixed charge per ton in order, presumably, to cover its terminal operations and the provision of wagons. This meant that the rate per ton mile fell sharply as the length of haul increased, and rail only became cheaper than road over about 120 miles. Yet the average haul for the steel which the Corporation dispatches to its customers by rail is only slightly longer, at 130 miles, and it seems likely that BR will lose a considerable part of its short-haul traffic during the next few years. The railways, as the marginal carrier, tend to retain their wagonload freight when trade is buoyant but to forfeit it permanently when conditions are adverse and spare capacity develops in road haulage.

It therefore seems likely that, despite the extra traffic that BR will obtain as a result of the Steel Corporation's programme of rationalisation, its carryings of finished and semi-finished steel will go on declining at a fairly rapid rate, although less fast than they have during recent years. It will therefore be assumed that by 1981 the rail tonnage will have fallen to 11 million tons; or, say, 12¼ million tons including pig iron. This compares with the 13¾ million tons of iron and steel products that BR carried in 1973.

THE OVERALL PICTURE

It can be seen from Table 4.2, in which the various forecasts for iron and steel traffic have been brought together, that by 1981

BR may be carrying around 30 million tons of materials and products, which is 5 million tons less than in 1973. In 1972 the average revenue per ton was £1·09 but it seems likely that, granting existing pricing policies and ignoring inflation, this figure will by 1981 have fallen to around £0·95. There are three reasons for expecting a decline. First, by 1981 iron ore, which is now largely carried in BR wagons, will be transported in wagons that belong to the Steel Corporation. This will involve BSC in considerable expense and, as a quid pro quo, the rate per ton for iron ore is likely to be reduced. Second, there is almost bound to be a sharp decline in wagonload traffic, but in 1974 the rate for finished and semi-finished iron and steel in wagonloads was nearly 40% higher than for trainload traffic. Third, traffic between steelworks is likely to comprise a larger proportion of carryings of finished and semi-finished steel, but in 1974 the revenue per ton was 85% higher for traffic to customers than for inter-works transfers.

If during 1981 British Rail carries 30 million tons of iron and steel at a rate of £0·95 per ton, it will earn £28½ million (at 1972 purchasing power). As it received nearly £36 million during 1973 this represents a considerable decline but is in line with the historic reduction in real receipts. In 1964 revenue from iron and steel had been £61½ million and in 1970 £45½ million.

CHAPTER 5

Coal and Oil

In 1973 about half the railways' freight revenue came from coal and oil, which together produced over £90 million (at 1972 purchasing power). Of this £80 million was accounted for by the 100 million tons of coal that was carried.

THE DEMAND FOR COAL

How much traffic British Rail will obtain during 1981 will largely depend on the tonnage of coal that is consumed. In 1973, as Table 5.1 shows, 134 million tons were used at home or shipped abroad, of which over 75 million tons (or 55%) was burnt at power stations.

As late as the summer of 1974 the Electricity Council was forecasting that electricity consumption, as measured by the amount available, would increase by just under 5% per annum between 1972–73 and 1981–82, which was about the rate at which it had increased over the previous decade. It seems extremely unlikely that the rise will be anything like as large, in view of the large increase in electricity prices and the slow rate of economic growth. The Electricity Council seems to have been assuming that the gross domestic product (GDP) would increase by almost 3% per annum but, as we have seen, a rise of only 2½% appears more likely. If so, the demand for electricity is, after making some allowance for special fuel-saving measures, only likely to increase by around 3½% a year between 1974 and 1981, or by a total of 27% between 1973 and 1981. If demand does increase at this rate it appears, from the evidence of the Central Electricity Generating Board to the Select Committee on Science and Tech-

TABLE 5.1: *UK Coal Supply and Demand (million tons)*

	Consumption			Demand	Supply
	1963	*1968*	*1973*	*1981*	*1981*
Power stations	67·5	73·2	75·6	*83*	*83*
BSC coke ovens		16·7	14·1	*13*	*12*
	23·7				
Other coke ovens		8·2	7·4	*6*	
Domestic	33·1	23·2	14·3	*8*	
Industry and other	69·7	43·2	19·9	*12*	*25*
Total home consumption, etc	194·0	164·5	131·3	*122*	
Exports	7·5	2·7	2·7	*5*	
Total consumption, etc.	201·5	167·2	134·0	*127*	*120*

nology, that the Board will in 1981 use about 120 million tons of primary fuel in terms of coal equivalent. Of this nuclear and gas-burning plant will account for 20 million tons or more, and the rest will be divided between coal and oil.

The Central Electricity Generating Board (CEGB) has said that a coal burn of up to 95 million tons would be practicable in the early 1980s. But it seems most improbable that it will want to use as much coal as this even if coal were to retain its present price advantage over oil. The delivered cost of power-station coal now ranges from 6·5p to 7·5p per therm and averages 6·7p. The price of oil, on the other hand, averages about 8·5p per therm, but the gap is slightly less wide than this suggests because coal is, for instance, more expensive to handle. Moreover it must be remembered that it will be worth using an oil-fired station if its thermal efficiency exceeds that of the best available coal-burning station by a greater percentage than the price of oil exceeds the price of coal. As most of the CEGB's oil-fired stations are modern and have a relatively high thermal efficiency this is a point of some importance.

Precisely how much coal the CEGB will want to consume in 1981 will depend on what happens to relative fuel prices. The most that can be prophesied with any confidence is that there is likely to be a considerable increase in the price of coal. The National Coal Board points out that output per man-shift (oms) increased by about 4% per annum in the ten years to 1972–73, and considers that forward increases of this order are perfectly feasible.[1] However most of this rise in productivity took place in the first half of the period and during the five years from 1968 to 1973 oms only rose by 1·5% a year. The spectacular rise in productivity during the period prior to 1968 was achieved only because numerous schemes for the modernisation and recon-struction of collieries came to fruition; because the National Coal Board (NCB) was rapidly closing down collieries at which oms was low; and because of the large-scale introduction of power loading and self-advancing pit props.

This has now been pushed to the limit and there is no sign that any corresponding technical advance will take place before 1981. It is true that the utilisation of the Coal Board's existing cutter-loaders is still very low and that faster and more powerful equipment is being introduced. However it would probably be wrong to expect that enormous gains will be made, as the Coal Board has been trying for years to increase the working time of its machinery. The root of the problem seems to be a lack of motivation on the part of the mining labour force which is unlikely to be overcome without the introduction of an effective incentive payment system.[2] This, if it is ever introduced, would cost a large amount of money. It would therefore be unrealistic to expect more than a modest increase in productivity by 1981 in the absence of a large increase in the industry's wage bill.

As a result there is likely to be a significant rise in staff expenditure per ton. As staff expenditure accounts for a very high proportion of the NCB's costs, and capital charges are likely to increase due to higher investment, it is almost certain that the price of coal will go on rising. It therefore seems likely that, other things being equal, the remaining price advantage which coal enjoys will have been more or less eliminated by 1981. Coal from the central fields may still be somewhat cheaper than oil but that from the peripheral coal fields is likely to be just as expensive. Any further increase in the relative pay of mineworkers is there-fore likely to lead to the closure of marginal mines in Wales, Lancashire and Scotland. It therefore seems unlikely that there will be any further large increase, especially as miners must, as a result of their latest award, have regained the relative wage lead that they enjoyed in the mid 1950s before the coal surplus developed. However it is possible that there will be a further rise in the cost of oil and that coal's price advantage will be restored, although if this happened the gap might be closed again as a result of big wage claims and a large increase in miners' earnings.

What will happen to the price of oil is almost impossible to tell. It is conceivable that, before many years are out, there will be a further large increase because demand is tending to outrun supply and the principal exporting nations wish to conserve their reserves. On the other hand it can be argued that there is likely to be a reduction because of the large surplus which will develop, partly due to the world recession caused by the previous rise, and partly due to greater economy in the use of oil. There is however no doubt that the conservationist motive is a strong one and that the largest exporters are already earning sufficient or more than sufficient revenue for the purpose of economic development. This makes it seem unlikely that, even though supply may tend to outrun demand during the next few years, price-cutting will develop and the Organisation of Petroleum Exporting Countries (OPEC) will break up. The weak spot of capitalist cartels has always been the difficulty of agreeing on the size and shape of the cut in production necessary if prices are to be maintained. The strength of OPEC is that so many of its members would be willing if need be to reduce their output.

However a further large rise in the price of crude oil might well lead to stresses and strains with which even OPEC would find it difficult to cope. Its members would fear that another major increase would lead to a world depression which, among its other adverse consequences, would reduce the earning power, and possibly even lead to the confiscation, of the enormous investments that are now being made. Moreover the present petroleum-exporting countries would not wish to give too great a stimulus to the development of alternative sources of supply and rival forms of fuel.

What may happen is that during the next two or three years the price of oil will fail to keep pace with the general inflation, partly because this will be extremely rapid, and partly because the demand for petroleum products will be exceptionally depressed. Subsequently there is likely to be some increase in the real cost of crude as the OPEC countries try to make up the ground that they have lost; and it is therefore assumed here, although this is no more than a hunch, that in 1981 the real price of oil will be about the same as it was at the beginning of 1974. If it is, and if the price of coal rises in the way that has been predicted, coal may have lost nearly all its current cost advantage by 1981. In this case it appears from the CEGB's estimates of its coal and oil burn in different price situations that it may by 1981 require 74 million tons of coal and 26 million tons of oil (in terms of coal equivalent). The other electricity authorities used 8½ million tons of coal in 1973 and if they need 9 million in 1981 the electricity industry's demand will total 83 million tons, as against 75½ million in 1973.

Coke ovens are the second largest market for coal. During 1973 they absorbed 21½ million tons, of which 14 million was used in the British Steel Corporation's ovens. It has already been estimated that by 1981 the Corporation will be producing 23½ million tons of crude steel, which is only slightly more than it produced in 1973. Before the jump in oil prices the Corporation believed that the quantity of coal used per ton of steel would decline from the present level of 0·6 tons to around 0·5 tons in 1981, because of the scrapping of old and inefficient blast furnaces and the construction of new furnaces with low coke rates. However after the rise in oil prices BSC estimated that during the early 1980s it would still require around 0·6 tons of coal per ton of steel. Because of the narrowing of the differential between the two fuels, and the prospect that coal will lose its remaining price advantage by 1981, it now seems likely that the Corporation will use about 0·55 tons of coal per ton of steel. If so, BSC will have a demand for about 13 million tons. There has been a slow decline in the amount of coal used at other coke ovens and some further reduction is to be expected because domestic and industrial coke is relatively highly priced in comparison with competing fuels. Nevertheless it seems likely that, in all, coke ovens will need as much as 19 million tons of coal in 1981.

The NCB anticipates a considerable decline in domestic coal consumption. In 1968 the domestic market took 23 million tons, but by 1973 consumption had fallen to 14 million, and the Coal Board expects that in 1985 the figure will be down to around 8 million tons. If anything this is probably on the high side. Anthracite and dry steam coal, which are smokeless, only account for 1¾ million tons of domestic sales and there will inevitably be a large reduction in sales of bituminous coal as smokeless zones are extended. By 1981 the area covered by smoke control is likely to have more than doubled and it will be assumed that domestic consumption will already have fallen to 8 million tons by then.

During 1973, 20 million tons of coal was consumed in smokeless fuel plants and by the general industrial and service sector. Although the tonnage used by patent fuel plants has been slowly increasing there has in general been a rapid decline in consumption, which totalled 43 million tons as recently as 1968. Some further reduction is to be expected because chemicals and other industries are switching over to natural gas and because coal is now viewed as an unreliable fuel. However the decline is unlikely to be as precipitate as it has been in the past because there is a firm demand from smokeless fuel plants and from the cement industry. The former consume about 4½ million tons a year while the cement manufacturers use around 3 million. The NCB believes that demand will come to something like 12 million tons in 1985, and this is the figure which we shall adopt for 1981.

Exports are the final element in demand. British coal is still cheap by world standards and, provided it is available, it should be possible to sell a considerable quantity abroad. The Coal Board's export estimate of around 5 million tons will therefore be accepted. This brings the total demand for coal to 127 million tons in 1981, which compares with 134 million tons in 1973. The overall level of demand is not however likely to have much practical significance because, unless it turns out to be much smaller than has been forecast, it will not determine how much coal will be produced. This is because there is little likelihood that the industry will be able to supply as much as 127 million tons.

COAL SUPPLY

The NCB believes that at present it has the capacity to produce 120 million tons of deep-mined coal, although experience since the miners' strike suggests that this is an overestimate. As the working party on the coal industry points out:

   like most extractive industries the NCB 'has to run fast to stay still'.Over the period up to 1985 it appears that a broad average of some 3–4 million tons capacity a year is likely to be lost mainly through exhaustion of mines and possibly also through exceptional mining difficulties. Thus deep mined capacity would decline from the notional current rate down to somewhere around 80 million tons by 1985.[3]

If so the Board would, in the absence of new capacity, and allowing for the fact that its present capacity is rather less than 120 million tons, only be able to produce about 90 million tons of deep-mined coal by 1981.

The NCB therefore proposes to bring some 42 million tons of new capacity into existence by 1985. Of this 9 million will be secured by the extension of pits which would otherwise exhaust, and a further 13 million tons a year from major schemes at other pits. Past experience suggests that these projects will take between three and five years to complete and it seems likely that a considerable part of this capacity will be in existence by 1981. In addition the Board plans to construct a number of new pits and hopes that by the mid 1980s they will be producing 20 million tons, of which about half will come from the recently discovered Selby coalfield. A small part of this capacity will be at drift mines which can be sunk relatively quickly and should be in operation by 1981, but it will be at least ten years before the big new pits are fully in production. They will not therefore be producing any great amount of coal by 1981, and it seems doubtful whether total deep-mined output will be any more than 110 million tons. The Board wants to expand opencast output from its present level of around 10 million tons a year to about 15 million tons. However planning procedures are an obstacle to expansion and the NCB believes that it will only be able to achieve this level if they are relaxed. Granted the present concern about the environment this seems unlikely and, even allowing for the small amount of coal which comes from miscellaneous sources, total output in 1981 is likely to be only about 120 million tons.

The Coal Board has itself virtually admitted that this is the case. The Generating Board states in its evidence to the Select Committee that:

Consultations with the NCB have indicated a likely range of coal availability to CEGB stations of 65 to 80 million tons in the early 1980s; this assumes the successful implementation of their investment plans, the best outcome of the manpower situation and redeployment of coal from exports to home power stations.

If to the mid-point of this range is added an allowance for other consumption derived from Coal Board estimates, one arrives at an output of 120 to 125 million tons. It must therefore be concluded that, unless a large tonnage of coal is imported or the Board is being pessimistic, only about this amount of coal will be available for consumption or export. However it is doubtful whether any great amount of coal will be obtained from abroad because, as the Generating Board has argued, the price is unlikely to fall much below the level required to make it competitive with oil. It will therefore be assumed that, although demand will be somewhat higher, supply will total around 120 million tons, of which the electricity industry will consume 83 million, BSC 12 million and other markets 25 million tons.

RAIL TRAFFIC

Now that coal consumption in 1981 has been forecast it is possible to begin estimating what tonnage will be carried by rail. As can be seen from Table 5.2, power stations accounted for 53 million tons out of the 100 million tons of solid fuel which BR transported in 1973. Some 40 million tons of power-station coal was delivered by merry-go-round (mgr) trains. There has been a very rapid build-up in mgr working, which five years before had only represented 8 million tons. During the next few years the CEGB will complete various stations which should take another 6 million tons of merry-go-round coal. In addition there is likely to be some increase in mgr deliveries due to the change in fuel prices and because of better performance at those stations where operating problems have been encountered. If these could be entirely eliminated, the mgr tonnage might be as high as 55 million tons, but considerable difficulties are still being experienced at stations which should by now have reached maturity. It will therefore be assumed that some of the Generating Board's big stations will never be fully efficient, and that in 1981 deliveries to power stations by mgr will be restricted to 50 million tons.

British Rail will also go on conveying a considerable tonnage

TABLE 5.2: *British Rail's Coal Traffic and Revenue*

	Tons (million)			Revenue per ton (£)
	1968	*1973*	*1981*	*1972*
Power stations: [a]				
Merry-go-round	8	40	*50*	0·57
Other	37	13	*14*	0·77
	45	53	*64*	0·66
BSC:				
Merry-go-round	—	—	*5*	—
Other	16	13½	*6*	0·95
	16	13½	*11*	0·95
Other consumers:				
Merry-go-round	—	2	*2*	..
Other	61½	30½	*12*	..
	61½	32½	*14*	1.18
Totals:				
Merry-go-round	8	42	*57*	..
Other	114½	57½	*32*	..
Total rail deliveries	122½	99½	*89*	0.88
Total deliveries by all modes	165½	131½	*120*	—
Rail deliveries as % of total	74·0	75·5	*74·2*	—
Revenue per ton (£, 1972 purchasing power)	0·98	0·80	*0·74*	0·88
Total revenue (£ million, 1972 purchasing power)	120½	79	*66*	77½

[a] Excluding coal railed to the port and then delivered by ship.

of power-station coal by ordinary trainload methods. During 1973 it carried 13 million tons of electricity coal excluding merry-go-round working. This represented about 45% of all deliveries apart from mgr and coal delivered by ship. It seems unlikely that this percentage will rise, partly because a considerable tonnage will continue to be moved direct from pit to power station by conveyor belt, partly because some pits and power stations are not rail-connected, and partly because the rate per ton for coal which is transported by road (and canal) is significantly lower than that for rail-borne coal, because the average length of haul is considerably shorter. (In theory the CEGB is committed to transport all coal by rail where both pits and power stations are linked to the railway system, but in practice the contract seems to be interpreted fairly freely.) If BR continues to carry 45% of that part of power-station coal that is not delivered by road or ship, it will transport about 14 million tons in 1981, virtually the same figure as in 1973.

During 1973 BR moved around 13½ million tons of coal to BSC's steelworks, which represented well over 90% of the total tonnage they received. As the proportion will probably stay about the same, and the Corporation's coal consumption has been put at 12 million tons, it appears that in 1981 around 11 million tons may arrive by rail. At present the Corporation does not receive any coal by merry-go-round, but by 1981 Scunthorpe will be served in this way and so will the new blast furnace installation which is being constructed at Redcar. However it seems unlikely that mgr will be used elsewhere, partly because of constraints at the colliery end, and partly because the Corporation does not regard mgr as the ideal method of transport. Nevertheless by 1981 this method of transport should have built up to about 5 million tons per annum.

During 1973 the railways carried 32½ million tons of general industrial and domestic coal. This was equivalent to 67% of total consumption, which was a slightly lower figure than five years before. By 1981 there is likely to have been a considerable reduction both in consumption and in BR's share of the market. A very high proportion of the miscellaneous coal that the railways carry is accounted for by wagonload working and it seems likely that part of this traffic will be lost, or should be given up. There must come a point where the flow of traffic falls to such a low level that it is not worthwhile for consumers to maintain private sidings and where operations become completely uneconomic for BR. It will therefore be assumed that by 1981 the railways will only be carrying 14 million tons of miscellaneous coal, which represents about 50% of consumption.

In total, it appears that BR may have about 89 million tons of coal traffic in 1981, 10 million tons less than it carried in 1973. This implies that there will be a slight reduction in the railways' share of total coal deliveries from 75½% in 1973 to 74% in 1981 because of the loss of wagonload traffic.

In 1972 BR's revenue per ton averaged £0·88; although by 1973 it had, after allowing for the general rise in prices, declined to

£0·80, due, presumably, to the combined effect of price restraint and the large increase in merry-go-round working. In 1972 British Rail appears to have received only about £0·57 per ton for the coal it moved to power stations by mgr trains, though this is a very rough-and-ready figure. Due to the continued switch to merry-go-round, which is likely to increase from 42% to 64% of the total tonnage, there will almost certainly be a further reduction in the average revenue per ton. It is estimated, largely on the basis of the rates quoted in the final column of Table 5.2, that this will have fallen to £0·74 by 1981 in money of 1972 purchasing power. As a result BR should earn about £66 million from the 89 million tons of traffic which has been forecast. This compares with the £79 million which it received during 1973, at 1972 purchasing power.

OIL

During 1973 British Rail carried over 20½ million tons of petroleum products and earned £12 million from this traffic, at 1972 purchasing power. Hitherto, oil has been an important growth area, although, as Table 5.3 shows, the increase in volume has been far more spectacular than the increase in receipts. Until the energy crisis it seemed likely that oil consumption and rail traffic would go on rising at a rapid rate. However, the situation has been completely changed by the enormous increase in the price of oil, which has transformed it into the marginal fuel and reduced the rate at which the overall demand for energy will increase. How much oil will be used in 1981 will therefore depend on the total demand for energy and on the availability of the other primary fuels.

In the past, inland energy consumption has been growing at around 2% per annum. This was, for example, the rate at which it increased between 1961–63 and 1971–73, after adjusting for differences in temperature. However, the growth in consumption between 1971–73 and 1981 is almost certain to be smaller, partly because national output will, as a result of the energy crisis, rise more slowly and partly because the enormous increase in the cost of energy is likely to lead to some economy in its use. It has

TABLE 5.3: *UK Consumption of Primary Fuels and Rail Transport of Oil*

	1963	1968	1973	1981
Inland energy consumption (million tons of coal equivalent):				
Natural gas	0·2	4·3	39·7	90
Nuclear and hydro-electricity	4·3	12·3	11·9	25
Coal	193·8	164·6	131·3	120
Oil	85·3	125·9	159·4	140
Total energy consumption	283·8	307·0	342·3	375
Oil consumption (million tons of oil)	50·2	74·0	93·8	82·4
BR carryings of petroleum products (million tons)	6·1	15·0	20·7	16·5
BR traffic as % of consumption	12·2	20·3	22·1	20·0
BR revenue (£ million, 1972 purchasing power)	9·2	10·9	12·0	9·5
BR revenue per ton (£, 1972 purchasing power)	1·52	0·73	0·58	0·58

already been forecast that GDP will rise by 2½% per annum between the last nine months of 1974 and 1981 which would, it so happens, mean an increase of the same size between 1971–73 and 1981. Although there is obviously some relationship between the rise in national output and the growth of energy consumption, the relationship between the two has been anything but stable. Over the period from 1961–63 to 1971–73 the demand for energy, on a coal-equivalent basis, grew at 75% of the rate at which the GDP increased. It will be assumed, since some assumption has to be made, that this relationship will hold for the future. This suggests that if the GDP rises by 2·5% a year between 1971–73 and 1981, energy consumption will increase by about 1·9% per annum.

However, no allowance has yet been made for any reduction in the demand for fuel as a result of the rise in energy prices. Estimates by the Organization for Economic Co-operation and Development suggest that the rise in oil prices will, even if the increase in national output remains the same, depress the growth in Common Market energy consumption from 5% per annum to 3·7% over the period 1972–80.[4] This means that the rate of increase in demand will be only 75% as great as it would otherwise have been. If this is also the case in the United Kingdom, the annual growth in energy consumption between 1971–73 and 1981 will be reduced from 1·9% to 1·4%. With such a rate of increase, consumption will rise from 342 million tons of coal equivalent in 1973 to 375 million tons by 1981, which is more or less in line with the private estimates of one of the fuel-producing industries.

From total energy consumption at 375 million tons must be deducted coal, which has already been estimated at 120 million; nuclear and hydro-electric power, which will represent about 25 million tons; and natural gas, which should be around 90 million tons of coal equivalent. This leaves oil with a market of 140 million tons which would mean that consumption would be 20 million tons less than it was in 1973. Such a reduction may seem improbable because, as transport is a big and growing market, our forecast implies a substantial reduction in the general industrial and domestic use of oil. This is unlikely if it will involve the scrapping of a large amount of relatively new oil-burning equipment, but it will not, because industrial equipment can be converted from oil to gas use very cheaply.

The 20½ million tons of petroleum products that British Rail carried during 1973 represented 22% of consumption. This was a much higher figure than in 1963 when the proportion was only 12%, but was not very much greater than during 1968, when it had been 20%. The danger of traffic being eroded by the construction of pipelines has receded, because the prospective decline in oil consumption makes it unlikely that movements from place to place will increase to the point at which the construction of a pipeline would be justified, and because oil companies must now be very reluctant to reduce their flexibility by building pipelines. Some reduction in rail carryings is, however, likely to occur because of the line from Milford Haven to Manchester, which was only opened during the summer of 1973; and the commodity composition of petroleum sales will probably alter in such a way as to depress British Rail's traffic. At present black oils account for a high proportion of its tonnage because they are more difficult to carry by pipeline than white oils. Now the reduction of sales of petroleum products is likely to have its main impact on fuel oil because it is here that competition from gas will really bite. It therefore seems likely that there will over the years be a slight decline in the proportion of oil that is delivered by rail, so it will be assumed that in 1981 rail traffic will be equivalent to 20% of consumption. If so, BR will carry 16½ million tons of oil during 1981, which is 4 million tons less than it moved in 1973.

After allowing for inflation, there has over the years been a large decline in the revenue per ton. In 1963 the railways earned around £1·50, in terms of 1972 purchasing power, but by 1968 the figure was down to £0·73, and by 1973 it had sunk to only £0·58. This reduction was the consequence of the long-term contracts which were negotiated with the oil companies in 1963 and 1964. In return for extra traffic in trainload quantities British Rail agreed to an immediate reduction in tariffs, and revenue per ton has continued to decline partly due to the decline in wagon-load traffic and partly to the introduction of large trains for which the charge is particularly low. It has also been British Rail's policy to reduce its charges in order to counter any decision by the oil companies to construct pipelines. However, the decline in revenue per ton may now have come to an end: because wagon-load traffic has shrunk to negligible proportions, because now that traffic is falling it is unlikely that there will be any great increase in the size of the average train, and because the threat of pipeline construction has greatly diminished. It will, therefore, be assumed that receipts per ton will be the same in 1981 as they were in 1973. If so, British Rail will earn £9½ million from carrying the 16½ million tons that have been forecast, which is £2½ million less than it received during 1973.

This brings the total estimated revenue from coal and oil to £75 million in 1981 as against the £91 million that BR earned in 1973, at 1972 purchasing power.

CHAPTER 6

General Freight
and the Overall Position

In 1973 British Rail earned £50 million at 1972 purchasing power from carrying 38 million tons of general freight. The breakdown of this traffic can be seen in Table 6.5 on page 90. In 1971, the latest year for which full figures are available, earths and stones were the most important item. They produced £12 million of revenue at 1972 purchasing power, and building materials yielded a further £5½ million. Vehicles and parts yielded approximately £6 million, chemicals £9¼ million, and agriculture, food and drink, and miscellaneous traffic a further £19 million. The balance of £6¾ million was what BR received for running trains on behalf of Freightliners Ltd. To discover what the railways are likely to earn in 1981 it is necessary to investigate each of these items in turn.

BUILDING MATERIALS

In 1971 BR carried about 4½ million tons of building materials apart from aggregates. By far the most important item was cement, which, as can be seen from Table 6.1, constituted around 3½ million tons. Between 1961 and 1973 rail carryings of cement rose rapidly from 1½ million tons to around 4¾ million tons. Part of this rise was due to the increased consumption of cement, but what was more important was that BR's share of deliveries doubled. At the beginning of the period, a large part of rail cement traffic was still being carried in bags, which meant that loading and unloading was very laborious. The modern method of

77

TABLE 6.1: *Deliveries and Rail Transport of Cement*

	UK cement deliveries[a] (million tons)	Rail carryings (million tons)	BR's proportion of deliveries (%)	BR revenue, 1972 purchasing power (£ million)
1961	13·5	1·6	12	. .
1963	13·6	2·0	15	2·9
1964	16·5	2·9	18	. .
1965	16·4	3·0	18	. .
1967	17·2	3·4	20	3·7
1968	17·6	3·2	18	. .
1969	17·0	3·2	19	. .
1970	16·8	3·3	20	. .
1971	17·3	3·5	20	. .
1972	17·6	4·1	23	4·5
1973	19·5	4·7	24	. .
1974	17·1	. .	. .	. .
1981	*20·0*	*5·2*	*26*	*4·8*

[a] Excludes exports.

carrying cement, which the railways themselves pioneered, was by tank wagon, and it was this development which paved the way for the great upsurge in rail traffic. This is mainly explained by the introduction of trainload working and by the cement companies' decision to construct much larger works in order to secure the considerable economies of scale which were to be had. Hitherto, it had been their policy to locate their works near the market, which meant that very little use was made of the railways, but from the giant works at Northfleet, and from the other big works, cement is now railed in bulk to distribution depots from which it is delivered by road.

To discover how much cement BR is likely to carry in 1981, it is necessary to forecast cement consumption. Between 1973 and 1974 the volume of cement deliveries in the United Kingdom fell by 12·4%, and a further decline is expected in 1975. Deliveries appear to move roughly in line with the output of the construction industry. If this industry revives in 1976, and then continues to grow at the same rate as we have assumed for gross domestic product (GDP), cement deliveries may reach 20 million tons by 1981. This is only slightly higher than their record 1973 level.

It does not appear likely that there will be any sharp increase in BR's share of deliveries, which stood at 23% in 1972. There would probably be an increase if another giant works was constructed, but as the industry already has a capacity of 21 million tons and has scrapped much of its old plant, it is difficult to see how another 4 million tons plant could be fitted in if consumption is only going to increase to 20 million tons. However, production is likely to become gradually more concentrated due to the installation of extra equipment at the larger and more modern works, and as a result the rail share of deliveries may slowly increase to, say, 26% in 1981. If so, the railways will by then be carrying around 5·2 million tons of cement. Allowing for some further decline in wagonload traffic, which yields twice as much per ton as trainload, BR may by 1981 be earning £4·8 million from carrying cement, as against roughly £4½ million in 1972.

BR's carryings of other building materials appear to have totalled only about 1 million tons in 1972, of which about 450,000 tons was bricks for the London Brick Company. This traffic is disappearing as the Company is switching to Freightliners. If a notional £½ million is included to cover the transport of other building materials, the railways' total revenue from this source adds up to £5·3 million in 1981 at 1972 purchasing power.

EARTHS AND STONES

Production of earths and stones in Great Britain is shown in Table 6.2. Of the total production of around 300 million tons in 1970, about 200 million tons was aggregates used in the construction industry and in roadworks. Transport of earths and stones by rail has been expanding in recent years, and in 1971 BR earned £12 million, at 1972 prices, from the carriage of 14·3 million tons. There appears to have been a slight fall in the tonnage carried between 1971 and 1972, and then a substantial increase between 1972 and 1973.

The most important component of BR's traffic is aggregates for the construction industry. Demand for aggregates has been growing steadily. In 1973 the Department of the Environment (DoE) forecast that demand for all aggregates would rise from 220 million tons in 1970 to 330 million in 1980. The latter figure needs to be revised downwards in view of the lower expected rate of

TABLE 6.2: *Production and Rail Transport of Earths and Stones*

	UK production[a] (million tons)	Rail carryings (million tons)	BR revenue, 1972 purchasing power (£ million)
1966	270·9	10·3	10·5
1968	304·6	10·4	10·5
1969	308·4	11·2	10·8
1970	305·8	13·3	12·4
1971	315·7	14·3	12·0
1972	333·1[b]	. .	. .
1981	. .	*20·0*	*15·0*

a Includes production of chalk, chert and flint, china clay and stone, other clays, shale, gravel and sand (including marine-dredged material), igneous rock, limestone (except that used by the iron and steel industry), sandstone, slate, gypsum and rock salt.

b Provisional.

growth of construction industry output, but demand for aggregates can be expected to increase. BR's growth prospects depend, however, not so much on the general growth of demand, but on the trends which have in the last few years enabled the railways to win an increased share of the market. Between 1972 and 1973 BR's transport of aggregates increased from 6·2 million tons to over 8 million, and rapid growth is likely to continue. This has been due in particular to the growing awareness of the aggregates industry of the economics of trainload rail movement. Half of the output of aggregates is now in the hands of twenty large firms, and a substantial part is now supplied from quarries which produce sufficient tonnages for rail movement to be cheap and convenient. An important trend in the industry is the setting-up of rail-served distribution depots in centres of population, from which dry stone and processed materials are distributed by road to local markets. The depots are linked to the quarries which serve them by regular trainload rail services, and the industry believes that this method of working has reduced the break-even distance at which rail transport becomes cheaper than road from 80 miles to 30 miles.[1]

Aggregates traffic on BR includes limestone, granite, and inland and marine-dredged gravel and sand. The most important of these items is limestone. A number of large quarries have been connected to BR in recent years, and these are generating a large and increasing tonnage of traffic. For example, Foster Yeomans' quarry at Merehead was linked to BR in 1970 and provided the railways with 2 million tons of limestone in 1972. This rail tonnage is projected to rise to 3–4 million tons by 1981. Other large firms are also forecasting substantial increases in rail traffic, and BR is continuing to sign new long-term contracts with the industry.

As well as aggregates, BR carries significant tonnages of other earths and stones. Limestone for the steel industry has been discussed in Chapter 4, but BR also carries large quantities of limestone for the chemical industry. In 1972 the railways hauled 2·5 million tons of lime and limestone for ICI. This traffic is expected to increase to about 4 million tons by 1981. Another traffic is rock salt, of which 200,000 tons was moved in trainloads from Cheshire to distribution depots throughout the country in 1972. The anticipated increase in production should lead to an increase in rail carryings. In 1972 BR moved 0·6 million tons of china clay, although 70% of this was short-distance traffic to the port of Fowey. Some increase in traffic is expected. Rail haulage of fly ash from power stations is expected to continue at about 1 million tons per annum up to 1981. Finally, in 1973 about 1·6 million tons of sand and 0·35 million tons of limestone were carried by BR into glassworks owned by United Glass Containers, Rockware Glass Company, and Redfearn National Glass Company, which together control 95% of the glass container market. Though the industry's demand for rail traffic is likely to rise slightly, much of this traffic is carried in wagonloads and so may decline for commercial reasons. The same applies to some of the rail transport of gypsum used by the cement industry.

Because of the loss of wagonload traffic, carryings of non-aggregates, earths and stones may remain at about their present level. However, the transport of aggregates is likely to increase fairly rapidly, and we estimate that by 1981 BR's total traffic in earths and stones may amount to about 20 million tons. This is about 2 million tons less than BR was forecasting in mid-1974, but because of slower economic growth the aggregates industry may be less willing to finance investment in new distribution systems. Allowing for the expected increase in carryings in private wagons and the decline in wagonload traffic, we estimate that this traffic will earn £15 million in 1981.

CHEMICALS

Over the past decade there has been, as can be seen from Table 6.3, a significant decline both in the volume of chemicals traffic and in the revenue which it yields. In 1972 the ton mileage was 18% less than it had been in 1963, and receipts at 1972 purchasing power were down from £16 million to £8 million. The explanations for the substantial fall in real revenue per ton seem to be partly the increase in the private ownership of wagons and partly the move from wagonload to trainload working.

TABLE 6.3: *Rail Transport of Chemicals*

	Tons (million)	Ton mileage (million)	Revenue, 1972 purchasing power (£ million)
1963	6·3	783	16·4
1964	6·7	836	15·6
1965	6·3	822	14·7
1966	5·8	785	13·1
1968	4·7	689	10·2
1969	4·3	688	9·9
1970	4·4	749	10·3
1971	4·0	702	9·3
1972	4·2	645	8·1
1981	7·5	600	8·0

Note: There was some reclassification of former chemicals traffic from chemicals to petroleum products between 1971 and 1972.

Growth of BR's chemical tonnage over the next decade appears likely. In 1972 BR signed a contract to move caustic soda liquid for ICI over a distance of 13 miles, and this particular flow could grow to 1·2 million tons by 1978. It is also planned that 1 million tons of potash will be hauled from Old Boulby mine to Teesport. The production of liquified oxygen and nitrogen is now being concentrated at large-scale plants, with the output being distributed in bulk by rail at very low temperatures. In 1970, BR signed a ten-year contract with British Oxygen, which believes that by 1981 its traffic will grow to nearly 1 million tons, and this figure will be higher if it decides to build another rail-connected plant. Over the next few years, there will also be a considerable increase in the movement of acids and other products for BP Chemicals, and by 1981 rail traffic could be up by 350,000 tons, depending on where new plant is located. However, fertiliser traffic on BR has been declining in recent years, and there will also be some further loss of wagonload traffic carried for the chemical industry.

BR is expecting that by 1978 its chemicals traffic will have risen to 6½ million tons. In view of the growth areas which have been identified, this seems perfectly reasonable, and it will be assumed that by 1981 the figure will have risen by a further million tons. But much of BR's new traffic will be moved over a very short distance, and there will therefore be a sharp reduction in the average length of haul. This is likely to be accentuated by the loss of much of the existing wagonload freight which passes over a long distance. As a result it is quite possible that, as measured by ton miles, the volume of traffic will not increase and may even fall slightly. Although the rate per ton mile tends to be relatively high for short-haul traffic, it would be unrealistic to expect that there will be any great increase in revenue, and it has been assumed that receipts will remain about the same as in 1972.

THE MOTOR INDUSTRY

Revenue from the motor industry was about £6 million at 1972 purchasing power in 1971 and £6¼ million in 1972, as can be seen from Table 6.5. The railways have had considerable success in gaining business and the number of cars carried rose from 300,000 in 1968 to 500,000 in 1972, which represented 26% of all cars produced in the United Kingdom. This is a high percentage because a considerable proportion of cars are sold near where they are made, or are exported through ports which are close to the car factories. On the other hand, BR's potential traffic is enlarged because some car bodies are moved between works during the course of production. BR may gain some additional traffic because of changes in the road haulage industry; many road haulage firms engaged in the transport of vehicles use BR for the trunk haul to distribution depots, and the trend towards fewer firms means that there will be more individual traffic flows suitable for trainload movement. BR's share of the market for built-up cars should therefore increase, but probably only slowly. There ought also to be a rise in the transport of components where the fastest growth in traffic has been taking place, and where new contracts are continuing to be won.

However, it seems unlikely that BR's revenue will rise much faster than the growth in vehicle production. During the past decade the growth in car output has been very modest, although there have been large year-to-year fluctuations. When, in 1972, United Kingdom car production reached its highest level, 1·92 million cars were produced, but the previous peak was as long ago as 1964, when 1·87 million were manufactured. Although large variations in the railways' vehicle traffic are almost bound to occur, it seems unlikely that there will be any great under-lying increase in output, and it will be assumed that by 1981 2 million cars will be produced. The slight rise in output, together with some increase in BR's market share, might push the rail-ways' revenue from the motor industry up to £7 million by 1981.

AGRICULTURAL, FOOD AND DRINK, AND OTHER MISCELLANEOUS TRAFFIC

The remaining group of traditional freight traffic includes agricultural traffic, transport of food and drink, and other miscel-laneous traffic. In 1971 carryings totalled 5 million tons and earned BR £19 million at 1972 purchasing power (see Table 6.5). This comprised £5·7 million of agricultural traffic (2·2 million tons), £4·9 million of food and drink (1·0 million tons) and £8·4 million of miscellaneous traffic (1·8 million tons). This freight earned a very high rate per ton because the average length of haul for all these groups was over 200 miles and because most was carried in wagonloads.

The wagonload traffic has been declining at a rapid rate, from about 9 million tons in 1966 to 4·6 million tons in 1971. Over this period, agricultural traffic fell by 21%, carryings of food and drink by 68%, and miscellaneous traffic by 65%. One of the explanations for the fall is the decline of conventional docks traffic. Rail facilities were withdrawn from the London docks in 1968–69 and from the Liverpool side of the Mersey in 1973. In addition, some traffic, particularly from the food and drink industry, has been transferred to Freightliners. Other traffic has been relinquished because BR has found it to be unprofitable, or has been lost because the railways' standard of service is inferior to that by road. Though we expect the fall in this traffic to continue, the rate of decline should slow down. This is because there is a stable element of about ¾ million tons, much of it agricultural produce, carried to and from Europe on train ferries. Moreover, the quality of service should improve with the introduction of the TOPS (Total Operations Processing System) computerized wagon information system, and of the air-braked wagonload services offering overnight transits. Two air-braked routes were in operation at the end of 1973, and BR hopes to have eight by 1976.

It seems likely that the wagonload element will have declined to 2 million tons by 1981, but trainload traffic, including alumina and aluminium, and household refuse, might by then have increased to about 2 million tons. We estimate that these traffics will together earn BR a revenue of around £10 million.

FREIGHTLINERS

Freightliners constitute the final item in the railways' general freight. In 1973, BR earned nearly £7½ million from running trains for Freightliners Limited, the company in which they have a 49% stake. Freightliners handles marketing, owns and operates most of the terminals, and provides containers and undertakes road collection and delivery where customers so desire. The first service was only inaugurated in November 1965 but, as can be seen from Table 6.4, traffic had risen to nearly 6½ million tons by 1973. This was due to the extension of the system which by the end of that year comprised 29 depots and 175 services per day.

Despite their rapid growth, Freightliners as yet play only a modest part in the long-distance market. Although they have captured half of the traffic which travels over 300 miles between main centres, their share of such freight over 100 miles is but 11%. Some of the remaining traffic moves by conventional rail services but as BR only accounts for about a third of the total

TABLE 6.4: *Freightliner Traffic and British Rail Revenue*

| | Containers (thousand) | | | Tons (million) | BR revenue, 1972 purchasing power (£ million) |
	Inland	Maritime	Total		
1966	27	0	27	0·2	. .
1967	105	3	108	0·9	. .
1968	243	38	281	2·4	4·9
1969	310	87	397	3·9	6·5
1970	364	116	480	4·9	6·8
1971	. .	. .	505	5·1	6·7
1972	339	215	554	5·5	6·8
1973	. .	. .	634	6·3	7·3
1981	*640*	*570*	*1 210*	*12·1*	*15·0*

tonnage which moves more than 100 miles the great bulk of inter-city freight must move by road. Because Freightliners have such a small share, the growth in their traffic depends not so much on the expansion of the market, which has only been growing at about 3% per annum, as on the comparative costs of using Freightliners and road haulage.[2]

This subject has been examined by Warner and Joy, who investigated the relative direct costs, excluding administration but including capital charges, of Freightliners and of road haulage at the beginning of 1971.[3] Their initial assumption was that the collection and delivery points for the goods being transported were nine miles from both the Freightliner terminal and the road haulage depot, and that the road and rail trunk hauls were the same. Under existing regulations, the maximum load which can be moved by road is only 5% heavier than the maximum which can be carried in a large 30-foot Freightliner container, but the latter has a capacity of only 1650 cubic feet whereas the flat trailer can be loaded with up to 2840 cubic feet of goods provided they are sufficiently light. This is partly because, due to the rail-ways' loading gauge, the standard rail containers have a somewhat restricted height. But the main reason is that the Freightliner container only has an effective length of 29½ feet whereas the largest trailer has one of 39½ feet.

As a result, the minimum distance at which Freightliners become competitive with road haulage is much greater for bulky than for heavy commodities. Warner and Joy found that for heavy products—steel, bricks, glass, wines, spirits and many foodstuffs—

the break-even distance is about 130 miles. But for commodities like glass bottles, meat, and paper and textiles in rolls, the break-even point rises to around 200 miles, and for products which occupy a large amount of space in relation to their weight, such as earthenware, clothing and cornflakes, the figure is 300 miles or more.

These break-even mileages would have been significantly greater if the distance between the collection (or delivery) point and the Freightliner terminal had been slightly longer than the distance from the road haulage depot, a situation which must often occur in practice where firms own their own lorries and no collection is involved. The break-even distance increased by about 40 miles for every 10 miles by which the collection (or delivery) point was further from the Freightliner terminal, even though the trunk haul was the same by road and by rail.

In the reverse situation, the break-even distance falls by only 20 miles for every 10 miles by which the road haulage depot is further off than the Freightliner terminal. This assymmetry arises because, other things being equal, the amount of local roadwork is less for road haulage than for Freightliner operations, because, where road is being used throughout, the lorry can be driven straight from the collection to the delivery point, and does not have to return to base like the Freightliner vehicle.

Fortunately it is sometimes possible to reduce the costs of cartage, which constitutes about 40% of the total expense of using Freightliners, through triangular working, e.g. by waiting at the delivery point while the container is unloaded and then taking the vehicle straight to a collection point where it is re-loaded. Despite this, only a little over two containers are carried each day per vehicle, although it is hoped to push the figure up to three.

This would make Freightliners more competitive but what would appear to be even more important is that 40-foot containers should be introduced on an extensive scale. At present there are very few and they are all privately owned. A 40-foot container has the advantage that its volume, at 2300 cubic feet, would more nearly approach the carrying capacity of the lorry with a 40-foot flat trailer (2840 cubic feet). Despite this, Freightliners has no plans for the general introduction of 40-foot containers, because it believes that there is no real demand for them.

It is to be expected that sooner or later big containers will be provided, but in their absence Freightliners are only competitive for heavy goods or where hauls are, by British standards, very long.

Another important reason why the tonnage which Freightliners can hope to capture is smaller than it appears, is that a two-way Freightliner service needs to carry at least 125,000 tons per annum in order to break even. Only about 25 million tons of traffic moves each year between major centres containing over 400,000 people which are over 150 miles apart, and the average per route is about 350,000 tons per annum.[4] Allowing for traffic which is already on rail or which is unsuitable for container transport, it seems likely that the *average* available inter-city flow is not very much greater than the amount necessary to support a Freightliner service. This means that a considerable part of the inter-city traffic which moves over 150 miles is too sparse to support a liner-train service. It must also be remembered that although Freightliners have a speed advantage on very long routes, and damage a negligible proportion of the goods carried, they are in some ways less reliable and convenient than road haulage. In the past, congestion and delays have occurred at their terminals, and are difficult to avoid because of the need to achieve a 70–75% load factor in order for their services to yield a profit. The flat road trailer also has the considerable advantage over the container (or the box trailer) that it can be loaded from the side as well as the end.

In view of the limited market which is available and the fact that, excluding maritime containers, there was very little growth in Freightliner traffic between 1969 and 1972 it will be assumed that over the period 1972–81 general traffic will rise at only 3% per annum. If so, it will, on the assumption of ten tons per container, increase from 3·4 million tons in 1972 to 4·4 million in 1981. To this will be added 2 million tons to cover the special traffic which Freightliners should pick up over the period. As we have seen, it should gain a considerable amount of parcel and letter-post traffic from the Post Office, and the London Brick Company is starting to use liner-trains on an extensive scale. By 1981 the London Brick Company will probably be sending about 1 million tons each year by Freightliner, and Freightliners is investigating the construction of private terminals for other concerns.

During the past few years there has been a rapid build-up in Freightliners' maritime container traffic, about which nothing has so far been said here. Its growth has been due to the large-scale containerisation of foreign trade and to the fact that Freightliners are far more competitive for maritime than for domestic traffic. The break-even distance for maritime containers is only about 50 miles, because they require either collection or delivery but not both, because the goods must be packed in a container so there are no volume advantages in the use of road, because only one extra terminal-handling is involved by using rail instead of road, and because disciplined rail movement of containers at ports reduces congestion.

As a result the movement of maritime containers by Freightliners has increased from virtually nothing in 1967 to around 215,000 in 1972, when they constituted nearly 40% of the company's total business. From estimates of total container traffic provided by those ports at which Freightliners has, or is likely to have, terminals, it seems likely that by 1976 the volume will have built up to around 450,000 containers per annum. By then the containerisation of imports and exports will, apart from trade with South Africa, be more or less complete. It has therefore been assumed that from 1976 to 1981 Freightliners' maritime traffic will only increase by 5% per annum: the rate at which the tonnage of imported and exported manufactures has been growing.

Our estimates suggest that in all Freightliners will carry 12·1 million tons of goods in 1981. If so, BR will earn about £15 million at 1972 purchasing power from running the trains.

GENERAL FREIGHT: THE GENERAL PICTURE

Now that each item of the railways' general freight traffic has been investigated, we must gather our estimates together and consider the general picture. BR's general freight traffic declined sharply from around 35 million tons in 1963 to about 29 million in 1968. Since then it has slowly recovered, and as can be seen from Table 6.5 it was up to nearly 38 million tons by 1973. This has been largely due to the advent of Freightliners, whose traffic

TABLE 6.5: *Composition of British Rail's General Freight Traffic*

	Tonnage (million tons)					Revenue, 1972 purchasing power (£ million)			
	1968	1971	1972	1973	1981	1971	1972	1973	1981
Traditional general freight:									
Earths and stones	10·4	14·3	18·9	22·3	20·0	12·0	..	..	15·0
Building materials	4·6	4·6			5·6	5·4			5·3
Chemicals and allied	4·7	4·0	4·2		7·5	9·3	8·1		8·0
Vehicles and parts	..	1·1			1·2	6·0	6·3		7·0
Agriculture, food and drink, and miscellaneous	..	5·0	5·0		4·0	19·0	..	..	10·0
Total	27·0	29·0	28·1	31·5	38·3	51·7	46·6	42·8	45·3
Freightliners	2·4	5·1	5·5	6·3	12·1	6·7	6·8	7·3	15·0
Total	29·4	34·1	33·6	37·8	50·4	58·4	53·4	50·1	60·3
Revenue per ton, 1972 purchasing power						£1·71	£1·59	£1·33	£1·20

had built up to 6½ million tons by the end of the period. It is forecast, as Table 6.5 shows, that over the period 1973–81 carryings will grow from 38 million tons to 50 million. The great bulk of this increase is accounted for by Freightliners and by earths and stones, which yield a relatively low revenue per ton. Moreover it is forecast that there will be a decline in the rate for most of the individual traffics due to changes in their composition (e.g. in earths and stones), to a reduction in the average length of haul (chemicals), to more privately-owned wagons (e.g. earths and stones), and to the decline of wagonload traffic. It is anticipated that as a result the overall revenue per ton for general freight will fall from £1·59 in 1972 to only around £1·20 in 1981. Because of this, BR's receipts from general freight are only likely to increase from £53½ million in 1972 to £60½ million in 1981.

AN INCREASE IN RAILWAY RATES?

Our revenue estimates allow, as far as possible, for changes in what the railways will earn per ton due to alterations in the composition of traffic. But as yet no allowance has been made for any variation in the relative price that British Rail charges for traffic of the same type. (General inflation can be ignored since it will have an equal effect on the costs that British Rail has to bear.) The railways' scope for making a price increase of this type will largely depend on the rates set by its principal competitors, the road hauliers. What little information is available suggests that in the past their rates have at least kept pace with inflation. Over the period 1972–81 they will probably increase rather more rapidly. By the spring of 1974 the price of diesel oil was about 45% higher than it had been in 1972, after allowing for the loss of most of the discount that large consumers were receiving. As the general rise in prices was 19½%, the real increase appears to have been only about 21%. The explanation is that excise duty represents such a large part of what the customer pays for derv that even a large rise in the price of crude has a relatively small impact. As fuel only constituted about 15% of general hauliers' costs in 1972, the relative increase in the price of derv appears to have led to an increase of only something over 3% in their overall expenditure.

As we have seen, no further rise in the relative cost of oil is to be expected. On the other hand there is likely to be a significant rise in labour costs. The present ten-hour driving day in road haulage will, under Common Market regulations, be replaced by an eight-hour day, and drivers will no longer be permitted to drive more than 280 miles a day. It is expected within the industry that as a result output per worker will fall by about 5% in long-distance haulage. Moreover, in the past the construction of motorways has made an important contribution to the growth of productivity, but this will more or less come to an end now that the principal routes have been completed and building is slowing down. It has been assumed that, for this and other reasons, there will henceforth be an increase of 1% a year in wages and salaries per unit of output. Staff expenditure constitutes half of road haulage expenditure and it is estimated that this increase, together with the adverse effect of the Common Market regulations, will push up operating costs by 7%.

Thus, long-distance haulage costs should, allowing for greater expenditure on both fuel and labour, rise by over 10% between 1972 and 1981. If, as will be assumed, British Rail increases its freight charges in line it should earn an extra £17 million in 1981. However, the railways probably have additional scope for raising their rates because in 1971–72 they were already on the low side. This is shown by a comparison between what road hauliers would have had to charge and the rates that BR received for its train-load traffic, where it provides a comparable standard of service.

The estimated road rates given in Table 6.6, along with BR's charges, were calculated on the basis of information from hauliers and the *Commercial Motor*'s widely used Tables of Operating Costs for goods vehicles. In order that the rates might be the minimum possible it was assumed that derv was obtained at a discount of $3\frac{1}{2}$p per gallon, that the largest lorries would be used, and that they would clock up 55,000 miles per annum, although the average for heavy goods vehicles is only about 37,000. After other costs had been calculated a margin of 20% was added to cover general overheads and provide a profit of 10% on net assets. The figure suggested by *Commercial Motor* is over twice as great, but this is on the high side.

TABLE 6.6: *Comparison of Rail Charges for Trainload Traffic and Road Haulage Rates*

	Actual rail charge per ton (£)	Actual or estimated average haul (miles)	Actual or estimated rail charge per ton mile (p)	Actual or estimated road haulage rate per ton mile (p)	Estimated road haulage running costs per ton mile[a] (p)
Coal and coke (1971)	0·61	30	2·0	2·4	1·5
Iron ore (1974)	0·58	47	1·2	3·2	2·0
Finished and semi-finished steel (1974)	1·63	103	1·6	2·3	1·3
Earths and stones (1971)	0·69	75	0·9	2·4	1·5
Cement (1971)	0·83	100	0·8	2·4	1·5
Petroleum (1971)	0·54	100	0·5	2·4	1·5

[a] Fuel, lubricants, tyres, maintenance and depreciation.

For each of the six commodities the rail charge was significantly lower than the estimated road haulage rate. The difference
was less than 0·4p per ton mile for coal but appears at first sight
to have been as much as 1·6p for cement and 1·9p for petroleum.
With the exception of coal and steel, the rail charge was lower
than the running cost for road haulage. However all the petroleum
and a substantial proportion of cement and earths and stones are
carried in privately-owned wagons. The extra expense in terms of
maintenance, depreciation and interest where wagons were
privately owned seems to have averaged something like 0·5p per
ton mile. If so, the true cost of using railways may have been
around 1p per ton mile for petroleum, cement, and earths and
stones. These are only back-of-an-envelope figures but they do
indicate that, although the discrepancy between the costs of road
and rail was less great than it appeared, it must nevertheless have
been very large.

However, for petroleum the real competition which the railways face comes not from hauliers but from pipelines. It appears
that in 1971 the cost of moving petrol or other white oils by pipeline would have been around 0·8p per ton mile, assuming a
throughput of over a million tons; and for black oils, which form
about 60% of British Rail's oil traffic, the figure would be around
20% higher. Furthermore, oil companies are not going to construct a pipeline unless their estimates suggest that there is going
to be a cost saving of at least 10% in comparison with rail.
Construction involves considerable time and trouble because of
the need to get agreement from landowners, and because major
projects are normally carried out on a co-operative basis and
companies have to reach agreement among themselves. Construction is also comparatively risky because a line is inflexible and oil
companies are always changing their production schedules and
making unplanned movements. It therefore appears that BR's
average charge for carrying oil in 1971 was roughly equivalent
to the cost by pipeline where a million tons or more was being
carried.

There are considerable economies of scale for pipelines, and
the cost per ton mile is around 60% higher when there is a
throughput of half a million tons than when it is a million. BR's
scope for raising its charges will therefore largely depend on the
size of the flows that it handles. Most are relatively small. There

is one flow of about a million tons per annum, and one or two of around half a million, but most are considerably smaller; the most common size being from 100,000 to 150,000 tons. This could give a misleading impression because refineries are sometimes located together, and the joint flow to a particular destination is likely to be greater than the amount consigned by the individual company. Hence, if firms co-operate the cost of a pipeline may be less prohibitive than it appears. If the railways raised their rates there would also be a tendency for companies to exchange business, so that a particular place would be supplied in bulk from a particular refinery in order that a pipeline might be constructed. However, there would probably have to be a considerable increase before this happened on any appreciable scale because of the difficulty the oil companies would have in reaching agreement, as some have more to gain than others.

For some of the commodities the use of rail instead of road may involve additional expenditure on terminal facilities. Greater storage capacity and more sophisticated loading equipment may, for instance, be necessary. Moreover in the case of steel products the road haulier usually undertakes or assists with loading, whereas British Rail does not. On the other hand rail is likely to be more convenient where output is on a very large scale and enormous tonnages of materials and products are flowing in and out of a works. It is here that rail, with its advantage of more disciplined working, and its ability to transport in bulk, really comes into its own. For instance in steel a large shift from rail to road for the movement of iron ore and semi-finished products would, as well as causing an environmental outcry, almost certainly result in serious congestion within the works and on approach roads. No doubt this could be mitigated by careful planning and by working round the clock. This, however, would be expensive both in terms of managerial time and extra payments for night and weekend work. Moreover for existing steelworks a switch from rail to road would sometimes involve extensive capital expenditure on new facilities and the modification of plant.

It is possible that if there were a large increase in rail charges, patterns of production would be altered in such a way as to reduce the demand for transport. For instance, cement manufacture has been concentrated in large works because, although this

involves extra transport, it has enabled substantial economies of
scale to be secured. This process could in theory be put into
reverse but it seems unlikely because of the size of these economies, and the fact that the cost by rail is at present so much
lower than the cost by road. Moreover, alterations in the pattern
of production in response to an increase in rail charges would
only take place slowly. In steel even a large increase in BR's
charge for moving ore would be insufficient to warrant the ending
of steel-making at the British Steel Corporation's inland works.
The avoidable costs of production at those plants which are being
retained are so much lower than the total costs for new coastal
capacity that no conceivable increase in the rail charge, which is
a relatively small item, would lead to premature closure.

British Rail might nevertheless be unwise to jack up its rates
if this meant that it would forfeit a large amount of new business.
There is little risk of steel business being lost as any major
expansion of capacity will take place at a coastal site. Again in
cement (and vehicles) it does not appear that there is much scope
for BR to increase its share of the market. In coal the introduction of merry-go-round working from pit to power station is now
more or less complete. It is only for earths and stones that a
general increase in the rate for trainload traffic might have a
damaging effect. British Rail is still in the process of inducing
firms to place greater reliance on rail and, as there are no great
economies of scale, the ability of a rail-connected quarry to
compete from a distance with the local road-based concern often
depends on what the railways charge.

Although British Rail ought to be able to increase its prices for
most of its trainload traffic it could have tied its hands by signing
up long-term contracts. However, the ten-year contract between
the Generating Board and BR which covers the merry-go-round
movement of coal can now be terminated, providing that twelve
months notice is given; and although the ten-year agreements
with the oil companies have just been renewed there is provision
for their terms to be varied at the end of five years. The inclusion
of such a break clause appears to be a standard feature of British
Rail's long-term contracts for steel and other commodities. Hence
the Board should have the opportunity before 1981 to raise its
rates for any type of traffic where it considers that the customer
is prepared to pay more.

Although it is clear that much of BR's freight traffic is under-priced it is very difficult to make any estimate of the extra revenue which it ought to be able to obtain. However, we assumed that in general BR would be able, without significant loss of traffic, to increase its charge by half the amount by which the road cost appeared to be higher than the railway rate on which our revenue forecasts were based. However for power-station coal it was simply assumed that the railways could increase their rates by 10%, and for oil, where the competition is from pipeline, a rise of 50% was built in. The other traffics which were included in the calculation were coal for steelworks (23% more), iron ore (+ 80%), inter-works movements of steel products (+ 20%), steel sold to customers (+ 25%) and cement (+ 60%). The estimate was confined to trainload traffic, with the exception of steel that is moved between works by wagonload working. The overall increase in revenue through repricing turned out to be about £21 million, but this was rounded down to £20 million. If this is related to BR's total estimated receipts from trainload traffic, it is equivalent to a price rise of only about 15%.

Our guesstimate of extra revenue is probably on the low side. One of the railways' largest customers is expecting that by 1981 it will have to pay nearly 25% more than the rates which lie behind our revenue estimates. However the customer was not assuming that the railways would make any determined effort to charge what it would be prepared to pay, despite the scope which it knows to exist. Moreover our revenue forecasts for 1981 were based on what BR charged in 1972 when it was subject to price restraint and its freight rates were somewhat lower than they might otherwise have been. As a result BR received £27 million of compensation from the Government, of which it appears that £12 million was in respect of freight.

TOTAL FREIGHT TRAFFIC AND RECEIPTS

Now that an estimate has been made for each type of freight traffic, and for repricing, it is possible to present the overall picture and see how it compares with British Rail's portrait of the future. In 1963, as Table 6.7 shows, BR carried over 230 million

TABLE 6.7: *British Rail's Freight Tonnage and Revenue Summarised*

	1963	1968	1969	1970	1971	1972	1973	1981
Freight tons (million):								
Iron and steel	39½	38½	39½	39½	33½	31	35	30
Coal and coke	151½	122½	119½	112½	107½	88	99½	89
Oil	6	15	16	18	19	21½	20½	16½
General freight[a]	35½	27	27	28½	29	28	31½	38½
Freightliners	—	2½	4	5	5	5½	6½	12
Total tonnage	232½	206	205½	204	194	174½	193	186
Freight ton miles (billions):	. .	14·5	15·0	16·1	14·6	14·0	15·3	14·1
Revenue (£ million, 1972 purchasing power):								
Iron and steel	55½	44	45	45½	35½	34	36	28½
Coal and coke	175	120½	116	112½	94½	77½	79	66
Oil	9½	11	11½	12½	12	12½	12	9½
General freight[a]	98	61½	58	57½	52½	47	43½	45½
Freightliners	—	5	6½	7	6½	7	7½	15
Total revenue	337½	242	236½	235	201	178	177½	164½/ 201½[b]
Revenue per ton (£, 1972 purchasing power)	1·45	1·17	1·15	1·15	1·04	1·02	0·92	0·88/ 1·08[b]

[a] Excludes estimated freight sundries in 1963 and 1968 but includes a little miscellaneous freight not included in Table 6.5.

[b] The second figure allows for a relative price increase worth £37 million.

tons but by 1968 the figure was down to about 205 million, and by 1973 had slipped to 193 million tons. This fall was almost wholly explained by the sharp reduction in the movement of coal, for other traffic remained about the same during the first half of the period and increased by 10 million tons between 1968 and 1973.

It is estimated that by 1981 British Rail will be carrying a total of 186 million tons, which is 7 million tons less than in 1973. Due to the rise in oil prices and the improvement in the coal industry's prospects the decline in coal traffic is likely to be somewhat slower in future than it was in the past. In 1981 BR's traffic will probably be 10 million tons lower than it was in 1973, as against a reduction of 23 million tons over the shorter period 1968–73. However it is forecast that oil, which has until recently been a growth traffic, will fall by about 4 million tons between 1973 and

1981. It is expected that steel will go on declining and will drop by 5 million tons. For general traffic and Freightliners prospects remain good and it seems likely that by 1981 an additional 13 million tons will be carried. But this rise will, if our estimates are right, be almost offset by the reductions in oil and steel; and for non-coal traffic as a whole there is likely to be only a small increase. Between 1968 and 1973 the average length of haul rose from 70 miles to 79 miles which meant that, despite the reduction in tonnage, there was a 5% increase in ton miles. However it seems likely that by 1981 the average haul will have fallen back to around 76 miles and that BR's total ton mileage will decline from 15·3 billion in 1973 to 14·1 in 1981, which is a fall of 8%. In its Interim Strategy BR predicted that the ton mileage would remain about the same and that in 1981 it would carry 191 million tons. It now seems to be expecting that it will carry around 200 million tons. Our forecasts are therefore slightly more pessimistic, which is just as well since British Rail is always over-optimistic.

In 1963 BR earned nearly £340 million at 1972 purchasing power (or around £1·45 per ton). By 1968 its revenue was down to about £240 million (£1·17 per ton), and in 1973 it only totalled around £180 million (or £0·92 per ton). Thus the railways' real earnings fell by approaching half during the course of the decade (and revenue per ton by well over a third). A large part of this decline was attributable to coal, where there was an exceptionally sharp reduction in revenue; to the switch from wagonload to trainload traffic which is carried at a much lower rate; and to the very large reduction in receipts per ton during 1973. This meant that revenue failed to increase between 1972 and 1973, although there was a considerable rise in the tonnage, partly because 1973 was a boom year and partly because coal traffic had been exceptionally low during 1972 as a result of the first miners' strike.

It is estimated that BR's earnings from freight will, at 1972 prices and purchasing power, decline from £178 million in 1973 to £165 million in 1981. Not only is there likely to be a reduction in tonnage but it also seems probable that, due to changes in the composition of traffic and the shift to train and merry-go-round working, the railways' earnings per ton will fall from £0·92 to £0·88. Since BR was receiving an exceptionally low rate during 1973, and had earned £1·02 per ton during 1972, this gives a rather misleading impression of the size of the fall. It has been estimated

CHAPTER 7

Railway Investment

Investment in the nationalised industries is expected to conform to the Government's rule that projects should earn a rate of return of at least 10% in discounted cash-flow terms; that is, they should show a positive net present value using a discount rate of 10%. Discounting costs and revenues accruing at different points in time to a common period is necessary because a given sum of money will be worth more now than in the future since it can be invested to yield a rate of return. The Government's test discount rate of 10% is intended to reflect the opportunity costs of investment, in terms of the returns which might be obtained from investing funds in projects other than the one under consideration. Rates of return from projects are generally calculated on normal profitability criteria. However, when projects are expected, as in the case of investments in rail commuter services, to yield social benefits not reflected in the investing agency's revenue, then cost-benefit analysis can be used. This technique involves the estimation of all the costs and benefits of a project, whether they accrue to the investing agency or to the rest of society.

Unfortunately the past record of investment in British Rail has not been a good one. Much investment which has been used to replace existing assets has failed to produce a satisfactory rate of return because the activity being invested in was unprofitable. Railway management has often taken the continuance of existing operations for granted, and has therefore distinguished between replacement investment, often termed as 'essential renewal', and other investment. Now 'essential renewals' will only yield a 10% rate of return if the section of the system of which they are a part is itself profitable. If this is not so, and if renewal really is unavoidable and not just the result of conventions about when assets should be replaced, then the 10% rule would imply closure rather than replacement of assets. Even effective discounted cash-flow appraisal of the non-renewal investment would then not be sufficient to ensure that rail investment as a whole was yielding a satisfactory rate of return to the community.

In this chapter we consider BR's investment programme for the period from the end of 1972 to the end of 1981. In 1972 BR invested £87·2 million in railway operations. In addition, investment of £15·5 million was made by leasing companies set up to hire rolling-stock to BR. In June 1973 BR's Interim Rail Strategy proposed total rail investment of £1787 million over the period from the end of 1972 to the end of 1981. This programme, shown in Table 7.1, represents an annual rate of investment of nearly £200 million, almost twice the 1972 level. The rail investment programme approved by the Government in November 1973 envisaged that rail investment, at 1973 prices, should rise from £140 million in 1973–74 to £225 million in 1977–78, excluding the Channel Tunnel rail link. Effectively this would have meant annual investment levels over the period from the end of 1973 to the end of 1978 which were 60% above the 1972 investment level.

TABLE 7.1: *British Rail's Proposed Investment, 1973–81*
(£ million, 1972 purchasing power)

	Com- mercial	London and South-East	PTE	Other	Total
Passenger	284	203	92	3	582
Freight and parcels	71	0	0	0	71
Systems and operations	705	250	93	45	1093
Office services, computers etc.	40	1	0	0	41
Total investment	1100	454	185	48	1787

Note: These figures exclude investment in the rail link to the Channel Tunnel.

We shall now consider BR's investment plans in detail. It will be assumed in this chapter that there will be no significant withdrawal of passenger services, and that sufficient investment will take place to enable BR to carry the passenger, freight and parcels traffic that has already been estimated to be available. Given these constraints we seek to determine the optimal level of investment for BR. Removal of the constraints would result in a lower optimal level of investment, because of the unprofitability of some parts of the railways' business. Nevertheless, accepting the constraints, we shall discover that over 40% of the investment proposed by BR can still not be justified, even when social benefits are taken into account. Table 7.6, at the end of this chapter, summarises our proposals.

TRACK RENEWAL

The most important single item of railway investment, accounting for a fifth of BR's planned investment between 1974 and 1978, is track renewal. There are a number of categories of track on BR related to the density and speed of traffic over the lines concerned. Renewal takes place when the existing track deteriorates below the standard which has been set for each category. Two main types of track can be used for renewal, traditional jointed track on wooden sleepers with 60-foot lengths of rail joined together by fishplates, and continuous welded rail (cwr) on concrete sleepers with rail joints welded together. Maintenance costs are lower for cwr because there are no joints under which ballast must be regularly packed and because fractures of rail around bolt holes are avoided. Cwr will last for 50 years, during which time the rails themselves, but not the sleepers, will need replacing once or twice, while jointed track needs complete replacement on average every 20 years, and as frequently as every 12 years on the most heavily used lines.

The mileage of cwr on BR has been increasing at a rate of about 600 miles per annum in recent years, and, by the end of 1972, totalled 6400 track miles. However, BR still had 16,700 miles of jointed track on running lines which, on the assumption of a 20-year life, would need replacing at a rate of 840 miles per annum. In fact, BR was expecting to replace 870 miles in 1973, 650 miles by cwr and the other 220 miles by jointed track.

The capital cost of installing cwr, including administration and ballasting costs, was £56,000 per mile in 1972, while the capital cost of jointed track was £52,000 per mile. Savings in maintenance costs from using cwr vary according to the speed of trains and density of traffic. In 1973 the cost saving at current prices varied from £2650 per mile per annum for track carrying over 18 million gross tons of traffic per annum at speeds up to 100 mph, to £600 per annum for track carrying under 6 million tons at speeds below 50 mph. These savings in maintenance costs ensure an *incremental* rate of return above 10% from installing cwr rather than jointed track even on the lowest category of track. However, because of the high cost of track renewal the only case where premature renewal of jointed track by cwr is justified is on lines where BR intends to run high-speed diesel trains or advanced passenger trains, as BR believes that jointed track is unsuitable for speeds above 100 mph. By the time these trains are introduced, however, the mileage of such track will be negligible on the routes in question.

BR has claimed that the present rate of installation of cwr is too slow. Indeed the fact that BR continues to replace some track with jointed track seems to suggest that BR is installing too little cwr. However, on lightly used or freight-only routes, where the maintenance cost advantage of cwr is lowest, the capital costs of installing jointed track can be reduced considerably by using second-hand materials retrieved from elsewhere in the system. At the beginning of 1972, BR's track mileage carrying less than 6 million tons per annum at speeds below 50 mph totalled 5196 miles. If this all has a 20-year life, an average of 260 miles would need to be replaced each year, although because of its light use a longer life and somewhat smaller replacement might be expected. Most, if not all, renewal with jointed track would therefore appear to have been economically justified. Nevertheless, it is possible that some track was replaced by jointed rails even though cwr would have yielded a higher rate of return, because until the end of 1974 cwr was financed from investment funds, on which there are government constraints, while jointed track was financed from revenue.

We assumed that one-twentieth of the remaining jointed track will be replaced each year, with 75% being renewed with cwr and 25% with jointed track. Allowing for the reduction in track mileage through singling discussed below, BR will need to lay 4700 miles of cwr and 1600 miles of traditional track over the period 1973–81. The cost of the cwr after allowing for the prospective rise in the cost of labour would be about £270 million at

1972 purchasing power and the re-railing of existing cwr might cost a further £14 million. What BR spends on the installation of jointed line is not known because the published figures also include the cost of partial renewal through re-railing and re-sleepering. However, average expenditure on traditional track cannot have exceeded £35,000 per mile during 1972, and it can be estimated that, again allowing for rising real wages, the complete and *partial* renewal of jointed track will cost BR £56 million between 1973 and 1981.

Total expenditure on track renewal therefore comes to £340 million for the period from the beginning of 1973 to the end of 1981. There have been suggestions by BR that no more renewal will be made with jointed track. Complete renewal with cwr would add some £25 million to our figure of £340 million but given the low capital cost of second-hand jointed track it is very doubtful if this additional investment would be justified. One important question which we are not qualified to discuss, however, is whether BR's criteria for determining when track needs replacing are correct. Prolonging the life of track before renewal takes place could lead to very large savings in railway investment.

TRACK RATIONALISATION

Investment in track rationalisation can reduce track maintenance costs by reducing the number of running lines. In 1967 the Joint Steering Group considered that BR was operating with surplus track and signalling capacity, and proposed a tapering grant to cover the costs of this surplus capacity while BR took steps to eliminate it. Provision for these grants was made in the 1968 Transport Act and BR planned to eliminate 4314 track miles between the end of 1968 and the end of 1973; 1320 of these miles were to be eliminated on 'grey' lines not scheduled for development, 1068 miles in connection with multiple-aspect signalling schemes, and the remaining 1926 miles on other parts of the Network for Development. The potential annual savings were estimated at £16·3 million at 1968 prices. However, the full programme was not implemented, and between the end of 1968 and the end of 1973 track mileage fell by only 2710 miles despite the complete closure of 1121 miles of route.

Track rationalisation can be expensive since, although the cost of physically lifting track is recouped from its scrap value, resignalling is often needed in order that trains can travel in different directions over the same stretch of track. From figures for two recent schemes on the Scottish Region it appears that the cost of singling may be about £6600 per route mile.[1] If so, the saving in expenditure on track maintenance when lines are singled would justify the necessary capital expenditure for all of BR's categories of track. The critical question is whether the capacity of the newly singled route will be able to satisfy the traffic demands upon it. The capacity of single-track routes depends on a large number of interrelated factors, including the speed and length of trains, the speed differences between different types of train, their distribution throughout the day, the distance between passing loops, the type of signalling in operation, and the amount of delay which might be acceptable for commercial reasons. Consequently, there can be no easy rule-of-thumb guide.

With loops spaced every five miles, a regular interval service of two passenger trains per hour in each direction would be feasible if all the trains operated at the same speed. In practice, there will often be different types of train operating along a line at irregular intervals. Nevertheless, in Cumberland 14 slow-moving freights and 10 diesel multiple unit (dmu) trains operate in each direction along a single-track section during a 16-hour working day. In practice, maximum capacity may therefore lie in the range of 1½ to 2 trains per hour in each direction. A line by line investigation revealed that in 1974 there were 1350 miles of double-track passenger route over which not more than about 20 passenger trains passed daily in each direction, but where it was known that there was a considerable amount of freight, lines were only regarded as candidates for singling if there were something less than 20 passenger trains. Assuming that one track could be removed for 80% of the distance, leaving the remainder for passing loops, we estimated the additional single-track mileage at 1080 miles. The cost of this programme would be of the order of £7 million.

SIGNALLING

There are a number of types of signalling in use on BR, of which the most important are semaphore signalling, three-aspect colour-light signalling, and four-aspect colour-light signalling (multiple-aspect signalling or mas). Traditional semaphore signalling is usually operated mechanically by means of wires connected to manual signal-boxes, although sometimes the more remote signals are electrically operated. Points are operated either mechanically, or electro-mechanically over longer distances, and mechanical interlocking devices prevent a signalman setting conflicting movements. Because of the limited distance over which mechanical operation is possible, and because the levers and interlocking take up a lot of space, signal-boxes are usually closely spaced. Hence semaphore signalling is labour intensive.

The use of electrical rather than mechanical control makes it possible to concentrate signal control in a very much smaller number of large power boxes. There are no physical limits to distances between boxes and signals, and the electrical control equipment takes up much less space than that of the mechanical system. In addition, electrical operation permits the automation of signalling by means of track circuits. A small current is passed down each rail so that when a section of track is occupied by a train there is a short circuit, and the signals are automatically set at danger. With an electrical system, a single switch can set a path through a section of line with a number of points and signals, in contrast to the mechanical system where each point and signal has a separate lever. Hence, it was possible for the new Motherwell power box to replace 91 manual boxes, and to control 123 route miles and 545 signals.

The first colour-light signalling schemes used a three-aspect system, but the present standard BR system for main lines uses four aspects, red, yellow, double yellow and green. The addition of a fourth, double yellow, aspect is important for high-speed running, since it can be used to give advance warning to the faster trains so that they can stop without difficulty. The system also increases line capacity with the faster trains, since the double-yellow aspect helps to keep dense traffic moving smoothly. BR regards the existing four-aspect system as necessary for high-speed running over 100 mph. The improved braking capabilities of the high-speed diesel and the advanced passenger train will allow them to stop comfortably from 125 mph in the distance between their driver sighting a double yellow and his train coming to rest at a red light two signals further on, but for speeds beyond 125 mph an entirely new and very expensive cab signalling system is thought to be required.

In recent years BR has been converting about 500 single-track miles per annum to multiple-aspect power signalling. By the end of 1972, 8600 miles of track, or 37% of the total, were controlled by colour-light signals. However, BR does not regard the present rate of conversion as sufficiently fast, and its Interim Rail Strategy plans envisaged that by 1986 colour-light signalling controlled from large power boxes would have been extended to all parts of the country apart from a few fringe areas. When the resignalling schemes in this National Signalling Plan are complete, 19,000 to 20,000 track miles will be controlled by about 75 large power boxes, each controlling on average 250 single-track miles. This compares with the present situation where about 3000 track miles are controlled from large power boxes. BR's plans therefore imply that about 5000 track miles presently controlled by colour-light signals operated from smaller signal-boxes (some of which have been built fairly recently) will be operated from large power boxes. The total cost of BR's proposed signalling investment is roughly £400 million, of which some £225 million would be incurred by the end of 1981.

The main saving from power signalling comes through staff reductions due to the replacement of many small electro-mechanical signal-boxes by a single large power box. Most electro-mechanical cabins require one signalman per shift to control their own short section of line, whereas one of the large power boxes opened recently requires only seven signalmen and supervisors per shift to control 250 track miles. However, staff savings by themselves are not sufficient to justify the introduction of power signalling because it is so expensive. According to BR the cost of installing mas and the associated power boxes averages about £30,000 per track mile at 1972 prices. It appears that the labour savings from the Saltley–Derby resignalling scheme, which should be fairly typical, can only have provided a rate of return of 2½%, despite the fact that when it was completed in 1969 BR made a staff saving of about 480 because 180 small boxes were replaced by three power units. Power resignalling schemes therefore have to be justified on other grounds, such as increased train speeds, greater track capacity and/or track rationalisation. For example, the recent Bristol resignalling could only be justified financially because of the extensive track rationalisation which accompanied it.

There is a danger that the return from power signalling may be exaggerated. For example, when a power signalling scheme is proposed, consideration is given to the prospects for track rationalisation in the area to be controlled. Some of this rational-isation might have been possible even without resignalling but it only comes to light when the track requirements in the area are surveyed when the project is being prepared. Similarly, resignal-ling might increase track capacity, but this will only be a benefit if BR is prevented by a lack of capacity from running potentially profitable services which cannot be fitted into the system on another route or at a different time of day. This is, of course, not to deny that there may be other benefits apart from those due to staff reduction, but there may well be a tendency to over-estimate the more intangible benefits of resignalling to support the financial case for such schemes.

Unfortunately, even with such benefits from resignalling included, the rate of return from many schemes is still low. In 1967 Foster and Joy noted that 'very few multiple-track resignal-ling schemes have shown substantially more than an 8% return on investment', and that 'the return on investment in many proposals in the National Signalling Plan suggests that they are largely a trade-off of capital for labour, and a change in the type of labour required.'[2] With rising real labour costs, the position may now be a little more favourable, but in 1973 BR quoted an average rate of return for resignalling schemes of only 13%. Given the difficulties in estimating benefits, many of these schemes must either fail to yield 10% or at best be of a very marginal nature. Indeed, BR failed to satisfy the Department of the Environment that extensions of the Weaver–Glasgow re-signalling onto secondary routes would be financially justifiable.

This analysis of the returns from resignalling suggests that large-scale investment in a National Signalling Plan, which aims to control nearly the whole of the railway system from large power boxes, is misjudged. Major resignalling schemes cannot be justified on labour saving alone, and the benefits in the form of increased speeds and increased track capacity are difficult to evaluate and will decline as BR's resignalling programme moves from the most heavily used main lines onto more lightly used routes. BR should therefore only resignal where a clear case can be made out for a *particular* scheme. This probably means that major resignalling should be confined to the remaining unresignalled main routes where four-aspect signalling is required for 125 mph running. These are the East Coast main line, where resignalling is at present in progress, the section of the Midland main line between St Pancras and Loughborough, and the Reading–Totnes section of the London to Plymouth line. Their total mileage is 600 route miles and about 1800 track miles. Resignalling would cost roughly £55 million, require the construction of 6 new power boxes, and permit the closure of 400 conventional signal-boxes.

The Southern plan to control their whole Region from only 13 power boxes, and estimated in 1969 that in order to achieve this it would be necessary to invest a sum equivalent to about £64 million at 1972 purchasing power. Some of the 13 boxes are already open, while work is proceeding on the London Bridge scheme. Most of the Region is already controlled by colour-light signals, and the advantages of major renewals seem doubtful, except for resignalling of the approaches to the London termini where the original colour lights were installed 35 to 50 years ago and where there are capacity problems. The labour savings which will be made cannot justify the capital costs, and because services are so intensive there will be no track rationalisation.

The total cost of major resignalling schemes which we believe to be justified over the period 1973 to 1981 is about £75 million. This includes schemes started before the end of 1972 but not completed, resignalling of the three main lines which still have semaphore signals, and of the approaches to the Southern Region's London termini, and Southern Region's Feltham scheme. The only other capital expenditure which will be justified is replacement of life-expired equipment, and minor rationalisation of existing signalling. For example, it is sometimes possible to close some manual boxes and install colour lights which are operated from the remaining boxes. To cover this, £15 million has been added, bringing total signalling investment to £90 million, as against BR's planned £225 million.

British Rail's plans

British Rail wishes to embark on a major electrification programme. Most of BR's proposals are for the standard main-line voltage of 25kV ac collected from overhead wires, though there are other schemes for extensions of existing third-rail systems on the Southern Region and on Merseyside. There is also the scheme to create a Tyneside rapid-transit network with a 1500 volts dc lightweight overhead system. The only schemes firmly agreed by the Government at the end of 1974 were the Great Northern suburban electrification into London Kings Cross and the Tyneside electrification.

The capital costs of fixed works for electrification included in the Interim Rail Strategy for the period 1973 to 1981 were £120 million. BR's plans for the years 1974 to 1978 envisaged total expenditure on fixed works for electrification of £58 million at 1972 purchasing power. Of this only £8 million was to be for main-line electrification, with the other £50 million covering the electrification of commuter services which included not only the Great Northern scheme, but also St Pancras–Bedford, Bishops Stortford–Cambridge and South Croydon–East Grinstead/Uckfield.

Although the only important main-line electrification envisaged before 1978 is the extension from Colchester to Harwich and Felixstowe, BR would then like to begin a major programme of inter-city electrification, starting with the East Coast main line from Kings Cross to Leeds and Edinburgh. This would eventually be followed by electrification between York, Sheffield and Bristol (the North-East–South-West route), Swansea and London, and Sheffield and London.

Costs and benefits of electrification

Electric traction has higher initial capital costs than diesel. Costs of electrification on the 25kV ac overhead system averaged £39,200 per track mile at 1971 prices.[3] The major item of this cost was the provision of power supply and overhead line which averaged £24,160 per mile. There have been considerable reductions in the cost of this item over the last decade. The cost of immunising colour-light signalling against electrical interference averaged £8160 per track mile if carried out when the signalling was being installed. However, if immunisation has to be carried out on existing colour-light signalling systems the cost increases to £20,400 per mile, and increases the total costs per track mile of electrification by 30%. Finally, expenditure on bridge clearances averaged £6880 per track mile, though this item will vary considerably depending on the route being electrified. Although expenditure on bridge clearances is not required for third-rail systems, such systems have costs per mile similar to those of the 25kV ac systems because of their need for expensive sub-stations every 3 to 4 miles instead of the cheaper switching stations every 30 to 40 miles on 25kV ac systems.

The cost of motive power is, on the other hand, slightly lower for electric than for diesel traction. In 1971 the price of a 2500kW ac electric locomotive was £150,000 while a less powerful 2200kW diesel type 4 cost £160,000. The price of a four-car electric outer-suburban multiple unit set was £145,000 compared with £160,000 for a diesel set. Electric stock also has a longer life expectancy, and less stock may be needed because of the greater time that diesels are out of service for maintenance, and because electrics may operate at faster speeds.

Despite this, electrification requires on balance a considerably greater capital outlay than diesel traction. Moreover, due to the time required to install the overhead line and to raise bridges a considerable period will elapse between the start of any large electrification project and its completion. This is of great significance when account is being taken, as it should be, of the timing of expenditures and receipts. What must also be allowed for is the disrupting effect that electrification schemes have on existing services. The lost revenue when they are curtailed or

slowed down must be regarded as part of the price of electrification.

Although the initial cost is high, electrification eventually
produces a saving in operating expenditure, although the upkeep
of the fixed works is fairly costly. The manpower requirement for
the maintenance of BR's overhead line and power-supply equipment is 0·32 men per single-track mile, implying a total maintenance cost of £1200 per annum per track mile at 1972 prices.
Locomotive maintenance costs are, however, much lower with
electric than with diesel traction. In 1971 such costs were 7·5
pence per mile for electrics and 23·3 pence per mile for diesels.

Until the energy crisis, fuel costs in Britain favoured diesel
traction. In 1973, fuel costs were 14·5 pence per mile for electric
locomotives and 10·4 pence for comparable diesels. However,
rapid increases in diesel oil prices relative to those of electric
power reduced the ratio between electric and diesel fuel costs
from 1·4 in 1973 to about 0·7 in the late summer of 1974. The
future trend of fuel prices is obviously subject to considerable
uncertainty. Our own view, discussed at some length in Chapter 4,
is that diesel oil prices will remain constant in real terms after
1974 but that electricity prices will rise because the cost of coal
will continue to increase. The gap between diesel and electric
fuel prices will therefore narrow, but electricity will retain its
price advantage since the rate of increase in its price will eventually slow down as nuclear generation becomes more important.

As well as reducing operating costs, electrification may also
increase revenue. On BR Inter-City services, electric locomotives
have had a maximum speed of 100 mph, compared with a top
speed of 90 mph for all but a few diesel locomotives. With the
125 mph high-speed diesel train, however, electric traction will no
longer have any speed advantages, while maximum speeds are
expected to be the same for the electric and gas-turbine advanced
passenger trains. Future Inter-City electrifications cannot therefore be justified on grounds of speed improvement.

BR has also argued that there is a 'sparks' effect which arises
because travellers prefer electric to diesel traction even if speeds
are exactly the same. It is claimed that growth of traffic on newly
electrified lines has been faster than on non-electrified routes.
However, the two main routes to be electrified had both had very
poor services prior to the introduction of electric trains. On the

London–Birmingham–Liverpool/Manchester route, service standards failed to improve and even grew worse after the commence-
ment of electrification in 1959 until its completion in 1966 and
1967. On the London–Bournemouth line a fast regular-interval
service of electric trains replaced an infrequent and much slower
service still operated by steam. On the other hand, dieselised
lines did not suffer from the kind of delays which are caused by
pre-electrification engineering work, while service improvements
were more gradual though often no less marked. Over the period
from 1964 to 1971, revenue from the diesel East Coast line, on
which 100 mph running was possible, rose by the same proportion
as did revenue from the electric West Coast line. This suggests
that the 'sparks' effect may be largely an illusion.

Main-line electrification

We concentrate our appraisal of BR's main-line electrification
plans on the proposals for the East Coast line, running from Kings
Cross to Edinburgh, with a spur from Doncaster to Leeds. The
London end of this line is currently being electrified from Kings
Cross to Hitchin as part of the Great Northern electrification,
but the new scheme would involve the electrification of a further
1340 track miles over a period of eight years at a total cost for
fixed equipment of £60 million.

Using the cost data which have already been quoted, it is
possible to estimate the discounted cash-flow rate of return from
this project. It was assumed that the capital cost of £60 million
would be incurred evenly over a period of eight years starting in
1980, and that there would be no additional capital costs for
rolling-stock above those which might be incurred in the absence
of electrification. Overhead line and locomotive maintenance
costs were based on the figures discussed above, projected forward
by 2% per annum to allow for rising real labour costs. The price
of diesel fuel was assumed to remain constant in real terms after
1974, with some increase in the real price of electricity. The
savings through electrification in the costs per mile of locomotive
maintenance and fuel were multiplied by the train mileage on
the routes to be electrified. The passenger-train mileage on these
routes in 1973–74 was about 9·5 million, and we assumed that
total train mileage on these routes was double this, say 20 million

miles. It was further assumed that this train mileage would grow by 1% per annum. Finally, we postulated that half the operating-cost savings would be achieved from 1984, and that the full savings would be realised from 1988, and would continue until 2010.

On this basis the net present value of the project was clearly negative, using a 10% rate of discount and making the most likely assumption about future energy prices. It appears that the net present value of electrification would only become positive if the price of oil were to rise by a further 30% in real terms. Moreover, these calculations exclude the loss of revenue which would result from the disruption of existing services, which would occur just when the Eastern Region would be hoping to gain the full revenue benefits from the high-speed diesel trains.

Given that the case for electrification of the East Coast main line is so dubious, it seems reasonable to assume that other main-line schemes, to which BR accords lower priority, will have even less justification, especially as a number of these schemes would have higher capital costs because of the need to immunise the existing signalling. However the investment required for some of the shorter extensions to the existing 25kV system would be relatively low, and a number might be justified. For example, when the electric advanced passenger train is introduced on the West Coast main line, some electric locomotives will become redundant and the construction of an electric link across North London and the extension of the Eastern Region system to Harwich and Felixstowe would enable them to be used.

Suburban electrification

A cost-benefit study of the Great Northern electrification indicated that it had a positive net present value greater than that of an alternative diesel scheme.[4] Electrification also appeared to have a higher benefit/net cost ratio. Gains to road users through reduced road congestion accounted for nearly half of the estimated benefit, and such gains are difficult to measure because of the possibility that other car owners will transfer onto the road-links once congestion is reduced. However, even when these gains are excluded, electrification still appears worthwhile, and the case has been strengthened by the increase in fuel prices.

There are two important ways in which the electrification of commuter routes differs from main-line electrification. Firstly, the electric suburban services will be faster and more comfortable than the diesel alternatives. They will therefore lead to substantial benefits to existing rail travellers, and to BR through the revenue gain from new travellers attracted by the improved service. We have seen that there will be little difference so far as Inter-City trains are concerned between future types of electric and diesel traction in terms of speed and comfort. Secondly, in urban areas a transfer of traffic from road to rail should lead to external benefits in the form of reduced road congestion. Again this will not apply to Inter-City services, because of the lack of serious traffic congestion on the motorways and dual carriage-ways that now link so many of Britain's principal towns.

Like the Great Northern line, the line from St Pancras to Bedford is a diesel-operated route running into the centre of London. Given the similarity, there seems a reasonable possibility that its electrification would also yield a satisfactory rate of return on cost-benefit grounds. However, the proposed electrifica-tions on the Southern Region involve routes beyond the Greater London area, where traffic congestion is less serious, so that the benefits from electrification might well fail to cover the costs. The same considerations apply to the Scottish Region's plan to electrify from Paisley to Ayr and Largs.

Conclusions on electrification

Our appraisal of the various electrification schemes proposed suggests that investment in fixed works for electrification should be cut by about two-thirds between 1973 and 1981, that is from £120 million to about £40 million. The latter figure would cover the completion of electrification to Glasgow, the Great Northern scheme, St Pancras–Bedford, the North London link, Colchester–Harwich/Felixstowe, and Bishops Stortford–Cambridge. Provided real oil prices do not rise substantially between 1974 and 1981, investment after 1981 should be cut even more drastically.

NEW CONSTRUCTION IN THE PASSENGER TRANSPORT EXECUTIVE AREAS

BR's June 1973 plans quoted a total investment in systems and operations on the Passenger Transport Executive areas' services of £93 million over the period from 1973 to 1981. This figure presumably includes investment in track renewal, and appears curiously low. In 1974 the PTEs in Tyneside, Merseyside, Greater Manchester and Glasgow were planning to spend £170 million on fixed works, excluding normal renewal of track and signalling, in the period up to 1981. However, actual expenditure depends not only on the PTEs' plans, but also on the availability of government finance, and on the speed with which construction programmes can be implemented.

There are two major uncertainties concerning the projected rail investments in conurbations. The first is the impact of such schemes on rail traffic. The projects considered have based their forecasts on relatively untested land-use and transportation studies which have predicted substantial increases in rail traffic. Even with such large increases in traffic, the resultant cost-benefit rates of return have been low. For instance, the Clyderail Report shows a benefit/cost ratio from the Glasgow scheme of 1·11, but this is achieved by excluding from costs the capital costs of the rolling-stock, and there is no justification for this. With all capital costs included, the benefit/cost ratio falls to an unsatisfactory 0·74. Secondly, there have been considerable increases in basic material costs since these studies were completed, so that actual capital costs are likely to be greater than originally projected. This suggests that, while the rail investment plans are an important attempt to solve city-centre transport problems, some caution should be exercised, and new schemes ought not to be approved until experience has been gained from those already under construction. This means that only the Merseyside and Tyneside projects should be undertaken before 1981, and that the proposed schemes in Manchester and Glasgow should be deferred. On Merseyside, work on the city-centre tunnels is well advanced, and approval of the associated electrification schemes is necessary to achieve full benefits from these tunnels. Though work is not so far advanced on the Tyneside rapid-transit system, this scheme constitutes an important and farsighted attempt to develop a new type of service better suited than the conventional rail system to the needs of the provincial conurbations. The rolling-stock will consist of articulated units similar to the modern trams used in many European cities. It is hoped that the units will be single-manned but will be in radio contact with a central control room. Outside the central areas, signalling will be by a simplified and relatively inexpensive two-aspect system operated not by signal-men but by the trains themselves. The rapid-transit system will be integrated with a system of feeder-bus networks. Our proposals imply that about £90 million would need to be invested in new construction in the PTEs over the period from 1973 to 1981, though none of this investment would be provided by BR.

PASSENGER STATION REBUILDING AND THE CONSTRUCTION OF
ROLLING-STOCK DEPOTS

In late 1973 BR was planning to spend £31 million between 1974 and 1978 on passenger stations and depots for Inter-City services; and £37 million on stations and depots for commuter services. This implies an expenditure of roughly £120 million at 1972 prices between 1973 and 1981. This seems high, particularly since major redevelopment schemes at main-line termini have been excluded. Though some new rolling-stock depots will be needed for the high-speed trains, the return from station rebuilding is difficult to measure even though some types of rebuilding can provide staff savings by reducing maintenance and ticket-checking re-quirements. In the absence of more detailed information, we suggest that the sums available for station rebuilding and rolling-stock depots should be reduced to £50 million.

One investment which will yield a high return, however, is the introduction of automatic fare collection (afc) systems. Following trials in the Glasgow area, BR has prepared a scheme costing £8 million which it expects will cover the London suburban network by 1982. Our own analysis of the prospects for afc systems, discussed in the following chapter, suggests a rapid extension of afc and an investment of £12½ million by the end of 1981.

THE HIGH-SPEED DIESEL TRAIN (HST) AND THE ADVANCED PASSENGER
TRAIN (APT)

By the end of 1981, BR plans to have 95 HST sets in operation,
but delays to the APT programme mean that, apart from the
prototype version, only 20 eight-car APT sets will be in operation
by the end of 1981; this compares with the 120 APT sets that were
included in the Interim Rail Strategy. At the end of 1974 the
capital cost of each eight-car HST set was reported by BR to be
£0·75 million at 1972 purchasing power. No precise figures are
available for the APT, though in 1972 BR claimed that the eight-
coach APT would cost 50% more than the seven-coach HST;
this gives a capital cost of about £1 million for each APT set at
1972 purchasing power. These figures imply a total investment in
HST and APT units of £88 million by 1981. In addition, BR
plans to spend £19 million at 1972 purchasing power on APT
development and on the construction of the electric prototypes
between 1974 and 1978.

As we have seen in Chapter 2, 125 mph trains should lead to
substantial revenue gains. In appraising these investments, it is
necessary to consider not only investment in rolling-stock, but
also the other expenditure which high-speed running will involve.
Additional capital costs include modifications to trackwork, the
installation of multiple-aspect signalling if the route concerned
has not already been resignalled, and the modification of level
crossings and automatic warning systems. The extra running costs
comprise additional track maintenance work, the expense of
retaining extra track capacity because of the greater differential
between the fastest and slowest trains, and the costs of running
additional parcels trains because of the lack of sufficient parcels
capacity on the new trains.

The HST

The first line on which the HST will be introduced is the Pad-
dington–Bristol–South Wales route, where 27 seven-coach train
sets will be operating from 1976 onwards. We calculated the net
present value (NPV) of the investment in these train sets on a

number of alternative assumptions. The full capital cost of £0·70 million for each train set comprises about £200,000 for each of the two power cars and about £43,000 for each of the seven Mark III coaches. In one of our NPV calculations these cost figures were used. However, our appraisal is concerned with the incremental impact of the HST on BR's revenues and costs, and use of the total capital cost of the train set implies that the existing trains operating on this route will not need replacement before 1987 (the year in which the HSTs themselves will require replacement). This is unlikely, and the alternative assumption was made that the Mark III coaches in the HST sets would need to be built in any case in order to preserve the existing revenue, so that only the cost of the power cars is properly counted as an incremental cost. Finally, because of their faster speed, the HST coaches will have a higher utilisation than those in conventional trains, and our third set of NPV calculations assumes a capital cost for the HST which allows for the reduced investment in coaches which this makes possible.

The capital costs of the train sets were assumed to be spread evenly over the years 1974 and 1975. A further capital cost of £0·75 million was included to cover civil engineering work in 1974 and 1975 to increase line speed to 125 mph. Track maintenance costs were assumed to increase by £350 a mile per annum, and £0·20 million per annum was included to cover the running of additional parcels trains. Since train mileage will increase with the HST, the additional operating costs were estimated by multiplying BR's average movement cost per mile for Inter-City services in 1972 by the difference between the train mileage which the HST sets should cover, and present train mileage on the route.

BR has claimed that operating costs per mile will be the same for high-speed and conventional trains. This must be treated with some caution, particularly since high speeds imply sharply rising fuel costs and higher maintenance costs. Driver productivity will be improved by faster speeds, but it appears likely that BR will have to pay its drivers extra for 125 mph running. We therefore calculated our NPVs on three alternative operating-cost assumptions: that operating costs per mile will be the same as for conventional trains, that they will be 10% higher and that they will be 20% higher. Our figures were calculated from annual train mileages for the HSTs and from the BR figures of average movement cost per mile for Inter-City services. It was assumed that the HST sets would have a life in revenue-earning service of twelve years. Revenue growth was derived from the forecasts of Inter-City traffic and revenue for the route which were estimated in Chapter 2, on the assumption that, in the absence of the HST, traffic on the route would grow at a rate of only $\frac{1}{2}\%$ per annum. This traffic growth was converted into a revenue gain by assuming that revenue per mile would be equal to the average fare per mile on BR's Inter-City services. No allowance was made for the possibility that BR will be able to increase fares on improved services more rapidly than on other Inter-City services. Finally, in order to cover the possibility that our forecasts may be over-optimistic, it was assumed as a further alternative that revenue growth will be only 75% of the amount predicted.

TABLE 7.2: *Net Present Values of High-speed Diesel Trains, London–Bristol–South Wales*

Treatment of capital costs	Operating costs: percentage above those of conventional trains	Net present value with full revenue gain (£m)	Net present value with 75% revenue gain (£m)
Full capital	0	+ 8·3	+ 1·9
costs of	+10	+ 5·3	− 1·1
train set	+20	+ 2·3	− 4·1
Capital costs	0	+14·7	+ 8·2
of power cars	+10	+11·7	+ 5·3
only	+20	+ 8·7	+ 2·3
Capital costs	0	+16·6	+10·1
of power cars,	+10	+13·6	+ 7·2
less allowance	+20	+10·6	+ 4·2
for increased			
coach			
utilisation			

Note: All costs and revenues have been discounted back to 1972.

All these costs and benefits were discounted at 10% per annum to yield NPVs in 1972. As Table 7.2 indicates, the HST will earn a satisfactory rate of return if we include the full capital costs of the train sets, unless revenue is much less than expected *and* operating costs increase. However, we have already argued that it is inappropriate to count the full capital costs as an *incremental* cost. If we include only the capital costs of the power cars, then NPVs will be positive for all combinations of our assumptions. Hence, it appears that investment in HST sets for the London–Bristol–South Wales route is economically justifiable.

On the East Coast main line 32 eight-coach HST train sets are to be introduced in 1977 and 1978. It has been estimated that in addition to their capital cost, £11 million will have to be spent on maintenance depots and on the preparation of track, signalling, and level crossings for 125 mph running. Nevertheless, if the revenue gains to be expected from the HST on this route are discounted at 10%, it appears that the HST power cars will yield a rate of return above 10% after allowance has been made for increased track maintenance and operating expenses. Therefore, investment in HSTs for the East Coast main line will also be justified.

The remaining 36 HST sets which BR plans to build will run on the London–South-West, London–Sheffield, and North-East–South-West routes. Investment in HSTs for these routes must be carefully appraised. Revenue and passenger loadings are lower than on the two previous routes, so that the revenue gain to be expected will also be lower. In addition, the configuration of these routes is much less suitable for 125 mph running. A careful appraisal therefore needs to be made, case by case, before expenditure on the last 36 HSTs is finally authorised. Such an appraisal might in turn cast doubt on the return from some of the power signalling schemes discussed earlier in this chapter.

The APT

We used the same method as for the HST to appraise the rate of return from introducing the electric APT onto the West Coast main line. The capital cost of the APT was taken to be the cost of its power cars, plus the additional cost of APT trailers over Mark III coaches, and three alternative assumptions about the relationship between the running costs of the APT and of conventional trains were made. Account was taken of the likely increase in track maintenance costs, and rough figures of £5 million for track improvements, and £0·4 million per annum for extra parcels trains were also included. Development costs were based on the forecasts BR made in late 1973.

TABLE 7.3: *Net Present Values of Advanced Passenger Trains, West Coast Main Line Services*

	Same as those of conventional trains *NPV (£m)*	*APT operating costs 10% above those of conventional trains* *NPV (£m)*	*20% above those of conventional trains* *NPV (£m)*
Excluding development costs:			
Full revenue gain	+44·4	+38·6	+32·8
75% revenue gain	+26·6	+20·8	+15·1
Including prospective development costs:			
Full revenue gain	+29·9	+24·1	+18·3
75% revenue gain	+12·1	+ 6·3	+ 0·6

Note: All costs and revenues have been discounted back to 1972.

The costs and benefits discounted at 10% per annum back to 1972 are shown in Table 7.3. It can be seen that the West Coast APT will yield a return sufficient to cover the anticipated development costs of the APT programme, even on the most pessimistic combination of our assumptions. These conclusions assume that the APT continues to run at 125 mph. Our preliminary calculations suggest a very low rate of return from increasing maximum speeds from 125 to 155 mph, because of the high capital costs of cab signalling and of track modifications, and the relatively small reduction in journey time which such a speed increase would permit.

The rate of return from introducing the gas turbine APT on the East Coast line appears to be much lower than that from introducing the electric APT on the West Coast line. This is because speeds on the East Coast line will already be high because of the HST. Nevertheless, East Coast revenue would show some gain because of the higher average speed of the APT, while the additional track and signalling costs would be very small since the HST will already be running at 125 mph. The rate of return from the APT on the East Coast line (excluding development costs) will be above 10% if the capital costs of the gas turbine APT are the same as those of its electric counterpart and if running costs are less than 20% above those of conventional trains. However, the major area of uncertainty lies in the feasibility and costs of a gas turbine APT, and any escalation of these costs would jeopardise the profitability of the East Coast APT. In view of the risk involved, it would seem reasonable to defer the decision on the gas turbine APT until more information is gained on the impact of high-speed trains on passenger revenue, and on the technical feasibility and cost of a gas turbine version. This appears to be BR's policy.

Conclusions on high-speed trains

Investment in both types of high-speed trains involves risks. Nevertheless, there appears to be a strong possibility that investment in HSTs for the London–Bristol–South Wales route and the East Coast main line, and in the electric APT for the West Coast main line, will yield a very satisfactory return. Other high-speed investments appear much more marginal, namely introduction of the HST on other routes, production of a gas turbine version of the APT, and acceleration of maximum speeds from 125 mph to 155 mph. The latter two investments fall outside our immediate period of consideration. If detailed appraisals of the HST on the London–South West, London–Sheffield and North-East–South-West line prove that its introduction there is not justifiable, then £82 million (including the cost of developing the APT) should be invested in high-speed rolling-stock between 1972 and 1981. This is less than half the figure implied by the plans outlined in BR's Interim Rail Strategy, and although most of the difference is accounted for by delays to the APT programme, our conclusions do suggest that this programme should be much curtailed after 1981.

LOCOMOTIVE-HAULED COACHES

At the end of 1973, BR operated 7152 locomotive-hauled coaches for passenger traffic. Of these 4459 were the older Mark I vehicles, 963 were Mark II vehicles without air-conditioning, 689 were Mark II vehicles with air-conditioning, 497 were catering vehicles, 398 were sleeping-cars, and the remaining 146 consisted largely of compartment stock. A further 286 air-conditioned Mark IIf coaches were on order at the end of 1973, and were to be followed by the Mark III coach designed both for the HST and for haulage by conventional locomotives. Construction of the first build of 300 Mark III coaches for locomotive-hauled services commenced in 1974.

BR's policy is to use its newest coaches on its most profitable services, and cascade older builds down onto secondary services and onto services which run on only one or two days in the week or only during the summer months. In 1974, about 2750 non-specialised coaches were in daily use on Inter-City services, and another 800 on grant-aided services and a few minor Inter-City routes. A further 1600 coaches were used either once or twice per week or only during the summer. Finally, 700 coaches, reserved for summer holiday traffic, were used very infrequently. Investment in new coaches will depend primarily on the ages of those in the first group, since it is traffic carried in these coaches which accounts for the great bulk of revenue. We estimate that, due to the introduction of the HST and APT, the numbers of these coaches in daily use on Inter-City services will decline from 2750 in 1974 to 2000 in 1981. To cover this requirement there will be 1275 air-conditioned Mark II and Mark III vehicles, all built after 1970, for services on the most important routes, and 725 of the non air-conditioned Mark II coaches, built between 1964 and 1970, for less important Inter-City services. Allowing for the other 240 Mark II coaches that would be available and for an expected reduction in the numbers of coaches used least frequently, 2300 Mark I coaches would need to be retained for seasonal time-tabled trains, for a few minor Inter-City services and for locomotive-hauled trains on non Inter-City lines. Assuming that the oldest Mark I coaches are scrapped first, these coaches will be 17 to 24 years old by 1981, but they will not be intensively used, and will mostly be operating unprofitable services. In any case, most can be withdrawn soon after 1981 as the APT building programme will permit large numbers of newer coaches to be cascaded downwards. We do not therefore believe that there is any justification in building further non-specialised locomotive-hauled coaches before 1981 once the present build of 300 locomotive-hauled Mark III coaches has been completed. The rate of introduction of new locomotive-hauled coaches in the 1980s will depend upon whether the HST is introduced on lines other than the London–Bristol–South Wales route and the East Coast main line, and on whether the APT runs on the East Coast main line.

So far as specialised vehicles are concerned, the high-speed trains will allow withdrawal of some 175 of the present 497 locomotive-hauled catering vehicles by 1981. The remaining locomotive-hauled coaches would then be 20 years old, but apart from those due to be replaced by the APT soon after 1981, the remainder would be operating on secondary Inter-City services and there does not appear to be any need for their replacement, at least before 1981. BR plans to begin replacing its 398 sleeping-cars, all built before 1965, with a Mark III version in the late 1970s, and again this replacement appears to be premature.

Our proposals suggest that investment in locomotive-hauled coaches before 1981 should be limited to the Mark IIe and IIf coaches built since the end of 1972, and to the first build of 300 locomotive-hauled Mark III coaches. The capital cost of these coaches is £33,000 for the Mark IIs and £43,000 for the Mark IIIs, giving a total investment of £29 million in locomotive-hauled coaches from 1973 to 1981. A precise figure of BR's plans is not available, but it appears to be of the order of £80 million over the same period.

ELECTRIC MULTIPLE UNITS

As Table 7.4 shows, the total number of electric multiple units (emus) operated by BR at the end of 1973 was 7150. At present the oldest emus on BR are 35 years old and a 35-year life for

TABLE 7.4: *Existing Electric Multiple Unit Stock*

	Number of coaches at end of 1973	*Number over 25 years old in 1981*	*Number over 35 years old in 1981*
Southern Region inner-suburban	2503	1727	0
Southern Region outer-suburban and express	2067	0	0
Other London and South-East	1511	301	28
	6081	2028	28
PTEs	1069a	246a	222a
Total	7150	2274	250

a Includes a few electric multiple units working on grant-aided services outside the London and South-East and PTE areas.

emus has in the past been usual on BR. Moreover this continues to be the standard life on London Transport. However, BR is now planning to reduce the average life to 25 years, and to replace its older inner-suburban stock with new emus whose capital cost will be substantially greater than that of conventional coaches.

On the Southern Region all the present outer-suburban and express electric units have been built since 1956, so that even with a 25-year life, none should need replacing before 1981. The Southern Region's inner-suburban units (numbering some 2500 in all) are older and with a 25-year life they will need replacing from the mid-1970s. BR is at present testing a new prototype inner-suburban train (known as PEP stock) which it originally hoped would be used to replace inner-suburban coaches at a rate of 200 units per annum from 1976 onwards. On other regions, and on the Southern Region's Isle of Wight and Waterloo and City lines, 547 emus will be over 25 years old by the end of 1981. Most of the 300 units operating in the South-East were rebuilt in 1960–61 and might well survive beyond 1981, but BR is planning to replace 200 units in the provinces. In all, therefore, 1200 emus would be replaced by 1981 if the necessary capital were made available. Retention of a 35-year life would require a very much lower level of replacement investment over the period from

1973 to 1981 because only about 250 units will reach the age of 35 by 1981.

BR's planned replacement programme is rather difficult to cost because of uncertainty about the capital cost of the new PEP stock. The stock incorporates many new features which are likely to increase its capital cost relative to that of conventional stock, including the powering of all axles to improve acceleration, and provision of automatic couplings and power doors. It appears that a conventional inner-suburban coach might have cost about £41,000 in 1972 and that the PEP stock might cost about 50% more. This puts its cost at around £61,500 per coach.

We can now consider whether BR's planned replacement programme is optimal. BR can adopt a 25-year life for emus, which implies that they must start replacing their Southern Region inner-suburban units from about 1976 onwards, or they can continue to base their emu replacement programme on a 35-year life. Once they have decided on their stock's length of life, they can choose to replace their stock with new stock of a similar design to the present, or they can build the more sophisticated PEP stock currently on trial. Alternatively, they could replace with stock fitted with power doors, but without the PEP stock's other expensive refinements. For instance, they might use a vehicle rather similar to the latest stock used by London Transport on its Metropolitan line. Such stock might cost around £47,000 per coach at 1972 prices.

The use of power doors means that station staff do not have to be employed to see that doors have been properly shut and to close those which have been left open. In addition, use of power doors prevents accidents which occur when doors are opened while trains are in motion. Thirdly, use of power doors on suburban trains would make it possible to dispense with guards. The Railway Inspectorate are permitting the introduction of one-man operation on London Transport, and there are no operational reasons why it should not be feasible on BR suburban services.

At the beginning of 1971, the Southern Region had 1950 station staff excluding those engaged on the sale, reservation and inspection of tickets. It seems reasonable to assume that 500 of these men could be saved by installing power doors on all inner-suburban stock, and this would lead to an economy of £0·95 million per annum. On the basis of experience in a recent year on the Southern Region, it can be estimated that power doors would lead to an accident-reduction benefit of £0·3 million per annum. Finally, we estimated the gains from the savings in guards through one-man operation. There are 1955 guards employed on this Region, of whom roughly 1000 are employed on inner-suburban operations, and so might be removed. This saving will involve some capital expenditure. If the Railway Inspectorate were to require BR to install equipment similar to that required for London Transport's one-man operation, then the total capital cost for Southern Region's inner-suburban services would be of the order of £14 million. We spread this cost over the period of construction of the trains. The saving in labour costs and the accident-reduction benefits were increased at an annual rate of 3% to allow for the increase in real wages. Besides the benefits which power doors will provide, PEP should yield extra revenue because it is more comfortable than conventional stock. The relationship between comfort and the demand for rail services is unknown, and we simply assumed that the PEP stock would increase revenue on the Southern Region's inner-suburban services by about 5%.

In order to compare the different types of coach, we assumed that a replacement programme would start in 1976 and continue at a rate of 200 cars per annum until its completion in 1987. The benefits from conventional and PEP stock were assumed to rise in line with the proportion of total inner-suburban units fitted with power doors. The costs and benefits for the 35 years from 1976 were discounted at 10% per annum back to 1972 to yield the net present values of the alternative stock-replacement programmes. The results indicated that the installation of power doors would be justified when coaches are replaced. Furthermore, the additional capital expense required for one-man operation would be justified by the extra savings. However, the revenue which might (hopefully) arise through the introduction of PEP stock would not justify the additional capital expenditure involved. It may be concluded that BR should replace with power-door stock, and that it will be worth switching to one-man operation. However, the likely revenue gain from introducing PEP would not, even on very optimistic assumptions, justify the heavy cost which would be incurred.

It now remains to consider whether BR is justified in introducing power-door stock from 1976 onwards, given that existing stock could continue in operation until the late 1980s. Premature replacement would be justified if the benefits from power-door operation, in the period before replacement would otherwise have been due, exceed the capital costs of premature replacement. Our net present value calculations suggest that they do not, and that if BR engages in premature replacement even of the most economical type (and BR's plans do not envisage one-man operation) then there will be a waste of over £20 million.

The conclusion is that the PEP stock programme should be discontinued; electric multiple units should only be replaced when they have reached the end of their life which should be kept at 35 years; and when new units do have to be purchased they should be equipped with power doors to permit one-man operation. If this policy is adopted, BR will only need to spend £10 million on replacing emus over the period 1973–81, in contrast to the £80 million which it wishes to invest. Even between 1982 and 1991, when extensive re-equipment will become necessary, capital expenditure should total no more than about £70 million, as against the £250 million which BR will spend if it goes ahead with its current programme.

We can deal with construction of emus for newly electrified lines, and to allow for traffic growth, more quickly. There is no length of life problem, and we have already determined that BR should use conventional stock, although on the inner-suburban services new coaches should have power doors. The Great Northern electrification will require 296 new units and a further 184 new units would be required for the St Pancras–Bedford electrification. On the Southern Region, electrification from Tonbridge to Hastings will, together with two smaller projects, displace 207 diesel units. A total of 687 new units will therefore be required as a result of electrification in the South-East. Of these, 376 would be inner-suburban units. The number of coaches needed because of the growth of traffic in the South-East is more difficult to determine. During 1973, 157 units were constructed for the Southern Region, and a further 76 new units are due to be delivered to the Liverpool Street and Fenchurch Street lines. We decided to assume a total requirement of around 350 outer-suburban units for traffic growth throughout the South-East.

In the conurbations, the requirement for new emus will be

dependent on how much progress is made with new construction. Assuming our suggestions concerning the rate of new construction in the PTEs are accepted, 100 conventional emu coaches will be needed on Merseyside, and 100 articulated units on Tyneside, by 1981. It is understood that the cost of the latter units will be £150,000 each. This very high figure is partly due to the fact that mass production is not possible in the United Kingdom because of the lack of a domestic market for this type of vehicle.

These plans imply a proposed net investment of £72 million in new, as opposed to replacement, emus. Our earlier conclusions, that the extra expense of the PEP stock is not justified, suggest that inner-suburban units should be conventional power-door stock. This will reduce the total capital requirement for new stock by £7 million. Refusal of approval for the Southern Region electrifications would reduce costs by a further £9 million. We estimate a final figure for replacement *and* net investment in emus on all lines of £66 million, compared with the sum of about £166 million implied by BR's plans. Most of this difference is accounted for by BR's desire to replace electric multiple units prematurely, and to use an unnecessarily expensive alternative.

FREIGHT WAGONS

Table 7.5 shows that, in August 1974, BR owned over 247,000 freight vehicles. In addition, some 19,000 privately-owned wagons, of which 13,000 were tank wagons, were permitted to operate over BR lines. BR has long been hampered by a fleet of wagons which includes a high proportion of slow, low capacity vehicles which limit freight-train speeds. The two most important factors determining maximum permitted freight train speeds are braking systems and length of wheelbase. Wagons are fitted either with air brakes or with the much less efficient vacuum brake, or are completely unfitted. Most of the privately-owned wagons have vacuum or air brakes. In 1974 BR owned only 12,201 air-braked wagons, which are used mainly for merry-go-round and Freightliner traffic. The remainder of BR's fleet consists of vacuum or unfitted stock. Though some of the vacuum stock is permitted to travel at 60 mph, the major factor limiting the speed of this fleet

TABLE 7.5:   *Number of Freight Wagons, August 1974*

	Air-braked	Vacuum-braked	Unbraked	Total
Owned by British Rail:				
Covered	1 020	29 931	1 199	32 150
Open	220	22 203	609	23 032
Mineral	8 223	32 332	118 943	159 498
Steel	525	15 084	9 647	25 256
Container-carrying	2 213	5 244	0	7 457
Total BR wagons[a]	12 201	104 794	130 398	247 393
Privately-owned wagons	8 478	8 036	2 492	19 006
Total	20 679	112 830	132 890	266 399

[a] Excludes departmental vehicles and brakevans.

is length of wheelbase. Because of the sharply rising trend of freight train derailments from 1963 onwards, all short-wheelbase wagons are limited to 45 mph. At the end of 1972, such wagons accounted for 63% of BR's total fleet. In addition, those wagons (mainly used for mineral traffic) which are not fitted with brakes are limited to 35 mph or even 25 mph, unless marshalled in a train containing a 'fitted head' of braked wagons next to the locomotive.

Freight train speeds with the non air-braked fleet are therefore generally low, with consequent higher train-crew and locomotive costs per mile. Most of the wagons have low capacities, so that train payloads are low in relation to maximum permitted train lengths and gross train weights. The large fleet required involves high maintenance costs, while increases in freight train speeds would increase track capacity and permit the complete closure of some routes. The replacement of the existing wagon fleet should also produce important improvements in the quality of service offered to rail freight users. Finally, most of the wagons concerned will, by the mid 1980s, be 30 or more years old.

BR has developed plans for the systematic renewal of its wagon fleet used by traffics which are thought to have a long-term future. These plans originally envisaged the expenditure of £71 million between end 1972 and end 1981, and of a further £12 million by the end of 1985, but the figures were revised upwards to about £114 million at 1972 purchasing power to allow for much higher future coal traffic levels. This expenditure would involve a rapid reduction of the BR-owned wagon fleet to about 75,000 vehicles, including departmental vehicles, by 1985. This reduction will be due to three main factors: the increase in average wagon capacity, the expected increase in the proportion of tonnage handled in private wagons from 19% in 1972 to 37% in 1985, and the decline of wagonload working.

The plans imply that by 1985 most coal and steel traffic will be carried in modern wagons, and that by that year the only non air-braked wagons in service will be used for some trainload services using vacuum-braked stock, and for what remains of the declining wagonload coal traffic. We believe that the plans to replace the wagon fleet are basically sound and that capital should be made available, but it is important that only wagons used for profitable services are replaced; that new wagons are not provided for traffics which do not have a clear long-term future; and that strenuous efforts are made to improve wagon turn-round times.

The utilisation of new wagons implied by BR's planned replacement programme does appear to be unsatisfactory. Firstly, on the basis of their forecast tonnages of traffic in 1985, BR appears to be assuming an average tonnage carried per wagon per year of about 1130 tons for those BR-owned wagons not used for merry-go-round (mgr) or Freightliner traffic. If each wagon made 60 loaded trips per annum, which was the average utilisation for the wagons of twenty European railways for which data are available in 1970, and if there were an increase in average loads per wagon of about 20% between 1974 and 1985, then each wagon should carry 1500 tons per annum. These loadings imply that by 1985 BR will require only three-quarters of the wagons for the non-mgr and non-Freightliner traffic which their own plans assume. Secondly, we do not believe that BR needs to build any further mgr wagons. BR estimates that it will require a further 2200 such wagons, of which 1000 have already been ordered, and this would imply a utilisation of 205 loaded trips per year. This implies there will be no improvement in utilisation, though in fact there should be a substantial improvement through the provision of rapid-loading facilities at collieries, the main bottleneck to efficient use of mgr wagons. In 1973–74, only about one-third of the coal carried in mgr wagons was loaded automatically, but by 1981 the National Coal Board expects this proportion to rise to

55–60%. This suggests that the existing fleet should be sufficient to cater for forecast mgr tonnages, and that any further orders for mgr wagons cannot be justified. We estimate that improved utilisation of wagons would reduce the required investment in wagon replacement between 1972 and 1985 from £114 million to about £85 million. Of this, about £73 million might be incurred before the end of 1981.

BRITISH RAIL'S OPTIMAL INVESTMENT LEVEL

We have now appraised investment projects accounting for 80% of the investment level of £1787 million proposed by BR in its Interim Rail Strategy. The remaining 20% of investment covers a wide variety of projects including replacement of level crossings, development of BR's National Telecommunications Plan and of the TOPS wagon information system, replacement of track maintenance vehicles, refurbishment of diesel multiple units and a wide range of minor projects. We cannot hope to discuss all these projects in detail, and so we will include a further £15 million per annum to cover any additional projects that are desirable. This gives total investment in BR's railway operations, excluding

TABLE 7.6: *Desirable Railway Investment, 1973–81*
(£ million, 1972 purchasing power)

	Total
Track renewal	340
Track rationalisation	7
Resignalling	90
Electrification, fixed works	40
Electrification, locomotives	10
PTE fixed works	90
Station rebuilding, rolling-stock depots	50
Automatic fare collection systems	13
High-speed trains, including development costs	82
Locomotive-hauled coaches	29
Electric multiple units	66
Freight wagons	73
Other	135
	1 025

only investment in private wagons, of £1025 million between the end of 1972 and the end of 1981. This investment is shown in Table 7.6. The main differences between our suggested investment figures and those implied by the investment plans in BR's Interim Rail Strategy, are in resignalling (about £135 million), high-speed trains (about £130 million), electric multiple units (about £100 million), electrification fixed works (about £80 million), station and depot rebuilding (about £70 million), locomotive-hauled coaches (roughly £50 million) and track renewal (about £25 million).

Excluding the investment in new construction schemes in the PTE areas, our investment proposals represent an annual rate of investment which is about 10% above the actual investment levels of 1972 and 1973. We will return to consider the financing of this investment in our final chapter.

CHAPTER 8

Manpower and Expenditure

In this chapter we shall try to determine what labour force British Rail will require in 1981. It will be assumed that it will carry all the traffic that has been forecast and that no significant line closures take place. Only when the minimum operating cost has been identified will it be possible to see which traffic, if any, it will be desirable to relinquish. It will also be assumed that railway workers and their unions do not obstruct the changes in operating practice which will be proposed. Consideration of the way in which co-operation can be obtained must be deferred until the changes have been identified and it is possible to see how much redundancy they would cause. However, nothing will be proposed which has not already been adopted in some other country, or which represents such a sharp break with existing practice that there is little hope of union agreement. For instance, no account has been taken of the possibility that drivers could act as guards when they would otherwise be idle. Improvements were also ruled out if they were so radical that a very high order of management might be necessary for their attainment.

TRAIN CREWS

To discover how many workers British Rail will need in 1981 each group of employees will be examined in turn. The size of the various groups and the order in which they will be reviewed can be seen from Table 8.9 on page 176. Train crews and associated workers numbered around 34,500 at the beginning of 1971, and constituted one of the largest blocks of railway workers. Their make-up is shown in Table 8.1. Drivers were the principal

TABLE 8.1: *Train Crew Staff*[a]

	30 January 1971	1981
Drivers:		
Passenger	7 490	
Parcel	660	
Freight	7 840	10 330
Departmental	780	
Training and route learning	1 320	660
	18 090	10 990
Second men and traction trainees	7 350	1 270
Guards	7 620	500
Training and route-learning miscellaneous staff	60	30
Rostering and miscellaneous salaried staff	1 520	1 020
Total employed	34 640	13 810

[a] Excluding passenger guards (see Table 8.4) and shunting (see Table 8.3).

Note: Any discrepancies between figures in the tables and figures in the text are a result of rather more drastic rounding in the text.

element and, excluding those engaged on shunting, numbered around 18,000. How many British Rail will require in 1981 will depend on the distance its trains cover, the speed at which they travel, and the amount of time that its drivers spend driving.

Train Miles and Loads

The train mileage which was performed in 1971 and is estimated for 1981 is shown in Table 8.2. By 1981 British Rail's passenger-train mileage is likely to be about 6% greater than it was during the early 1970s, due largely to electrification and the more intensive service to which it will lead. There is however likely to be a considerable fall in the distance travelled by other coaching trains because of the rationalisation of Rail Express, and the loss of Post Office and newspaper traffic. More important, there ought to be a significant reduction in the mileage performed by freight trains due to the reduction in freight traffic from 15½ billion ton miles in 1970–71 to 14 billion in 1981, and to an increase in the average train load.

The heaviest trains are used for merry-go-round coal, iron ore, and earths and stones; and our freight forecasts suggest that in 1981 they will together account for almost half the total tonnage,

TABLE 8.2: *Train Miles Performed by British Rail (million)*

	1970	1971	1981
Passenger:			
Inter-City		49·8	56·5
London and South-East	182·7	79·2	82·0
Other		55·3	57·0
Empty	9·5	9·5	9·5
	192·2	193·8	205·0
Other coaching[a]	13·2	13·4	8·5
Freight:			
Loaded	62·7	57·1	38·0
Empty	12·6	12·0	12·0
	75·3	69·1	50·0
Departmental[b]	11·2	12·0	11·0
Total train miles	291·9	288·3	274·5
Type of traction:			
Diesel locomotive	134·2	130·6	107·5[c]
Electric locomotive	19·9	19·8	26·0[c]
Diesel multiple units	61·3	60·9	54·0
Electric multiple units	76·5	77·0	87·0

[a] Trains exclusively for mail, papers and parcels (other than those for NCL)

[b] Trains to and from workshops, breakdown trains, etc.

[c] Including HST and APT at 11·8 and 3·25 million miles respectively.

compared with 38% in 1973. There will also be a considerable reduction in wagonload traffic, where the number of train miles per ton is about 4½ times greater than it is for trainload working, though this is partly due to the commodities involved. Furthermore by 1981 most of the constraints that have for so long held down the size of British freight trains ought to have been removed. The elimination of loose-coupled wagons should, for instance, end the situation in which the weight of freight trains has to be restricted because, in the absence of a proper braking system, they are very difficult to stop. Due to the low carrying capacity of the average wagon it is often impossible for the engine to pull sufficient wagons to accommodate a large load. However, the smaller wagons are being scrapped and the new air-braked stock has a high capacity in relation to its tare weight.

Between 1968 and 1973 the number of ton miles per train mile increased from just under 245 to about 285, and it will be assumed that it will go on increasing at the same rate to 370 by 1981. If so, BR's freight train mileage should, even with a generous allowance for empty running, decline from 72 million in 1970-71 to 50 million by 1981; a reduction of 30%. This is very important, because freight trains involve a much larger amount of work than their mileage may suggest.

Train Speeds

In 1971 the average speed of all freight trains was a pitiful 21 mph, and in 1973 it was still only 22½ mph. The average is so low because, due to the characteristics of the wagons they contain, a high proportion of BR's freight trains are restricted to a maximum speed of 45 mph or less. These trains averaged only just over 19 mph during 1973, whereas those that were permitted to travel at between 45 and 60 had an average speed of 30½ mph, and for those with a maximum of between 60 and 75 the average was 33½ mph. By 1981 a major part of British Rail's own wagon fleet ought to be capable of speeds of 60 mph or more, and so will the great bulk of privately-owned wagons, which are likely to carry about a quarter of BR's traffic.

By 1981 BR should, even with the reduced programme of investment that we have suggested, possess about 25,000 high-speed air-braked wagons out of the 75,000 wagons we estimate later that it will require. This air-braked stock, which should have a high rate of utilisation, will be capable of at least 60 mph, and the Freightliner flats and some of the other wagons are able to travel at 75 mph. A high proportion of those vacuum-braked wagons that will remain in service will be permitted to travel at 50 to 60 mph because they will be long-wheelbase stock. However the great majority of BR's mineral wagons will still only be able to move at a relatively low speed. The merry-go-round wagons are restricted to 45 mph when loaded (although they can travel at 55 mph when empty); well over half of the non-air-braked coal wagons will be limited to 45 mph, and the remaining vehicles are only capable of 50 mph.

This will have less effect on the average speed of British Rail's freight than might be expected. Coal and other low-speed mineral-wagon trains composed of BR stock tend to be very heavy. They will account for only about 17% of the total freight train mileage in 1981, and will be comfortably outdistanced by Freightliners. Moreover, a high proportion of mineral-wagon traffic is concentrated on a small part of the system where it does not conflict with other freight trains. At present, the railways' mineral and other slow-moving freight trains tend to impede those which are able to move relatively fast. Hence Freightliners average only 38 mph and oil trains average as little as 20 mph, although they are permitted to travel at 60 mph. However, if slow-moving trains become the exception and not the rule, it will be possible to programme trains which are capable of 60 to 75 mph at something more nearly approaching their maximum speed.

It therefore seems reasonable to assume that by 1981 freight trains should average at least 30 mph, although BR is only planning to increase the average speed to about 24 mph by 1985. Due to the positioning of the staging points, where drivers take over and exchange trains, BR considers that if any real speed-up is to take place it will have to be substantial and so, despite its large planned investments in high-speed wagons, it has settled for the status quo. On the passenger side there is less scope for an increase in speed. However, there should be a rise of about 15% on Inter-City services, because of the completion of electrification to Glasgow and the introduction of the HST and APT, and a slight increase in the pace of commuter services with electrification.

Driving Time

Like the speed of freight trains, the amount of time that drivers spend driving is incredibly low. On the London Midland Region the amount of productive time – the interval between the departure and the arrival of the train – averages only about $3\frac{3}{4}$ hours per driver during their 8-hour turn of duty. This includes shunting and it has been found in one Division that, when trains that involve shunting are excluded, the average driving time for diesel-hauled freight is less than $2\frac{1}{2}$ hours per turn of duty.

The most obvious reason is that when drivers have arrived at their destination there may not be a train for them to drive back, in which case their return journey will be merely as a passenger. Alternatively, they may have to pick up a train at a particular point, but not have any train to drive there. Although drivers will never be able to spend all their time productively, it should be possible to push up the amount of driving by concentrating freight traffic on as few routes and depots as possible. The greater the number of trains that are handled by a depot, or that pass over a route, the higher the probability that when a train is driven out there will be another train available for the driver to drive back. British Rail has already made some progress here, but it seems likely that there is still considerable scope for improvement. Moreover, as the speed of freight trains increases, the number of unproductive journeys should tend to decline, because there will be more destinations to which it is possible for drivers to drive out and back in a day.

Driving is also restricted by the wide margin of unproductive time which occurs before and after journeys. This is partly unavoidable, because some time must be allowed for drivers to read notices about temporary speed restrictions and other important matters, and it would be unrealistic to schedule drivers on the assumption that every train will arrive precisely on time. However, the delays which occur are often enormous, with a quarter of all company trains arriving over two hours late during a sample period, and the margin for late running now averages almost half an hour. Furthermore a high proportion of the freight trains which are scheduled never run, while others which have not been scheduled do run. Although BR knows that many trains will be cancelled and plans accordingly, it cannot make the best use of its drivers when trains are deleted and inserted at short notice, because the task of re-rostering is too complex to be undertaken in more than a very rough-and-ready fashion.

There are two ways in which the problem of rapid changes in demand can be tackled. First, it is possible to use computers to work out the best possible way in which drivers and locomotives can be redeployed. Considerable savings in locomotives have already been made, and it is hoped that in about three years time it will be possible to apply the same techniques to train drivers. This is less easy because the constraints on the use of men are more numerous. By the early 1980s it may be possible to combine the scheduling procedures for drivers and locomotives, and work out the best possible joint utilisation.

The second way of dealing with rapid shifts in demand is to attempt to reduce their magnitude by charging particularly favourable rates for traffic which does not vary in amount, destination or the time for collection. Under the original company-train contracts for oil and other commodities, the charge was linked to the ton mileage which was carried each year, with a low rate being charged for any amount above the minimum. Thus rail users have not had any encouragement to furnish truly regular traffic, but only to forward a certain minimum tonnage. British Rail is aware that the contracts need tightening up and reframing, but as yet comparatively little progress has been made. If the optimum use is to be made of drivers and engines, demand needs to be less peaky as well as more stable. It should be possible to make some progress towards peak-related prices by 1981, although it would be wrong to expect that enormous progress will be made because the troughs in demand are of relatively short duration.

Unfortunately, it does not always pay BR to use its drivers more productively, because of the penalties which it incurs as various time and distance limits are passed. Under the agreement of 1974, drivers receive a mileage-related bonus when they cover more than 200 miles in a day, and prior to 1974 bonus payments started at 125 miles. In addition, under the manning agreement of 1965 a second man must accompany the driver when the non-stop distance or time, or the aggregate distance or time exceed certain limits. Although the agreement probably leads to some restriction of drivers' hours, it would be wrong to exaggerate the extent to which they are limited. In order to secure the unions' agreement BR undertook that any footplate staff who became surplus to requirements as a result of the new arrangements would be allowed to remain at their existing depots. There are a considerable number of surplus second men, and where they exist there is no reason for British Rail to limit drivers' work. What may have a more serious restrictive effect is that most drivers are only conversant, or say they are only conversant, with a limited number of routes. They are only permitted to drive if they have signed a declaration saying that they know the route, and they can refuse if they have not been over a line for six months. This discourages management from training drivers for a large num-

ber of routes, especially as it takes about three weeks of route
learning before drivers are prepared to sign. Another obstacle
is that when there are any considerable number of drivers at a
depot they are grouped into links; drivers passing from one link
to another as they become more senior. As the most lucrative
routes are reserved for the top link, there is little point in training junior drivers for them. Moreover, there may not be anyone
at a particular depot who is permitted to drive over a route for
which somebody ought to be trained; and even if drivers are sent
to a depot where they can learn they may not be taught, because
depots jealously guard their route knowledge.

Because this knowledge is so restricted the railways are highly
inflexible. If a freight train is cancelled at short notice it may
be difficult to find the driver suitable alternative work because
he is only qualified to drive a few routes. In practice, duties are
shuffled around so that few men remain completely idle, but it is
often impossible to re-roster in such a way that everyone does a
full day's work. Similarly, if the pattern of business alters,
British Rail may well find that it has too many men with the
wrong experience at one depot, and too few men at another depot
which has a monopolistic hold on the routes where traffic has
increased.

This archaic system needs to be reformed if drivers are to
spend their time more productively. British Rail should be free
to reallocate work between depots; the link system also needs to
be made less restrictive; and, most important of all, the arrangements about route learning need to be thoroughly overhauled. It
should be possible to reduce the amount that the driver needs to
remember by lighting up speed restrictions or putting headlights
on trains. It would also be possible, although this could be more
expensive, to equip trains with radio so that when a driver takes
a train over a route he has not travelled for some time he can
obtain information. The excessive time that British drivers take
in learning routes also needs to be cut down by running special
trains (or films) so that drivers can get to know a route quickly.
Drivers also need to be provided with some financial incentive not
to plead ignorance and to maintain the maximum route knowledge. The restrictive arrangements which discourage BR from
increasing driving time also need to be relaxed. The bonus system
is completely out of date and ought to be brought to an end, as

the National Union of Railwaymen has recognised. This should not only lead to a more efficient use of manpower, but would also be more equitable, since there is no clear relationship between effort and the distance driven. Moreover, as the Board told the Railway Staff National Tribunal:

> the limitations on drivers' hours arise from negotiated agreements and Trade Union policies rather than inherent characteristics and stresses of the driver's job. This is not a safety consideration. Whilst the need to control hours is acknowledged this need not be as inflexible as present practice suggests, for example, turns longer than those presently rostered could be worked without in any way being unsafe or unduly arduous compared with other types of employment.[1]

All things considered, it does not seem unreasonable to suppose that by 1981 driving time on British Rail could be 20% higher. Assuming that the situation on the London Midland is fairly typical, this would bring the total driving time to about 4½ hours, which is less than the Dutch figure of 5 hours (out of an 8½-hour turn but ignoring shunting). It is now possible to estimate how many drivers British Rail will need in 1981. The increase in the speed of passenger trains should almost offset the rise in the mileage, and there ought to be little or no increase in traction hours. Hence, other things being equal, the need for passenger drivers should, at 7600, be only fractionally higher than it was in 1971; while the number of drivers required for other coaching trains will fall to about 400, even if it only declines in proportion to train miles. For freight it has been estimated that there will between 1970–71 and 1981 be a reduction of about 30% in the train mileage, and it has been assumed that the average speed will increase from 21 mph to 30 mph. If so, the number of traction hours will decline by over half, and no more than 3800 freight drivers will be required. If there is a slight reduction for departmental trains, British Rail's total requirement for drivers will, other things being equal, be about 12,400. But if driving time per worker rises by a fifth, the number of drivers that are needed will fall to 10,350. With a cut of, say, 50% in drivers engaged on route learning, there will therefore be a reduction in the number of drivers engaged on work other than shunting from 18,100 in 1971 to 11,000 in 1981.

Besides these fully qualified drivers, there will also have to be some trainees. If it takes about two years to train each driver, and if each driver who has been trained stays with British Rail about twenty years, then trainees would need to be equivalent to around 10% of qualified drivers. Allowing for drivers engaged on shunting, there will need to be about 12,700 qualified drivers in 1981, and hence 1270 trainees.

Second Men and Freight Guards

As we have seen, the manning agreement of 1965 requires that a second man shall accompany the driver where either his non-stop driving distance or time, or his total driving distance or time, exceeds various limits during a turn of duty. They must also be carried if a physical needs break, lasting a clear 30 minutes, is not provided during a period beginning 2 hours and 50 minutes after the start of the driver's turn and ending 6 hours and 10 minutes from its start.

Second men are almost completely unnecessary, except in the case of those diesel passenger trains where the carriages are steam-heated and the second man looks after the boiler. However, BR is planning to eliminate these boilers by 1977. None of the other arguments which might be used to justify the presence of second men have any substance. They are not there to take over the controls in order to relieve the driver because they are not required to be qualified drivers. Moreover, it is difficult to believe that the presence of a second man is an adequate substitute for a meal break. The argument that a second man is necessary to keep a look out for signals where the driver has been driving for a considerable period is slightly more plausible. However, if the driver is too weary to drive alone then he should not be allowed to drive at all, especially as the second man is also likely to be tired. If the rules governing single-manning had any rational basis a second man would only be required on lines where the automatic warning system has not yet been installed, as it has over one-third of the route system. That second men are not required is shown by the fact that they have already been eliminated in a number of other countries, including Switzerland, Austria and, for electric and passenger trains, Norway.[2]

The French and Dutch railways have gone further and have removed the guard from fully braked freight trains.[3] On trains where the wagons are loose-coupled, the guard applies the hand brake if a link breaks and the end of the train starts to run backwards, although this rarely happens except during stopping and starting. But if all the wagons on a train have power brakes, and they are in use, the brakes will be automatically applied and the guard's van is superfluous; as shown by the fact that on fully fitted trains it has been dispensed with and the guard travels in the rear cab of the locomotive.

By 1981 all wagons ought to have power brakes, or at least to have been fitted with brake pipes. British Rail should only need around 75,000 wagons, but it already possesses 105,000 vacuum-braked vehicles and ought to have at least 33,000 air-braked wagons. The only type of vehicle where there might be some problem is mineral wagons. It appears, from the braking characteristics and carrying capacity of the wagons that are now available for moving coal, that something like 4500 unbraked wagons may still be required in 1981, assuming that the average (non-merry-go-round) vehicle makes one loaded journey per week. It would be possible to eliminate this unbraked stock by providing slightly more air-braked mineral wagons than have been allowed for in our estimates of capital expenditure. Alternatively, it would be possible to fit any unbraked wagons that have to be retained (and the estimates of their number are necessarily crude) with brake pipes so that they can form part of fully braked trains.

Although unfitted freight vehicles should be a thing of the past by 1981, there will still be some loose-coupled trains. Where trains are engaged in trip working and a number of sidings are, for instance, being called at to pick up or deliver wagons, it is not always worth joining up the brake pipes. However, only about 1230 guards were engaged in trip working during 1971, and since it is mainly associated with wagonload working, the number of guards required for this purpose should decline roughly in line with wagonload traffic. If so, only about 430 freight guards would be necessary in 1981, but to be on the safe side the number will be put at 500.

Another safety duty performed by the guard is to protect the back of the train in case of derailment by placing warning detonators on the track. On ordinary double-track route the signalling system will prevent following trains from entering the section in which the derailment has taken place. If there are three or more tracks it is possible that the vehicles that have come off the line may obstruct the path of a train that is coming up from the rear. However, by 1981 continuous track circuiting will have been installed on virtually all multi-track line. This means that when the vehicles fall onto the track along which other trains are moving in the same direction they may well cause a short circuit and turn the signals to red. But even if this does not happen, the driver can clip a wire across the line, or lines, that are blocked, and in this way give warning through the signalling system. The detonator argument for freight guards is, therefore, very weak, and certainly does not justify their presence.

A small number of other workers has been classified with train crews. In 1971 about 1500 were employed on rostering and other miscellaneous duties. Although more computer programmers and other staff may be necessary if rostering is to become more efficient, it has been assumed that there will be some reduction because there will not be anything like as many men to roster. If so, train crews and associated staff will fall from about 34,750 in 1971 to about 13,750 in 1981, which is a reduction of 21,000 or 60%.

SHUNTING

As can be seen from Table 8.3, around 14,000 workers appear to have been engaged on shunting during 1971, of whom 8500 were involved in freight shunting. Because train load operations involve relatively little shunting, the number of engine hours absorbed in freight shunting has moved closely in line with the wagonload tonnage. BR's forecasts suggest that by 1981 it will be down to 24 million tons compared with 69 million tons in 1971. Although trainload working is responsible for some shunting, the amount of work is also tending to fall because of the increase in the size of the average wagon load, and British Rail is itself assuming that between 1971 and 1981 the number of shunting engines will decline by the same proportion as wagonload freight, i.e. by 65%. If the number of drivers and other staff engaged on freight shunting declines in step, it will be down to about 3000 by 1981.

TABLE 8.3: *Shunting Staff*

	30 January 1971	1981
Freight:		
Drivers	2 070	*720*
Ground staff	6 480	*2 270*
	8 550	*2 990*
Passenger:		
Drivers	1 110	*890*
Ground staff	1 810	*1 450*
	2 920	*2 340*
Parcel:		
Drivers	160	*80*
Ground staff	650	*320*
	810	*400*
Second men	1 110	—
Guards	690	*360*
Total employed	14 080	*6 090*

Although freight accounts for the bulk of all shunting, some 2900 workers appear to have been engaged on the shunting of passenger trains in 1971. By 1981 there should be a considerable reduction due to the introduction of the HST and APT, which will generate virtually no shunting because they can be driven from either end, and because the carriages will be permanently coupled. Their introduction will lead to a swift decline in loco-motive-hauled trains, which account for a high proportion of passenger shunting. Indeed, it appears that in 1971 only about a third as many workers were employed on shunting per train mile where multiple units were in use as where locomotives pro-vided the traction. If this relationship continues to hold there should over the period 1971–81 be a saving of 600 staff engaged in passenger shunting.

Relatively few are employed on parcels shunting, but there should be a worthwhile economy here, because the amount of work will be cut by half as a result of the reshaping of the parcels system. If there is a corresponding reduction in staff, 400 jobs will disappear.

So far no account has been taken of the considerable number of second men and guards who appear to be engaged on shunting. Although 1100 second men are recorded as having been so employed in 1971, it seems very doubtful whether many of these played any active or necessary role. It is most unusual for them to help couple and uncouple at marshalling yards and stations, and they only perform this work during the course of a journey at those small sidings and terminals where there are no railmen available. Guards play a more important part, as they not only help en route, but even do a certain amount of shunting at marshalling yards and other places where railmen are employed. It therefore seems reasonable to assume that the number actively engaged on shunting did not exceed 690, i.e. the guards attributed to shunting in 1971. If by 1981 employment declines in line with the amount of work, as previously estimated for freight, passenger and parcels, the figure will be down to about 360.

The total number engaged on shunting ought therefore to drop from just over 14,000 in 1971 to a little over 6000 in 1981.

FREIGHT TERMINALS

In 1971 4500 workers, apart from footplate staff and guards, were employed at freight depots and terminals. From studies which BR has made, it appears that the 2100 or so terminals which were wholly or mainly dependent on wagonload traffic will be down to 840 by 1981. However, the number of BR depots from which traffic is distributed by road will decline even more sharply, and it is here that the bulk of employment is concentrated. Freight which has to be delivered by road is unprofitable due to the cost of transhipment, and has declined rapidly. A further reduction will occur if only because British Rail is going to scrap the old and inefficient containers in which much of the traffic has been carried. All that is likely to remain by 1981 is some steel traffic into Birmingham and perhaps a few other towns where there are sufficient small customers for trainload working to be possible. In addition, some 20 depots will be needed for the new air-braked wagonload service.

It will, therefore, be assumed that there will be a reduction of 67% in the 3850 terminal staff engaged on wagonload traffic, which is a somewhat greater decline than the fall in the number of terminals. It will further be assumed that with fewer but larger terminals the number employed on trainload operations will remain the same. If so, the total employment at freight terminals and depots will fall from 4500 in 1971 to about 1920 in 1981, which is a reduction of 57%.

PARCELS

In 1971 the parcels service appears to have employed 7200, excluding train working and the maintenance of rolling-stock. By 1981 employment should be considerably lower, because British Rail's plans to reduce the network to about 100 depots, compared with the present 300, should lead to a better utilisation of sorting staff. A further gain in productivity will be secured through mechanisation.

BR has informed the railway unions that, due to the reshaping of the network, and the loss of much of the Post Office parcels traffic, employment will be cut by around 3000 by 1981. Excluding train crews and shunters, it seems likely that BR is planning to reduce employment by about 2000, but this does not allow for the saving in staff due to the possible loss of part of BR's letter and newspaper traffic. Moreover, its estimate of the number of Rail Express parcels which it will carry seems highly over-optimistic. Although it is only possible to make a very rough-and-ready comparison, it appears that our forecast for Rail Express and for letters and papers in 1981 represents only around 70% of the volume of traffic for which British Rail is hoping.

If BR is able to make an off-setting reduction in its parcels staff, it may find the service can be run with far fewer people than it believes. This may, however, be too much to ask in view of the difficulty which parcels organisations have in maintaining productivity when traffic falls. There is also reason to suppose that the railways' estimate of a cut of 2000 through rationalisation relates to a higher estimate of the number employed on handling parcels traffic. It will, therefore, be assumed that British Rail will only be able to prune its labour force down by a further 1000. This means that it will require 4200 against the 7200 which were employed in 1971, a reduction of over 40%.

PASSENGER STATIONS AND GUARDS

In 1971, as can be seen from Table 8.4, about 17,600 workers were employed on passenger work at stations and there were 5900 passenger guards. They close doors like porters, check tickets like barrier staff, and/or issue tickets like booking clerks. Thus, in all, about 23,500 railway workers, apart from drivers and firemen, are employed on trains and at stations in the running of BR's passenger services.

TABLE 8.4: *Staff Employed on Passenger Station Duties and as Passenger Guards*

	30 January 1971	1981
Ticket sales	3 630 ⎫	
Ticket inspection and collection	2 950 ⎪	13 060
Enquiries and reservations	1 420 ⎬	
Other duties	8 810 ⎭	
Station management	820	700
	17 630	13 760
Passenger guards	5 880	4 440
Total employed	23 510	18 200

It should, by 1981, be possible to eliminate all, or nearly all, of those station staff whose principal duty is the checking and collection of tickets; to cut down the number of other station workers; and to remove guards from some suburban and a few little-used stopping trains. In order to make these savings, a number of important developments and innovations will have to take place.

Power-Door Trains

On suburban services the only real function of the guard is to ensure that all passengers are safely on board and all the doors are properly shut when the train leaves the station. If there are power doors, the driver can undertake this function, and guards can be dispensed with as they have been by a number of railway undertakings, including Stockholm, the Philadelphia Transit Corporation and London Transport.

Although most of British Rail's suburban carriages have swing doors, the mileage performed by those trains which already have sliding doors, or which will have them, should add up to about 14 million by 1981. This is equivalent to 10% of the total loaded passenger-train miles in 1971 excluding Inter-City. If there is a corresponding reduction in the number of guards who man these trains, there will be a saving of 500. However, it would be necessary, where platforms are curved, to install closed-circuit television so that the driver could see that nobody was stuck half in and half out of the train as it left the platform.

Pay-Driver Trains

Although BR has for a decade or more had trains on which the guard issues tickets, there are no trains on which the passengers pay the driver. These, however, are by no means impossible, as the example of one-man buses suggests, and as the German railways have shown.

In Britain, where one-man buses have been introduced, it has been found that it takes about three seconds for the driver to collect a fare. Hence, it should be possible for a train driver to cope with something like 25 passengers in a minute, allowing for those who have their fares paid by others or already have season tickets. On services which are very lightly loaded, it should therefore be possible to switch to one-man operation without causing intolerable delays at stations; and it seems reasonable to suppose that it could be introduced where the number of passengers per train mile averages less than 30, because even if passengers travel as little as 15 miles, which represents about three stops in rural areas, only 10 passengers will on average board the train at each station. In 1972 those services where the average was less than 30 passengers accounted for 5 million train miles; and those where it was between 30 and 40, where it might be possible for the driver to collect the fares part of the time, for a further 6·4 million. If pay-driver trains had been operating in 1971 for all the former, and half the latter, they would have covered 8·2 million train miles, which was 6% of the non Inter-City mileage. With a corresponding reduction in the number of guards employed on such trains about 300 could have been dispensed with.

Pay-Guard Trains

At the end of 1972, British Rail had some 2360 stations, of which about 630, or rather over a quarter, had no staff. But much greater progress has been made in some parts of the country than in others, which suggests that there is scope for further pay trains. In Scotland, for instance, there are very few and 88% of the stations still have staff, whereas in the Western Region they have been withdrawn from approaching half the stations.

On buses, it has been found that on average it takes a conductor four seconds to collect a fare, and that on a bus containing 60 to 70 people tickets can be issued in about three minutes. These times might be slightly longer on a pay train, but if it takes a guard with a rapid-issuing ticket machine five seconds per fare he will be able to deal with up to 40 passengers in three minutes, which is about the minimum time between stations. Where there is four minutes interval it should be possible to issue tickets to up to about 50 passengers, when the interval is five minutes to 60, and so on.

This rule of thumb was applied line by line to discover at how many stations the booking office needs to be retained. It is of course possible, even when suburban trains are excluded, that loadings differ so greatly from one train to another, and from one station to another, that the key assumption is wrong. However, if traffic is concentrated to a very marked extent on one or two trains each day, or on a particular section of the line, there should be scope to de-staff some stations at which it has been assumed that booking-office facilities will need to be retained, and to introduce pay trains during off-peak periods on some services which, due to the high average loads carried, have not been considered as candidates for this method of operation.

If the guard is unable to make a complete check of tickets between stations, the scope for fare evasion will be greater, but it should be possible to offset any loss here, and in general to reduce fare evasion on pay trains, by making some arrangement for the display of tickets. On some American railroads, holders are provided in which passengers are expected to insert their tickets, and some similar pouch or clip system could be adopted in this country. This would also meet another possible objection to the extension of the pay train system, namely that passengers do not like being repeatedly asked to produce their tickets, and there is a limit to what guards can remember.

When the rule of thumb is applied, it looks from the average loadings in 1972 as if there are about 260 stations from which staff could be removed by 1981. If, on average, there are two railway workers at each of these stations this would lead to a staff saving of about 500.

Inter-City Ticket-Checking

At present, Inter-City passengers often have their tickets checked three or more times, viz. by barrier staff at the beginning and end of the journey and by the guard. Sometimes the final barrier check is omitted but, unless the guard makes an examination between every station, it is then possible to defraud British Rail. Thus BR's present ticketing arrangements not only involve much overlapping effort but are also inefficient.

The remedy for these weaknesses is to restrict ticket inspection on the Inter-City services to the train but to tighten up the examination of tickets by the guards. This is what happens on the continent and the system is not unknown in this country. As in the case of pay trains, it would however probably be necessary to make some arrangement for the display of tickets so that the guard does not have to keep troubling passengers, and is able to work through the train more quickly than at present.

Commuter Ticket-Checking

On commuter services it is usually impracticable to check tickets on the train, but it should be possible to reduce the number of station staff and the amount of fare evasion by installing automatic ticket barriers, which will henceforth be referred to as turnstiles. Barriers which open when a coin or token is inserted have long been in operation in foreign cities, but they have the disadvantage that a uniform fare has to be charged, so that if the commuter network is at all extensive a considerable amount of revenue is likely to be lost.

However, technological progress, and in particular the electronic scanning of magnetically encoded tickets, has now made it possible to introduce automatic barriers even though fares vary with distance. The first system of this type came into operation in 1966 on the Chicago commuter lines of the Illinois Central Railway, and in 1972 British Rail itself introduced automatic barriers on the service from Glasgow Central to Gourock and Wemyss Bay. Some automatic fare-collection systems are very advanced and sophisticated, but it would probably be best for BR to retain the existing point-to-point ticket-issuing arrangements, and simply to introduce turnstiles for inspection and collection. This would be relatively inexpensive, as suitable reversible barriers might cost as little as £1500, and do not cost very much to install and maintain. Since the encoded tickets would have the origin and destination of the passenger printed on them, automatic ticket-checking on commuter lines could readily be combined with manual inspection and collection on the rest of the system.

In view of the enormous rate of return shown by a specimen turnstile scheme covering the South Manchester area, it has been assumed that it would be worth installing turnstiles on those lines where it is virtually impossible to check tickets on the train because of the number of passengers they carry and the short time between stops. What is important here is not so much the average load as that at the peak, and some attempt was therefore made to identify commuter lines. Where, for instance, only one or two trains arrived at their destinations between 8 and 9 a.m., it seemed unlikely that traffic would be very peaky. A considerable amount of effort was also devoted to identifying those parts of the system where the services are reasonably self-contained.

Schemes were drawn up which together embrace 1250 stations, which is over half of the total. Nearly 800 of these possible turnstile stations are in London and the South-East, and the others are in the Black Country (50), the Liverpool–Manchester area (215), Tyneside (40) and central Scotland (150). Although the different barrier districts are more or less self-contained, there are some trains from outside. These present a considerable problem because, unless the passengers have been issued with encoded tickets, they cannot pass through the turnstiles. When trains from outside originate from or call at a limited number of outside stations, then the best course will be to enable these to issue encoded tickets. But to issue encoded tickets on a large scale outside would cause considerable difficulties, and it is probably best in most cases to tackle the problem at the receiving end. Where the station at which the problem train arrives has a number of platforms, it may be possible to divide it into barrier and Inter-City sections. However, where there are only two platforms, or where division would be very expensive, manned barriers would have to be maintained alongside the turnstiles so that some barrier staff would have to be retained.

Unfortunately the retention of manned barriers is not a perfect solution, because, unless special measures are taken, there will be nothing to stop passengers getting off Inter-City trains, and then boarding a local service without troubling to rebook with an encoded ticket. It seems doubtful, however, whether there are very many passengers who transfer from Inter-City to suburban trains except at terminal stations, where there would be no problem because certain platforms could be reserved for intra-barrier trains. It is only those indivisible stations where a large number of passengers transfer from Inter-City to local trains that would present a problem. This could be solved either by employing staff to shepherd passengers from Inter-City trains off the platforms so that they had to rebook, or by making any-one who failed to purchase an encoded ticket pay a surcharge when they arrived at their destination and had to summon help. Moreover, it appears that out of the 1250 stations covered by the projects there are only around 60 at which there would be any real problem. Although it would probably be possible to split some of these at little cost, it will be assumed that, except at the terminal stations, manned barriers would, in most cases, have to be maintained. By no means all of these problem stations are large, and it will be assumed that only about 200 ticket collectors will need to be retained.

The introduction of turnstiles would mean that all the stations that form part of the system will have to sell encoded tickets, and that the 40 or so stations that have been reduced to halts would have to be restaffed. Moreover, by 1981 there will be about 25 new stations on Merseyside and Tyneside, which it is convenient to take into account at this point. In all, the staffing and restaffing of stations would probably require the employment of about 200. When turnstiles are introduced, it may not be possible to make any saving at those small stations where staff spend part of their time selling and part of their time collecting tickets. From the way in which stations are staffed in one of our provincial turnstile districts, it appears that no reduction may be possible at about half the stations, and it seems possible that about 300 of those who appear as ticket inspectors and collectors in Table 8.4 could not in fact be dispensed with.

British Rail is planning to install turnstiles at 600 stations in and around London by 1982, and hopes that it will also have covered the major provincial centres by that date. However, BR does not anticipate that the introduction of turnstiles will lead to any great saving in labour, because it does not believe that it is possible to carve out areas which are sufficiently self-contained for manned barriers to be dispensed with at most stations. This is almost certainly wrong, and there is little doubt that large economies in manpower can be made. The widespread introduction of turnstiles should also produce a worthwhile increase in revenue as a result of reduced fare evasion. It is believed that 10% of revenue is being lost as a result of fraud, and it is estimated that receipts have risen by 11% as a result of the introduction of turnstiles on the line from Glasgow to Gourock and Wemyss Bay. By 1981 the services which move within the automatic-barrier system should have a combined revenue of about £175 million, and it will be assumed that there is a gain of £9 million through the reduction in fare evasion, which is equivalent to only 5% of receipts.

Other Economies

There are probably other ways in which economies could be made, for example, through the installation of ticket-issuing machines at larger stations, the closing of left luggage offices, and, more important, through further reductions in the number of porters. Although the carrying of cases is supposed to be incidental to other duties such as parcel work, the large number of men who are still to be seen standing around or plying for hire suggests that parcels are sometimes a convenient excuse for the employment of men who are felt to be necessary in order to lend assistance to passengers and answer their questions. Passengers obviously do need information and reassurance but it should be possible to meet this need in other and cheaper ways such as indicators on trains and/or platforms.

There is a considerable variation from one part of the country to another in the number of men per station. The Southern, Midland and Scottish Regions have an average of 6 to 7½ men at each station where staff are present, but on the Western Region the figure is 10½. In the Eastern Region the number is almost exactly the same, but here the stations are intensively used, whereas in the Western Region the number of journeys per manned station is less than half as great. If the number of staff per station on the Western Region was brought down to the level of the London Midland, where the stations are probably used more intensively, 575 staff would be saved. To this a token reduction of 425 will be added to cover the elimination of unnecessary porters, the other miscellaneous economies which have been mentioned, and a general tightening-up of efficiency.

Station Staff and Guards Required

In 1971 17,600 staff were engaged on passenger station duties, but by 1981, besides the economy of 1000 which has just been described, there ought to have been a saving of 500 due to the de-manning of stations. In addition there should, allowing for those stations inside turnstile areas at which manned barriers would still be necessary or a staff saving might prove impossible, be a net reduction of 2250 in the number of ticket collectors; and also some small saving in station and depot management. As a result the total number employed at stations ought probably to be down to about 13,750 in 1981.

There should also be a significant reduction in passenger guards. As we have seen it ought to be possible to save 500 by eliminating guards where the carriages have power doors and

300 by introducing pay-driving on those services which are very little used. The net saving from these measures, allowing for a few assistant guards, works out at 770. This, however, will be rounded up to 1000 to allow for the fact that it will not always be necessary to carry a guard when passenger trains run empty, as they do for about 5% of their mileage, and for the possibility that guards could be eliminated from some intra-barrier trains where loads are very light and only one or two carriages are necessary, as must sometimes be the case at week-ends.

It should also be possible to push up the amount of time that guards spend usefully employed while they are on duty. At present the amount of productive time averages just over 3½ hours per turn of duty on the London Midland Region. It should be possible to secure some increase by using computers to work out the best way in which guards can be deployed because it is virtually impossible, using manual methods, to investigate all the alternative ways in which guards might be scheduled. It would, however, be wrong to anticipate any enormous increase in the time that guards are actively employed as a result of computerisation, and there do not appear to be any other obvious ways in which productivity can be increased. It will therefore be assumed that the railways will only be able to increase guards' effective working time by 10%. After allowing for the savings already made, this would mean that 450 fewer guards would be needed in 1981 than would otherwise be required.

This brings the total saving in passenger guards to 1450, which means that by 1981 they should number about 4450 as against 5900 in 1971. When the guards and the station staff are brought together, our estimates suggest that employment should decline from 23,500 in 1971 to 18,200 in 1981, which is a reduction of 5300.

SERVICING ROLLING-STOCK

In 1971, as can be seen from Table 8.5, nearly 60,000 workers appear to have been engaged on the upkeep, repair and design of rolling-stock.

TABLE 8.5: *Staff Employed on the Cleaning, Inspection, Maintenance, Overhaul and Design of Rolling-stock, etc.*

	30 January 1971	1981
Inspection and repair of freight vehicles	12 310	3 810
Maintenance and overhaul of diesel and electric multiple units	14 410	14 270
Maintenance and overhaul of carriages and parcels vans etc.	5 740	4 620
Coaching vehicle examination	1 390	1 010
Coaching vehicle cleaning	4 870	4 250
Servicing, repair and overhaul of locomotives	18 890	13 810
Servicing and repair of outdoor machinery	1 390	1 390
	59 000	43 160
Design staff	720	550
		43 710
Allowance for higher productivity		−5 500
Total employed	59 720	38 210

Note: Some of the 1971 figures are only approximations.

In the case of wagons the volume of maintenance appears to be almost wholly related to the number in existence, i.e. wagon maintenance is a time cost. During 1973 the average wagon only made 38 loaded trips. Freight vehicles therefore spend the greater part of their lives standing around slowly decaying, and this, and the damage that they sustain during shunting, is the principal reason why they have to be repaired. As can be seen from Table 8.6 it has been estimated that the number of freight vehicles will decline from 370,000 at the beginning of 1971, and just over 250,000 at the end of 1973, to about 75,000 in 1981.

This reduction should come about due to the increase in private wagon ownership that is taking place, because of the trend towards large wagon loads, and as a result of the scope which exists for improving the utilisation of vehicles. It has been assumed that, excluding merry-go-round stock and Freightliner flats, the number of loaded trips per wagon will average one a week by 1981. This would represent a considerable improvement, but is a level of efficiency that has long been attained in most continental countries, and BR should be assisted in achieving better utilisation by TOPS, its new computer-based system for

TABLE 8.6: *British Rail's Traffic Rolling-stock*

	1 January 1971	1 January 1974	1981
Freight vehicles	370 917	253 442	76 500
Coaching vehicles:			
Diesel multiple units	3 621	3 468	3 100
Electric multiple units	7 358	7 173	8 200
Carriages, and HST and APT trailers	7 699	7 152	5 800
Parcel vehicles etc.	6 508	5 551	2 750
Total coaching vehicles	25 186	23 344	19 850
Main-line locomotives:			
Freight	2 290	. .	1 250
Passenger and other coaching	870	. .	660
Total main-line locomotives	3 160	2 850	1 910
HST power units	—	—	118
APT power units	—	—	20
Shunting engines	1 338	1 122	400

providing information on the whereabouts of its rolling-stock. The average wagon load, excluding coal and Freightliner traffic, has been assumed to increase from about 18½ tons in 1973 to 22 tons during 1981, which is a smaller absolute increase than took place over the shorter period 1968–73. BR's new air-braked wagons have capacities which range from 22 to 44 tons, and, granted the increase in utilisation assumed, BR will be able to scrap its smaller vehicles. On the other hand, some of its freight, such as iron ore, where the average load is already high, will by 1981 be carried in privately-owned wagons.

Although wagon maintenance is largely a time cost, it may be unrealistic to suppose that the volume of work will fall in step with the number of vehicles, because the new air-braked stock is somewhat more expensive to service and repair. During 1972 the cost per freight vehicle averaged just under £100, but for air-braked wagons the figure was around £150 and for Freightliner flats it was as high as £550. When the change in the composition of the wagon fleet is taken into account, it appears that the work load should decline by about two-thirds over the period 1971–81, which means that the number of workers engaged on wagon maintenance ought to be cut by 8500. If anything, this probably understates the size of the reduction that can be made, because the plan which British Rail Engineering (BREL) prepared in the early 1970s showed the number of wages-grade staff at its wagon works declining slightly faster than the wagon fleet, whereas we have assumed that it will fall more slowly.

In contrast to wagons, the cost of repairing and maintaining multiple units is very closely related to the mileage performed. It should therefore be possible to derive a passable estimate of the number of repair staff required in 1981 from the likely increase in the mileage which multiple unit trains will travel. However, in 1971 nearly 40 workers were engaged on the day-to-day maintenance and repair of diesel multiple units per million train miles whereas the corresponding figure for electric multiple units was only about 25. Cost data suggest that at the wagon workshops, where the bulk of maintenance labour is concentrated, diesel multiple units involve relatively more work than the previous figures suggest. It has therefore been assumed that diesel multiple units generate 75% more maintenance than electrical multiple units, on which basis it appears that there will be a slight decline in the number of staff that are needed.

The repair and overhaul of ordinary carriages is almost wholly a time cost, but it would be unrealistic to suppose that the volume of maintenance will fall in proportion to their number. Carriages are becoming more and more complicated and expensive to maintain due to factors such as the installation of air conditioning. In the absence of any better information it has been assumed that the amount of maintenance work generated by carriages of different types is proportional to their capital costs. This implies, for instance, that the new Mark III coach to be used by the HST will involve 75% more labour than the Mark I which is being retired. On this basis, the volume of maintenance was calculated from the actual composition of the carriage fleet in 1971 and its estimated make-up during 1981. Including parcels vans, it appears that the amount of work will be about 20% lower in 1981 than it was in 1971, and that there will be a reduction of about 1100 in the number of workers required.

The remaining staff engaged on the upkeep of coaching stock can be dealt with very briefly. Carriage examination is largely a time cost and it will be assumed that the number of workers declines in line with the number of vehicles. One passenger vehicle was treated as being equivalent to $2\frac{1}{2}$ parcels vans in order to reflect the amount of work involved. Although it seems difficult to believe that BR could have too many carriage cleaners, there will, if the number is not reduced, be one for every 3½ passenger vehicles in 1981. Some reduction has therefore been assumed.

The cost of maintaining main-line locomotives is partly a time cost, and partly a mileage-related expense, although the latter is if anything the more important of the two. An estimate of the distance cost for locomotives was derived from forecasts of the mileage that they will perform. Allowance was made for the fact that the cost per mile is about 3½ times greater for diesel than for electric engines; and also for the possibility that HST and APT power units will be relatively expensive to maintain. In order to determine the time component in locomotive maintenance it was necessary to predict the number of engines.

There ought to be a considerable reduction in engines engaged on freight work, partly because of a fall in train miles, but mainly due to a significant increase in the mileage performed by each locomotive. In 1971 freight engines appear to have covered an average distance of 42,000 miles, including light running and other miscellaneous mileage. By 1981 this should have risen to around 53,000, due to a large increase in train speeds and a small increase in utilisation. At present engines engaged on freight work appear to spend less than a quarter of their time on the move, and a significant improvement ought to be possible by, for instance, using computers to improve their scheduling and through better time-keeping. It has been assumed that BR will only be able to do without 10% of the locomotives that it would otherwise require.[4] On the passenger side it has been assumed that the number of locomotives will fall in line with the number of train miles, as services are taken over by the HST and APT, and that there will also be a reduction of 10% through improved utilisation. It is estimated that the total fleet of main-line loco-motives should decline from 3160 in 1971 to about 1900 in 1981. This is a substantial reduction, but past experience suggests that it ought to be within BR's grasp. Between 1968 and 1973 loaded-train miles per locomotive increased by 12½%, and if they go on increasing at the same rate up to 1981 a mere 1850 engines will be required. Although the fall in conventional locomotives will be partly offset by more power cars for the HST and APT, there should nevertheless be a large overall reduction in engines, and hence in the time element in the maintenance of main-line traction units. Moreover, there will be a large cut in the fleet of shunting engines, where maintenance costs are almost wholly a function of time. As a result, the total work involved in the servicing, repair and overhaul of locomotives and main-line power units should decline by approximately 27% over the decade, and employment should be cut by about 5100.

Finally, it has been assumed that there will be some reduction in design staff because by then work on the HST, APT and new types of wagon will be largely complete, but no change has been allowed for in the number of workers engaged on the servicing and repair of plant and equipment. There should be some scope for economy here due, for instance, to the contraction and rationalisation of the parcels sector which makes use of some of this equipment. On the other hand extra work will arise from the need to service and repair turnstiles and closed-circuit television. This brings the grand total for the upkeep and repair of rolling-stock to about 43,750 which represents a saving of 16,000 jobs.

However, by raising productivity it should be possible to do better than this. The survey which was made by BR work-study officers at the end of 1969 showed that, by tighening up efficiency and adopting better methods, it would be possible by the end of 1974 to eliminate 2800 jobs in mechanical and electrical engineering, which is the department in charge of servicing and minor repairs; and for the major workshops it was estimated that there ought to be a reduction of nearly 3800 over and above the cutback in employment which would have to be made because of the prospective decline in the work load. The adoption of the most up-to-date methods and the best practice is not a once and for all matter, because management and technology do not stand still; and BREL is expecting that it will be able to raise its productivity by 3½% per annum during the period up to 1981. However, it seems unlikely that it will be able to achieve this. Over the period 1968–73 output per man year in the railway vehicle industry, which is dominated by BREL, increased by less than 1% per annum, and it is always difficult to make gains in productivity in the face of declining output. Nevertheless, it should be possible to do better than this, and it will be assumed that a gain of 1½% per annum can be made over the period 1971–81. This implies that BREL will prune its labour force by about 3450 over and above the reduction due to the contraction in its work load. For the day-to-day maintenance and repair of rolling-stock and outdoor machinery it will be assumed that a saving of 2050 is possible. This is simply the old work-study target rounded down to allow for the lower level of employment.

When higher productivity is allowed for in this rough-and-ready fashion, it appears that the total work force employed on the upkeep and repair of rolling-stock should only be around 38,250 by 1981. As it was about 59,750 in 1971, BR ought to be able to save 21,500 jobs.

THE PERMANENT WAY

At the beginning of 1971 over 39,000 were employed on the maintenance and renewal of the route system as can be seen from Table 8.7.

TABLE 8.7: *Staff Employed on the Maintenance and Renewal of Track and Electrified Line*

	30 January 1971	1981
Maintenance of permanent way	17 620	*14 430*
Renewal of permanent way	5 960	*3 580*
Maintenance and renewal of earthworks, bridges and tunnels	7 340	*6 980*
Maintenance of electrified line	1 640	*2 210*
Look-out duties	2 160	*1 000*
Maintenance of civil engineering plant and machinery	870	*870*
Depots and workshops	1 700	*1 380*
Administration, planning and professional	1 950	*1 750*
		32 200
Allowance for higher productivity		*– 1 800*
Total employed	39 240	*30 400*

The largest single group of staff, numbering 17,600, was employed on the maintenance of the track and the road bed. The extent to which the volume of maintenance work declines

will largely depend on the progress that is made with the introduction of continuously welded rail (cwr). In 1972 the cost of
inspecting and maintaining the most intensively worked track
over which speeds of 75 to 100 mph were possible was about 60%
lower for cwr than for jointed track, and even on low grade line
there was a saving of 45% or more. In our estimates of desirable
capital expenditure, sufficient money has been provided to extend
the mileage of continuously welded rail from 5200 at the beginning of 1971 to around 11,300 in 1981. Since the most intensively
used track has already been converted, it has been assumed that
the bulk of the new continuously welded rail will be installed
where the traffic is moderately heavy and/or the maximum speed
is between 50 and 75 mph. The reduction in track maintenance was then calculated from figures showing the approximate cost of maintaining each category of track, where
continuously welded rail has been introduced, and where jointed
rail is still in existence.

The overall expense turns out to be 16% lower in 1981 than
it was in 1971, and the figure would have been much the same
even if rather different assumptions had been made about the
type of track which will be converted. If BR reduces its maintenance staff in proportion there will be a saving of about 2500
jobs. However, in order to make the introduction of the APT
and the HST worthwhile, around 3000 miles of track will have
to be upgraded from 100 mph to 125 mph, and we estimate,
again on the basis of cost data, that this will require 400 extra
workers.

Some allowance must also be made for higher speeds on other
routes, in particular for faster freight trains. It has been assumed
that their average speed will increase from 21 mph in 1970 to
30 mph in 1981. However, what tends to happen at present is
that they travel at something approaching their maximum speed
while they are hopping from one refuge loop to another, or until
they are held up by a signal. BR is therefore already paying a
large part of the price for a fast freight service without reaping
the benefit, and it should be possible to increase the average pace
at which trains travel without a corresponding rise in their maximum speed or the amount of fast running. Moreover, the wear
and tear that the track sustains is likely to be held down by better
designed rolling-stock, and by the restriction that is placed on the

axle load when speeds are high. Nevertheless, some increase in track maintenance is to be expected, especially as high speeds cause a disproportionate amount of damage. How great it would be is very difficult to tell, and it will simply be assumed that the pace at which the typical freight train moves will increase from 50 mph to 60 mph and, following the estimates of BR's former Chief Civil Engineer, that this will lead to an increase of about 25% in the amount of track maintenance.[5] If freight is responsible for something like a quarter of the work, higher freight speeds will mean that around 700 extra track-maintenance staff are required, although this is little better than a guess.

On the other hand, it should be possible to make savings by reducing some routes from double to single track. In 1972 the cost of inspecting and repairing the lowest category of track, over which less than 6 million gross tons passed, averaged £1200 per mile for jointed track. The cost for a line where there were two tracks would thus have been about £2400 per route mile. But the cost per track mile where between 6 and 12 million gross tons passed over the line was only £1600. It therefore appears that when a little-used passenger route is singled, and the traffic is doubled up on the remaining track, British Rail should save around £800 per annum in maintenance costs for each mile of track that is eliminated. If so, BR should be able to dispense with over 300 workers as a result of our programme for singling 1080 miles of its passenger route.

Although we have assumed that the route over which passenger trains pass is sacred, some of it has been closed since 1971, and there is a considerable mileage which is only used by freight trains. At the beginning of 1971 there were 2600 miles of freight-only route, but by the end of 1973 the mileage was already down to 2435, of which nearly half was double track. Both from what has been happening during recent years, and from the railways' own estimates, it appears that by 1981 there should be no more than 1700 miles of freight-only route. Allowing for the closure of some double-track route, and for the singling of half of what may remain, it appears that something like 1400 miles of freight-only track could be removed. If it is assumed that this, and the 625 miles of track which was closed during 1971 and 1972, figures in the lowest maintenance category, BR should be able to save 750 jobs.

A further economy in labour ought to result from the closure of what BR describes as sidings, although it also includes spur lines and marshalling yards under this heading. According to BR's estimates the number of private sidings and other freight terminals is likely to be cut in half between 1971 and 1981, and relatively few marshalling yards ought to remain open. Nevertheless, because it is the smaller sidings and yards that will be closed, it would be unwise to count on a saving in maintenance labour of more than a third, which represents something like 750 workers. In all, the number of workers who are engaged on the maintenance of the permanent way should, if the estimates are correct, fall by 3200, from 17,600 in 1971 to 14,400 in 1981.

A further 6000 workers were employed during 1971 on the renewal of track. It is to be expected that in 1981 fewer men will be required because the total mileage of continuously welded rail is steadily increasing and so the mileage of jointed track falling due for replacement will decline. Our estimates imply that there will be about 9500 miles of jointed track in 1981 as against 18,500 miles at the beginning of 1971. This is a reduction of almost half, but to allow for some extra replacement as a result of higher speeds it will be assumed that the volume of work and the number of workers engaged on renewal will fall by only 40%, i.e. by 2400.

The reduction in the number of workers engaged on the maintenance and renewal of earthworks, bridges and tunnels will not be anything like as large. As a result of closures the mileage of route, which is what largely determines the number of bridges and the length of earthworks to be repaired and renewed, should fall from 11,800 miles at the beginning of 1971 to 10,700 in 1981. This is a reduction of 9%, but it will be assumed that the volume of work only declines by 5% to allow for the fact that the route closed is little used, and there may be some relationship between the amount of traffic and the volume of work. On this basis there will be a fall of about 350 in the number employed.

Moreover, there is likely to be a positive increase in the next category of staff, namely workers engaged on the maintenance and renewal of electrified line. If employment on the upkeep of electricity installations in those regions which have third-rail and overhead line is increased in proportion to the estimated growth in the respective route miles, it appears that an extra 570 workers will be necessary.

No allowance has been made in any of these estimates of manpower requirements in 1981 for technical progress or greater efficiency. During the past decade the traditional pick-and-shovel methods of track maintenance have, to a large extent, been superseded by highly sophisticated machines. Although improved machines are being developed, it seems unlikely that there is going to be any innovation which will have a revolutionary effect on the present system of maintenance. Moreover, since British Rail has already equipped itself with the latest machines, there is no lost ground for it to make up. It would, however, be wrong to conclude that there is no scope for higher productivity, because BR does not appear to be making the best use of the equipment which it possesses.

The length of track that is levelled and consolidated by each tamper and its crew tends to be considerably higher on the continent. This may be partly because those who operate the machines here are not sufficiently skilled to get them back into working order quickly if they break down. Moreover, in other countries the tamping crews, in radio contact with signal-boxes, work during intervals which are considered too short in Britain. In general, they appear to have less difficulty in gaining access to the line, possibly because the responsibility for scheduling and operating trains and for track maintenance is not so sharply divided as it is in BR. Yet another factor which tends to depress productivity is that the necessary road transport is not always available to take track maintenance workers to where they ought to be working. As this shows, some tightening-up of efficiency is usually possible, and it will be assumed that this, together with some technical progress, will enable BR to raise the productivity of those engaged on the maintenance and renewal of track, and the associated electrical equipment, by 1% per annum: a figure with which BR's civil engineers do not appear to have any quarrel. If output per man does increase at this rate over the period 1971–81, a further saving of 1800 jobs will be made.

Although, in general, technical change is unlikely to lead to any great reduction in the amount of manpower required, there is one area in which a substantial economy should take place, viz. in look-out men. In 1971 2160 men were employed in permanent-way gangs to keep a look-out for approaching trains. Maintenance parties have about two look-out men, on average, and it should be possible to dispense with at least one of these by providing a radio link to the nearest signal-box, or by the use of sensors that would be placed up and down the line and would give advance warning of trains. Various problems, such as securing the necessary radio frequencies, would have to be overcome, but there is no insuperable obstacle. Nor need an on-line warning system be very expensive or difficult to develop, although it obviously will be if, like BR, one calls for a device that functions down to $-40°C$ and is able to tell how fast the train is moving. It will be assumed that the number of look-out men will be cut to 1000, which is a little less than half the 1971 figure to allow for a decline in the amount of maintenance.

Finally, it is necessary to make an estimate of the number of ancillary and general administrative staff. In 1971 something like 870 workers were employed on the maintenance of civil engineering plant and machinery, and the increasing use which is being made of sophisticated equipment suggests that the number may rise still further. However, because the figure is already surprisingly high and there is scope for a more intensive use of equipment, it will be assumed that there is no change. Employment at depots and workshops has been reduced in line with the fall in the number employed on the maintenance and renewal of track, earthworks and bridges; while for administrative, planning, and professional staff it has been assumed that there will be a small reduction. A large part of their work must be related to the number of staff that they have to control, and there should be a decline in the amount of work that they have to plan and manage.

The total employed on the maintenance and renewal of the route system should, according to these estimates, decline from about 39,250 in 1971 to 30,400 in 1981. which is a fall of approaching 9000 or 23%.

SIGNALLING

In 1971 16,250 railway staff were employed on signalling and related activities, while a further 6200 were engaged on the maintenance of signalling and telecommunications equipment, as **Table 8.8** shows.

TABLE 8.8: *Staff Employed on the Maintenance and Operation of Signalling*

	30 January 1971	1981
Signalling:		
Signalling	12 160	
		9 400
Crossing-keeping	2 390	
Control-office staff	1 690	*1 300*
Total employed	16 240	*10 700*
Maintenance:		
Maintenance and renewal of signalling	4 890	
		4 500
Maintenance and renewal of telecommunications	610	
Administration and planning	680	*630*
Total employed	6 180	*5 130*

During recent years there has been a marked fall in the number employed on signalling and crossing-keeping from about 14,500 at the beginning of 1971 to around 12,000 by the end of 1973. The reduction in signalmen has been mainly due to the extension of colour-light signalling which had led to the closure of a large number of signal-boxes. In our estimates of desirable investment, sufficient money has been allocated to resignal 600 miles of route (and 1800 miles of track) so that it will be possible for trains to travel at speeds of up to 125 mph. The recent colour-light signalling project on the West Coast main line permitted the closure of one manual box per 1·6 miles of route (and per 3·6 miles of track). This suggests that BR will be able to close about 400 boxes on the route that needs to be resignalled by 1981. At about 3½ men per signal-box these might have something like 1400 workers, but six big new power boxes will have to be constructed and they will have a complement of about 120. The resignalling on the Southern Region will not result in any great saving, so the overall reduction in manpower may well be only about 1400.

There are other reasons besides the extension of automatic signalling why the number of boxes should decline. BR should be able to dispense with traditional signalling over that part of the system which has relatively little traffic. There are at least two inexpensive substitutes for conventional signalling. First, it is possible where there are relatively few trains to have two-aspect signals controlled by track circuiting. At the end of Station A there will be a signal that will be switched to green by the passage of the preceding train over a short section of track-circuited line outside the next station B. Once the signal at A has changed to green it will therefore be safe for the train to travel as far as a signal on the near side of Station B, which will not turn to green until the station has been vacated by the preceding train. This, in essence, is the system which is already in use in Holland, and will be used on Tyneside. Second, it is possible to use radio signalling, which is employed on the line from Groningen to Roodeschool in Holland, and in Germany between Altona and Neumünster. In America, where extensive use is made of radio, there have been numerous accidents, but it has worked well in Holland, and there is nothing wrong with it if strict disciplines are observed.

In 1973 there were around 1750 miles of single-track passenger route, and it has been suggested earlier that by 1981 a further 1350 miles of line should, save for loops, be singled. It would not be possible to get rid of traditional signalling over all of this line, partly because this has already happened in some places, but it seems reasonable to assume that signal-boxes might be eliminated from 1500 miles of route. If there is only one box every 5 miles, BR would be able to close down 300, and a further 200 will be added to cover those that can be shut through minor rationalisation schemes, and because of the reduction in marshalling yards and in freight-only route. The number of signalmen per box averages $3\frac{1}{4}$, but if there are only 2 at the boxes that can be closed there might, after some allowance for radio-signalling centres, be a saving of 900 men. To this must be added the reduction in the number of crossing-keepers. Automatic barriers are now very expensive, and it seems likely that it will be worth installing only a relatively small number. Since they would be put in where the amount of manpower to be saved is above average, it will be assumed that 300 jobs will be eliminated.

Finally, in order to complete the estimates for signalling and related employment, a figure has to be inserted for the control-office staff who give advice to signalmen when difficulties arise

and trains get out of schedule. There has already been a significant reduction here, and it has been assumed that there will be
a further saving in labour. In all, it appears that employment
should decline by around 5500 between 1971 and 1981 from
16,250 to 10,750.

From the BR survey of its manpower requirements to which
reference has already been made, it appears that there should be
a drop of at least 450 in the work force engaged on the upkeep
of signalling and telecommunications. British Rail appears to
believe that from now on there will not be any great change in
employment. However, the use of radio and two-aspect signalling
on those lines which are little used, and the elimination of freight-
only route and marshalling yards, should lead to the closure of
a significant number of signal-boxes. If the saving in manpower is
somewhat less than the percentage decline in the number of
boxes (for reasons other than the extension of multiple-aspect
signalling) an additional economy of about 500 might be made.
Allowing for a small decline in the number of administrative
staff, the total number employed in the upkeep of signalling and
telecommunications should decline from about 6200 in 1971 to
about 5100 in 1981.

OVERHEAD STAFF

The final category of staff is British Rail's general administrative and overhead workers. The group contained 35,250 workers
at the beginning of 1971, but by the end of 1973 the number
appears to have been at least 1000 lower.

That there is scope for considerable economies in the number
of overhead and administrative staff is suggested by a comparison of BR with other railway systems. During 1973 about 40,700
were employed on British Rail at levels higher than that of the
station (the figure is larger than our general administrative and
overhead group in Table 8.9 because of the inclusion of civil
and mechanical engineering staff who work at headquarters, etc.).
This was a greater number than in any other major railway in
a developed country for which figures are available. When the
foreign systems are combined it turns out that 10% of their

employees work at levels above that of the station, whereas in Britain the figure is about twice as high. The contrast between British Rail and the other railway administrations is so great that it seems unlikely that it can be due to minor differences in definition or, except possibly for some of the smaller systems, to variations in organisation. All the figures, except those for BR, were taken from *International Railway Statistics*, and the definition employed by the International Union of Railways for administrative and general employment—staff employed by all authorities above station level—appears to be exactly the same as that used in Britain.

What is really wanted, however, is a comparison in which the number of office and overhead staff is related to the amount of work they have to undertake. In the case of those who plan and supervise the running of trains this will depend, among other things, on the number of train miles run, while the work to be performed in civil engineering offices will be largely determined by how much track there is to be maintained. Using these and other representative statistics, an index of administrative work was constructed; the various indicators being combined with weights proportional to the employment in the railway department whose work load it is intended to reflect. These weights were calculated from the number employed by British Rail in the various departments and fields of activity at its divisional, regional and central headquarters.

British Rail appears to require considerably more workers to perform a given amount of work. With the exception of the Swedish and Austrian railways, the continental systems all seem to have only between 50% and 70% of the staff which BR would employ. The three railways which are nearest to BR in size and probably in organisation came into this category, namely, the German, French and Italian state railways. Too much weight should not be placed on these results but they do strongly suggest that BR has far too many office and overhead staff.

The Railways Board planned to eliminate 4500 to 6500 jobs by replacing the present Regions and Divisions by Territories and thus removing a whole tier of management. After years of study and considerable expenditure on new office accommodation, this scheme was abandoned at the beginning of 1975, but there has been no suggestion that it was impossible to achieve a big reduction in staff. Our international comparisons indicate that a saving of at least 6500 should be readily attainable. When BR made its estimate, it cannot have allowed for the cut in administrative staff which will be possible if there is a substantial reduction in the general level of rail employment, because no great saving was then being planned. However, our estimates suggest that BR ought to be able to slim down its labour force by about a third between 1971 and 1981. If so, it should be able to make a large cut-back in the 16,000 or so overhead staff who were in 1971 engaged on such tasks as the payment of wages (2300), personnel work (3800), training (1800) and work study (1200).

There are other factors which are tending to reduce the managerial and administrative work load. A large group of overhead staff, which numbered 3500 in 1971, plans and controls the movement of trains and ensures that the necessary rolling-stock is available when it is wanted. Although the increase in passenger-train speeds and the reduction in rolling-stock will tend to make their job more difficult in some ways, it should on balance become easier because of the significant reduction in the number of trains; the elimination of most slow-moving freight, which greatly complicates the programming of trains; the more disciplined freight working that it should be possible to achieve; and the use of computers. The decline of wagonload traffic should also lead to a significant saving in administrative staff. The reduction in the number of small and irregular consignments should, for instance, enable BR to dispense with some of those who are engaged in freight billing; the reduction in damage, which is largely caused by wagonload working, should mean that fewer have to be employed on claims; and if freight keeps on the move there will be less opportunity for theft and fewer police will be necessary. Although the number of staff involved is in each case relatively small, a total of over 1000 were employed on such administrative work during 1971.

It is impossible to know exactly how large a saving in overhead staff BR should be able to make by 1981, but the international comparisons and the other evidence suggest that it should be able to reduce its work force by at least 10,000: a figure which the Board's more progressive managers believe to be capable of achievement.

AGGREGATE EMPLOYMENT

Our examination of BR's staff requirements in 1981 is now complete and the estimates for each activity are brought together in Table 8.9.

TABLE 8.9: *Summary: British Rail Staff by Activity*

	30 January 1971	1981	Reduction	Percentage decline
Train crews, excluding passenger guards and shunting	34 640	*13 810*	20 830	60
Shunting, including footplate and guards	14 080	*6 090*	7 990	57
Freight terminals and depots	4 500	*1 920*	2 580	57
Parcels	7 190	*4 200*	2 990	42
Passenger stations and guards	23 510	*18 200*	5 310	23
Repair, inspection and cleaning of rolling-stock	59 720	*38 210*	21 510	36
Maintenance of track and electric line	39 240	*30 400*	8 840	23
Signalling	16,240	*10 700*	5 540	34
Maintenance of signalling and telecommunications	6 180	*5 130*	1 050	17
Management and overhead staff	35 260	*24 260*	11 000	31
Total employed	240 560ᵃ	*152 920*	87 640	36

ᵃ The comparable figure at 1 January 1974 was about 219 600.

Note: These figures for rail employment do not correspond to those which appear in the Railways Board's *Annual Report* because those engaged on work charged to capital account have wherever possible been excluded. Corporate and common-service staff were included except where it was obvious that their work related to the Board's non-rail activities, or, in the case of the British Transport Police, were engaged on duties for London Transport, etc.

Between 1971 and 1981 rail employment should fall from 240,500 to 153,000, a reduction of 87,500 or 36%. The largest absolute reduction is in the maintenance and repair of rolling-stock, at 21,500, although because this is a large group the proportionate decline is no higher than average. The biggest cutback in relation to employment is the 60% fall in train crews, a decline of nearly 21,000. There should also be a large saving, amounting to 10,500 and 57%, in the number employed in shunting and at freight terminals. The reduction for track and signalling comes to 15,500; and there should be a cut of at least 11,000 in overhead employment.

It was stated in the Interim Strategy that British Rail was looking for a reduction of 40,000 over the period from the beginning of 1973 to 1981. As rail employment had already fallen to 225,750 by the start of 1973 our estimates imply that BR should have been aiming to cut its labour force by 73,000. What is the explanation for the gap of 33,000 between the railways' target reduction and the cut which it appears that they ought to have been aiming at? One important reason is that we have assumed that as second men and freight guards are almost entirely unnecessary they will be dispensed with, whereas BR is assuming that they will be retained. Moreover, the Board did not allow for any substantial increase in the speed of freight trains; for any significant saving in ticket collectors as a result of automatic barriers; or for any reduction in the number of passenger guards and station staff through the introduction of more pay-guard trains, and the removal of guards from those trains which have power doors or are very lightly loaded. Nor does the Board appear to have allowed for any saving in overhead staff over and above the reduction which it was hoped to achieve as a result of the reorganisation into Territories. However, to a large extent the discrepancy between the two estimates is illusory. What seems to have happened is that the Board estimated that it could prune its staff by 55,000 or more, but then added back 15,000 to 20,000 as a contingency allowance to cover a possible reduction in the length of the working week. Whether any staff need to be added back to allow for a fall in average hours will be discussed later.

REDUNDANCY AND UNEMPLOYMENT

It seems doubtful whether the reduction in rail employment which has been proposed would lead to any general redundancy problem because natural wastage will be more than sufficient to cover the rundown. At the beginning of 1973 British Rail had 55,000 employees over 55 years old. In addition a large contingent of younger workers will decide to find other employment. Between 1969 and 1973 wastage among rail staff as a result of death, retirement and resignation was equivalent each year to about 10½% of the number employed.[6] This means that about 125,000 workers will leave the railways voluntarily between the beginning of 1974 and the end of 1981. This is over 55,000 more than our estimate of BR's potential staff reduction.

Footplate staff appear to be the only category of workers where natural wastage would be significantly less than the desirable reduction in employment. According to our estimates, BR ought to be able to cut down footplate staff by 14,000 between the beginning of 1974 and 1981. However, between 1969 and 1973 natural wastage averaged only 2·4% per annum for this group of workers, and if it continues at this rate only 5000 drivers and second men will leave BR for reasons other than redundancy and dismissal during the period 1974 to 1981. In order to prevent a redundancy problem arising, the Government ought to introduce a special scheme to encourage footplate staff to leave the industry.

The reduction in railway employment should be spread throughout the country, and it seems unlikely that it will give rise to any acute regional problems. The railway workshops are the only possible exception, but some difficulty here is likely to arise regardless of whether rail employment is pruned by 40,000 or 73,000. Moreover, previous closures have led to remarkably little unemployment.[7]

Although the faster rate of rundown which has been proposed need not lead to serious redundancy, it will mean some contraction in employment opportunities in areas of high unemployment. Nevertheless, it is surely wrong to continue employing men who make little or no contribution to the functioning of the railways. It is one thing to keep a coal mine open in order that miners who would otherwise be out of work can produce coal, but it is quite another to retain men on BR who produce nothing. However, the necessary contraction of the railways' labour force does make it even more essential to ensure that extra jobs become available in areas of high unemployment.

EXPENDITURE IN 1981

It can be seen from Table 8.10 that during 1973 the railways' expenditure totalled £570 million before capital charges, and that staff expenditure accounted for £465 million or 82%. The size of the railways' pay bill in 1981 will partly depend on the number of railwaymen, which has already been estimated, and partly on the extent to which their earnings increase. If railwaymen have lost ground in relation to other workers they may, like the miners, catch up. Up to 1972 there was little or no reason to suppose that railwaymen were falling behind. Between 1963 and 1972 average hourly earnings for adult male workers on BR moved closely in line with those for all industries and services and there was never more than 2 pence difference between the two. For weekly earnings the relationship was slightly less stable. Between 1963 and 1965 the average weekly pay packet on BR

TABLE 8.10: *British Rail Operating Expenditure Before Interest and Depreciation*
(£ million, 1972 purchasing power)

	1969	1972	1973	1974	1981
Staff expenses	. .	466·5	465·3	499·7	*430·0*
Fuel and power:					
Oil	12·4	13·7	13·7	30·5	*31·5*
Electricity	17·1	14·4	13·3	17·9	*26·5*
	30·1ᵃ	28·1	27·0	48·4	*58·0*
Collection and delivery:					
Freight	8·6	6·7	6·5	6·0	*3·0*
Parcels	11·9	11·5	11·9	12·0	*14·0*
	20·5	18·2	18·4	18·0	*17·0*
Materials, supplies and services	. .	60·5	59·7	59·1	*50·0*
Total expenditure	580·3	573·3	570·4	625·2	*555·0*

ᵃ Includes coal (£0·6m).

Note: These figures differ from those given in Statement 4B of the Railways Board's *Annual Report* because staff costs include an allowance for British Rail Engineering, and because expenditure includes the surplus track grant, but excludes benefits to retired staff and BREL's depreciation.

was around 5% lower than the average for all industries and services. It then became slightly greater and, with the exception of 1967, stayed larger because the general decline in average hours did not affect the railways.

During 1973 railway workers do appear to have fallen slightly behind. The autumn surveys of earnings showed that both their average hourly and average weekly earnings were now slightly lower than those in industry as a whole. However, railwaymen must have more than caught up as a result of the special award which they received, with effect from April 1974, as a result of the Railway Staff National Tribunal. From what the Tribunal awarded, it appears that, even after allowing for the rise in prices, staff expenditure per employee must have been nearly 11% higher during 1974 than it was in 1973.[8]

It has been assumed that, for the rest of the period up to 1981, wages and salaries per railway worker will rise by 2½% a year, which is about the same rate of increase that is expected in real national income per worker. Although in the long run real earnings can be expected to move closely in line with productivity, they have in the past risen somewhat faster because employment income's share of the national income has increased while that of profits and other income has fallen. However, it seems doubtful whether this process can go much further, and it may well be reversed. It is possible that real income per worker will increase somewhat faster on the railways than in the economy as a whole. Salaried workers, who are relatively highly paid, will, even allowing for the large reduction in overhead and administrative staff, decline less rapidly than wage earners. On the other hand, there should be a large reduction in footplate staff, who are now an extremely well-paid group.

If BR is to reduce its labour force in the way that has been forecast, considerable changes in working arrangements will be necessary and will have to be paid for. The elimination of the restrictions on single-manning and the other impediments to the efficient use of drivers can be costed by discovering what BR had to pay under the productivity deal which it negotiated in the autumn of 1965. Up to that time most diesel and electric locomotives had carried firemen, but it was agreed that double-manning should be confined to the deep night hours and to situations in which time and distance limits of a less restrictive nature had been exceeded. In order to secure this concession, the Board paid the equivalent of just over £4 a week per driver, after adjusting the original sum to the wage levels ruling at the end of 1972. What BR had to pay in 1968, when single-manning was extended to the deep night hours, is impossible to tell, as this formed part of a wider deal. However, if the payment had been on the same basis as that of 1965, BR would have had to pay £2·20 a week more per driver, allowing as before for the subsequent rise in earnings. Some idea of the cost of the other alterations in operating practice can be obtained by examining what other employers have had to pay for similar changes. In 1972 the weekly rate for London Transport's automatic-train operators was £6·30 higher than that of its ordinary drivers, and when double-deck buses were operated without conductors the drivers received an extra £6·15 per week, although the rate was lower in the provinces.

In all the price for various alterations in working practice would appear, both from what BR has had to pay in the past and from what other employers are paying now, to represent about £6·25 per week for each driver (at the pay and price levels prevailing in 1972), which would mean a gain of 16%. If it is possible for the railways to make a productivity deal with their train crews along these lines, the cost in 1981, at 1972 purchasing power but allowing for the rise in real earnings over the period 1972–81, will be about £8 million.

It may be questioned whether the railway unions would be prepared to make such a bargain, and, in particular, whether BR would be able to regain the freedom to discharge those footplate staff who become surplus to requirements and are not prepared to move from their present depots. In view of the likely scale of redundancy if drivers and second men were reduced in line with our estimates, there might at present be no price which they would be prepared to accept. However, as we have already suggested, the Government should make special arrangements to encourage footplate staff, and if necessary guards, to quit the railways so that anyone who is willing to change his depot or booking-on point does not have to be sacked. Although it may still be doubted whether train crews would be willing to accept the radical changes in working practice that have been proposed, such changes have proved possible in other countries, and on BR far-reaching changes have in the past been successfully negotiated. In addition, it has been assumed that over the period 1972–81 there will be a very rapid increase in real earnings per employee. If a productivity deal is signed up the growth in *per capita* pay works out at over 3½% a year. This is the same rate that was being assumed by those engaged in railway planning prior to the energy crisis, when our economic prospects appeared far more rosy than they do now. The reason why the increase is as high as 3½%, despite the growth of only 2½% per annum which has been assumed for the period 1974–81, is the size of the award that railwaymen received during 1974. Although this has already taken place, it should be regarded as a productivity payment in advance, and it will have to be recognised that co-operation in securing higher productivity is necessary for the retention of the wage advantage that has been secured.

Allowing for the prospective increase in earnings and for the estimated reduction in the labour force, BR's staff expenditure comes to £430 million in 1981, at 1972 purchasing power. This is £35 million less than in 1973. It may be possible for the Board to make a further saving, and to provide extra employment, by reducing the amount of overtime that is worked. During 1973 manual workers on the railways appear to have worked an average of 46½ hours per week compared with the figure of 45½ hours for all industries and services. As overtime is paid at a rate of time and a half, the Board will, if it raises its efficiency, have the opportunity of cutting the amount of overtime and of reducing its labour force slightly more slowly. Whether BR will find this financially worthwhile depends on whether it will have to increase its basic hourly rates in order to keep the weekly pay packet at a reasonable level. This might well be unnecessary in view of the large rise in *per capita* pay that has been assumed to take place over the period 1972–81. This is why there is no need to allow for a reduction in overtime hours worked, and the extra workers that would then be required. If extra staff were retained to reduce the amount of overtime, the pay they receive should be offset, or more than offset, by the saving in overtime payments.

In order to complete our forecast, it is necessary to determine how much BR will spend on goods and services. In 1973 fuel and power cost £27 million, divided more or less equally between oil and electricity. The bill is now very much greater. By the spring of 1974 the railways were paying nearly two and a half times more for derv than they had in 1972, even when allowance is made for the general rise in prices. This was very much larger than the real increase of just over 20% which road hauliers had to face because BR obtains its oil almost entirely free of duty, so that when the pre-tax price of oil rises the railways feel virtually the full impact. As a result of electrification and the fall in mileage, there will be some reduction in the amount of derv that BR uses, but it will not be very great because the HST is likely to have a high consumption. Hence, it is likely that, even in the absence of any further rise in the cost of oil, BR will be spending over £30 million in 1981.

By the end of 1974 the railways were paying about 32% more for electricity than they had in 1972 after allowing for general inflation, and the cost of the fuel which the power stations burn will continue to rise. There has already been another substantial rise in the price of coal and miners' wages are likely to go on increasing faster than productivity. As fuel now constitutes such a large part of the costs of generation, this will have a marked effect on the price of electricity, and it has been assumed that it will be 55% higher in 1981 than it was in 1972. This, together with some increase in the quantity that BR consumes, may push up expenditure to something like £26½ million in 1981. In all the railways' bill for fuel is likely to more than double from £27 million to £58 million.

In 1973 British Rail paid National Carriers £18 million for the collection and delivery of freight and parcels on its behalf. By 1981 the amount of freight on which the railways bear the costs of cartage will almost certainly be very much smaller. However, the number of parcels which have to be collected and/or delivered should be about the same, while the reduction in the number of depots will lead to some increase in the amount of road work. Moreover, there is likely to be a significant increase in the rate which National Carriers charge. The work it performs is labour intensive, and there is little scope for gains in productivity. The reduction in expenditure on cartage as a result of the decline in the amount of freight which has to be collected or delivered is likely to be more or less offset by the other factors which are tending to push up costs, and the overall figure is likely to remain about the same.

The final item in the railways' running costs was the £60 million which they spent on miscellaneous goods and services. Of this the materials that BREL purchased seem to have accounted for well over half. After allowing for inflation, there has, over the years, been some decline in expenditure, and as the volume of maintenance work on railway vehicles is likely to fall it is likely to continue. There should also be a reduction in the railways' other expenditure. As we have seen, there ought by 1981 to have been a significant decline in the number of freight stations, in parcels depots, in manned passenger stations, in signal-boxes and in the mileage of track. This should lead to a reduction in the amount spent on the upkeep and repair of buildings and works; and the pruning down in the number of administrative staff ought to be accompanied by some reduction in the cost of office supplies and services. It will therefore be assumed that by 1981 overall expenditure on miscellaneous goods and services will be down to £50 million.

When the various cost estimates are brought together, it appears that British Rail's operating expenditure will fall from £570 million in 1973 to £555 million in 1981. Although there should be a saving of £35 million in staff costs, it has been estimated that this will be largely offset by an increase of £30 million in expenditure on fuel.

analysis can be used. We therefore need to investigate the reasons why the private benefits and costs of rail passenger services, as measured by British Rail's revenues and costs, might be expected to differ from the overall social benefits which the community derives from those services and the social costs which the services impose on the community. Before doing so, however, we should note that even using cost-benefit analysis there are considerable problems involved in securing optimal allocation of investment funds throughout the economy.

These problems arise, firstly, because projects in many sectors are appraised not by cost-benefit analysis, but by financial criteria. Rates of return estimated by these two alternative methods are not comparable with each other, and, moreover, there is no general rule whereby financial rates can be converted into cost-benefit rates, or vice versa. Difficulties therefore arise in choosing between projects appraised by the different methods. Secondly, there are usually constraints on total investment within each sector of the economy, which means that not all projects earning rates of return above 10% can be carried out. Instead some form of capital rationing has to be introduced to choose the best projects. The total amount of investment funds in any given sector of the economy is not, in practice, usually determined by economic techniques. However, it is possible that if cost-benefit analysis came into more general use in sectors other than transport, such as health and education, then it might generate pressure to allocate more resources to these sectors. Conversely, if large increases in the subsidies required to support rail services became necessary, this might lead to greater realisation that any increase in resources used in the transport sector must inevitably lead to fewer resources being available for other purposes. In practice, therefore, the test discount rate is mainly useful in determining optimal allocation of funds within a given sector of the economy, and has been less successful in determining inter-sectoral allocations. Because it is desirable that all projects within a sector should be appraised by the same method, and because cost-benefit analysis encompasses all benefits and costs where social and private benefits and costs diverge, its use is preferable to the use of financial criteria. While some projects earning a rate of return above 10% may still not be justified, because of budget constraints, those earning less than 10% can clearly be rejected.

The case for subsidisation

There are a number of reasons why it may be desirable to subsidise unprofitable rail passenger services. It is possible that the reduction in welfare that their users would suffer if they were withdrawn is greater than the loss from keeping them open. Secondly, in urban areas, rail closures would divert traffic onto the roads, and this might impose social costs in the form of increased traffic congestion and accidents on existing road users. Thirdly, some of the labour and other resources that are employed on these services may not have any alternative uses. Fourthly, it is possible that unprofitable lines should be retained because of the damage that a region's economy will sustain if its rail links are severed. Finally, it is sometimes believed that the subsidisation of railways has a favourable effect on the distribution of income. Each of these arguments will now be examined, and we shall try to discover by means of cost-benefit analysis how far BR's loss-making passenger services are worth retaining.

As a general rule, and ignoring external effects, the benefits which an industry's customers receive from its products or services should be sufficiently large to cover that industry's costs of production. If this is not so, it is not desirable either from the industry's or society's point of view that it should continue to produce, since the resources used should be transferred to the production of some other commodity where they are valued more highly. So long as the value received by consumers is less than the value of the factors of production, it is evident that a social loss will be incurred. However, the benefits which consumers receive will not, except on the marginal units which the industry sells, be measured simply by the industry's revenue. On intra-marginal units consumers obtain a surplus equivalent to the difference between what they are charged and the higher price that they would be willing to pay. The total benefits that consumers receive will therefore be equal to this consumers' surplus, plus the revenue paid to the firms in the industry.

In most circumstances consumers' surplus has no great significance, and firms will be able to cover their costs of production. Though this may not always be possible in the short run if sales are less than expected and fixed costs are high, in the long run capacity can be adjusted to demand. However, there are some industries, or sections of industries, where the minimum scale of operation is so large in relation to the market that there is no output at which fixed costs can be covered. In this situation, it may nevertheless be socially desirable for production to commence or continue, if the total amount that consumers would be prepared to pay rather than go without the commodity in question exceeds the total cost of producing it. To put the same point another way, the commodity should be produced so long as the consumers' surplus is greater than the loss. However, since the undertaking that is providing the good or service will often be unable to determine which consumers are willing to contribute more, or how much extra they would be willing to pay, it has to charge a uniform price. It will therefore make a loss, and production can only continue if it receives a subsidy, or is able and willing to practice cross-subsidisation.

There is probably a considerable range of activity that is unprofitable but where the deficit is smaller than the consumers' surplus. This will, for instance, be true of theatres, cinemas, bank branches and bus routes, in places where there are too few customers to make them profitable, and on a national scale it may apply to newspapers that cater for minority groups. Railways are another possible candidate for subsidisation, because the minimum cost of keeping a line open and providing a passenger service is high, and the number of passengers is often too small to cover this cost. To what extent services should be maintained, or possibly increased, will therefore depend, among other factors, on whether the costs of operating them are greater or smaller than the benefits to users, as measured by the maximum amount these users would be prepared to pay.

The amount that rail users would be prepared to pay over and above what they do pay will depend upon the alternative forms of transport available. In Figure 9.1, AD is the demand curve for travel between two points by those who initially use the rail service. As a simplification, it is assumed that in the event of closure, former rail travellers will either transfer onto an alternative bus service, or will no longer travel. Fares by rail and by bus, which are assumed to be the same, are shown by OF_1. This does not, however, represent the full cost of travel, because this takes time, and time has a value. The distance F_1G_1 indicates the time cost of using the railway, while F_1G_2 measures that of

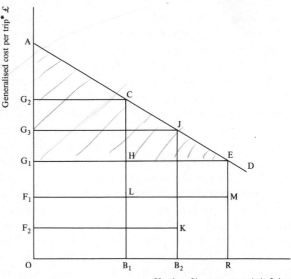

Number of journeys per period of time

*Generalised cost includes both money costs and time costs measured in monetary units.

travelling by the slower bus service. Hence, while there is a rail service, OR rail journeys will be made, but no traveller who finds it faster to use the railway will travel by bus. If, however, the railway line were closed, its former users would make OB_1 journeys by bus.

So long as the rail service is maintained, its users will enjoy the consumers' surplus G_1AE, which is the difference between the total amount they would be prepared to expend on their rail journeys, whether in money or in time ($OAER$), and the total cost they bear in payments to the railway (OF_1MR) and in travelling time (F_1G_1EM). Now, if the line is closed, the surplus will re reduced to the triangle G_2AC, because of the cost in terms of extra time that is incurred by those passengers who switch to bus (G_1G_2CH) and because of the loss of welfare sustained by those who no longer travel (HCE). For the latter group the time cost of travelling by bus is discouragingly high, and they decide to use the money that they formerly paid the railway (B_1LMR) for some other purpose. So far it has been assumed that rail and bus fares are equal, but if they differ this can readily be allowed for. Let us assume that the bus company only charges OF_2, half as much as the railway. The overall, or generalised, cost of travel by bus is now only OG_3, so that more former rail passengers will switch to bus, and the loss of consumers' surplus will, at G_1G_3JE, be smaller than it was at G_1G_2CE. In both examples, the benefits of retention to former rail travellers are measured by the difference in the generalised cost of travel for those who switch to the alternative bus service. Those who are dissuaded from travelling altogether must value their trips at a lower rate than those who switch to the bus service, and assuming a linear demand curve, their loss of welfare can be measured by valuing their trips at half the difference in generalised cost.

In practice, some former rail travellers will transfer to private cars instead of to an alternative bus service. The loss to these former rail travellers will be measured by the difference between the generalised cost of their trip by rail and that by car. The fuel taxation element of the generalised cost of their trip by car should, however, be excluded from the costs of rail service withdrawal, since it represents a transfer payment from motorists to the Government, and not a consumption of resources.

If the analysis described is to be of practical use it is necessary to ascribe a money value to time. In the case of journeys in working time, this presents no great difficulty because the value ought to correspond to the cost, including overheads such as National Insurance contributions borne by the employer, of hiring the worker for the appropriate period. However, surveys show that journeys of this type represent only a small proportion of the total travel on most grant-aided services. Empirical work by Beesley and Quarmby has thrown some light on the value of leisure time.[1] When they investigated commuters' willingness, or unwillingness, to pay extra for a quicker journey to work they found that in-vehicle time was valued at 25% of the wage rate and walking and waiting time was valued at 50% of the wage rate. The Department of the Environment use what they term an 'equity' value of leisure time equal to 25% of the average wage in the whole economy, which is used for all in-vehicle leisure-time savings irrespective of the income of the particular traveller. This means that leisure-time savings to the rich do not attract a higher weighting than similar time savings to the poor. The DoE's equity time value will be used later when various cost-benefit analyses are reworked and updated.

Having examined the benefit which rail users derive from the retention of a loss-making railway line, i.e. the reduction in welfare they would sustain if it were withdrawn, we must now turn to the cost society incurs in keeping it open. Since the benefit has been taken to be the surplus remaining after the amount that users pay to BR, the cost to society of maintaining the rail service must exclude what BR receives in fares. This means that the cost of retention is the loss from operating the rail service, less any deficit that is incurred on a replacement bus service. In some studies the cost of retention has been regarded either implicitly or explicitly as the difference between what the railways spend in running their service and the amount that it would cost to operate replacement buses. This is incorrect, however, since not all of the rail users will transfer if the rail line is closed. Resources will be required to produce the goods they will buy with the money they save, though if they buy goods bearing indirect taxation the taxation component of their spending will represent a transfer payment and not a real resource cost. Hence, ignoring for the moment the problem of indirect taxation, the reduction in the cost of operating public transport services exaggerates the resource saving that society secures by the extent to which bus revenue from former rail travellers falls short of what the railways earned. In Figure 9.1 this is indicated by the area $B_1 LMR$ if rail and bus fares are equal, and by OF_1MR less OF_2KB_2 if bus fares are lower.

The extent to which losses on public transport are reduced when a rail line is closed will partly depend on the quality of the alternative bus service that is provided, and the assumption made about this can have a major impact on the results of the cost-benefit study. For example, in the Ministry of Transport's study of the Cambrian Coast line, the costs of the alternative bus service account for 77% of the benefits of complete retention of the line.[2] A less satisfactory alternative bus service would therefore reduce this element of benefit, though it would increase the time-saving benefit of retaining the rail line. The problem is to determine the optimal type of alternative bus service in terms of minimising the social loss of closure, subject to the usual condition for Ministerial approval of closure that alternative bus services be provided. In the Cambrian study the principal replacement bus service was a service to cater for long-distance passen-

gers, despite the fact that the study notes that the line is predominantly used for local journeys and that most long-distance
rail passengers would not be likely to use the bus in the event of
closure. In addition, the assumption often appears to be made
in cost-benefit studies that only displaced rail travellers will use
the replacement bus services. However, in practice, it is likely
that former non-travellers will now use the new buses and so
derive some benefit from them over and above the price they pay.

The second argument for the subsidisation of rail services is
that where roads in areas served by the rail service are congested,
the increase in road traffic which would result from rail closure
will increase congestion, and thereby impose increased travel
costs on all existing road users. These increased congestion costs
may be an important element of the benefits of rail services in
urban areas. However, as we shall argue later, the subsidisation
of rail services is not the most effective way of dealing with these
congestion costs, and once the existing pricing system for urban
roads has been reformed, the case for subsidising urban rail
services will be weaker.

When the saving through closing a railway service is being
estimated, no charge should be made for resources which have no
alternative use. This will be true of capital equipment that cannot be moved elsewhere, even though, if kept in use, sooner or
later it will need to be replaced and a cost will then be imposed
on society. In addition, railway employees who would be made
redundant on closure of the line may be unable to find alternative
employment. BR will usually be able to reabsorb such men elsewhere on the system. However, on some lines this might require
them to move house, and if they were unwilling to do this they
might have difficulty in finding alternative employment if local
unemployment were high. Where labour would be unemployed,
society is losing nothing by paying such men to work on the railway, since the community is not forgoing any goods and services
which they might otherwise produce. Their wage costs should
therefore be excluded from the railway's operating expenditure in
the cost-benefit appraisal. Since loss-making railway services are
scattered around the country, there is no reason to believe that
railwaymen would have any general difficulty in finding alternative work. However, the withdrawal of certain services might
create difficulties. For instance, if the Cambrian Coast line were

closed, some former rail staff might become unemployed because of the high average age of the work force, the isolation of the line from alternative BR sources of employment, and the high level of unemployment in the area. However, the assumptions made in the Cambrian Coast study about the employment prospects of the railwaymen who would become redundant were pessimistic, while no allowance was made for the increase in employment which would be created by the replacement bus services.

It is also argued that a region's economy will suffer if its rail links are severed. Loss of rail transport facilities could affect regional prosperity in a number of ways. Some industries may be directly dependent on rail freight facilities, so that withdrawal of these facilities would lead to industrial decline. However, there are few industries of this type in the United Kingdom, and most of those grant-aided lines which do carry freight serve light industries whose dominant mode of transport is by road. Thus, a survey of rail freight users of the Cambrian Coast line found that, though closure would be regretted, it would be unlikely to influence the level of industrial activity in the area. Tourism is a possible exception, since closure of a rail service may reduce the accessibility of an area to holidaymakers. However, only a small proportion of holidaymakers now travel by train, and where rail services are withdrawn they may switch to coaches where the choice of service is usually much wider or, indeed, visit an alternative resort still served by rail. It has also been suggested that rail closures may lead to rural depopulation. Little is known about the relationship between the lack of transport facilities and depopulation, but it seems unlikely that the railways' remaining rural services can have much of a retaining effect. The railways have, ever since the advent of the bus, played a small and restricted part in rural transport, and with the spread of car ownership there has been a further decline in their role. For example, in Merioneth, where the Cambrian Coast line has been retained, a recent travel survey has shown that only 1·9% of the residents of the county use the rail service. Perhaps the only area where alternative roads are not adequate, and where regional development costs might be important, is the Highlands of Scotland.

The distribution of income

As well as the regional distribution of benefits, governments are also interested in the distribution of costs and benefits between different income groups. Cost-benefit analysis ignores this because costs and benefits are usually evaluated on the basis of how much money the sufferers or beneficiaries would be prepared to pay to avoid costs or obtain benefits, and these monetary valuations must inevitably be based on the existing distribution of income. Therefore, gains to those better off are given a greater emphasis than gains to those less well off. We shall however assume that, other things being equal, the welfare of the community is promoted by a more equitable distribution. It is therefore important to discover whether the less affluent sections of the community benefit from rail passenger subsidies, as is sometimes popularly supposed.

Railway passenger revenue consists of both personal expenditure by households and expenditure by firms and government agencies for travel by their employees. In 1972, railway passenger revenue earned by British Rail, London Transport, Northern Ireland Railways, the Glasgow Underground and various minor lines totalled £352 million. Personal expenditure on rail travel in the United Kingdom was equal to £289 million, military expenditure to about £11 million and business expenditure to about £52 million. Business expenditure is concentrated on BR's Inter-City services, since only about 5% of journeys on grant-aided services and on London Transport lines are accounted for by journeys in the course of work. This means that in 1972 non-personal expenditure accounted for about 40% of Inter-City revenue.

Figures for the income distribution of rail users not travelling on business are available from the Family Expenditure Survey. This is a survey of personal expenditure in the United Kingdom, derived from data from a representative sample of about 7000 households selected each year. Table 9.1 shows the proportion of personal rail expenditure which different income groups accounted for in 1972. For comparison, the shares of these income groups in total expenditure are also shown. Personal expenditure on rail travel is heavily weighted towards the highest income group, with just over 50% of personal rail expenditure contributed by the top 20% of households although they account for

TABLE 9.1: *Personal Expenditure by Income Group in the United Kingdom, 1972*

Households	All goods and services %	Rail %	Bus %	Car %	Rail season-tickets %
Poorest 20%	7·9	5·0	9·3	1·7	0·6
Second quintile	14·7	8·8	18·6	11·1	6·0
Third quintile	19·0	13·5	20·9	17·5	12·9
Fourth quintile	23·8	21·7	24·4	27·5	23·3
Richest 20%	34·6	51·0	26·9	42·3	57·2
Total	100·0	100·0	100·1	100·1	100·1

Note: Totals do not always add to 100% because of rounding.

only a third of all expenditure. The highest income groups must also be responsible for the great bulk of business expenditure on rail travel and derive extra satisfaction from this source. In contrast, the poorest 20% of households accounted for only 5% of personal expenditure on rail travel, although their share of all expenditure was around 8%. Data for the years 1968 and 1970 show similar results, which suggests that the picture presented has not been affected by sampling errors.

Also of interest is a comparison between expenditure on rail and on the other means of internal transport. As Table 9.1 shows, the lower income groups account for a much higher proportion of expenditure on bus than on rail travel. This might be expected, but even more interesting is a comparison between expenditure on rail and on the purchase and running of motor vehicles. While a higher proportion of rail than of car expenditure is accounted for by the lowest income group, which includes few car owners, the three middle income groups each account for a larger share of car than of rail expenditure. Hence if we were to rank the three modes of travel in relation to the extent to which they were used by the lower income groups, the order would be bus, car and finally rail. It is also noteworthy that among the 94 items distinguished in the Family Expenditure Survey, there is only one where the highest income group accounts for a greater propor-

tion of household spending, namely education and training
expenses, which must largely represent expenditure on public
schools.

   Although it is clear that the top income group is responsible
for an exceptionally high proportion of expenditure on rail transport, it is just conceivable that they make exceptionally little use
of the services which were subsidised under the 1968 Act. If so,
rail subsidies could have a favourable effect on the distribution
of income, although this argument appears less plausible now that
the Government is subsidising the whole of BR's passenger business. It is, in any case, a weak one. No breakdown by income or
social class appears to be available for those who use the grant-
aided services. However, detailed information is available for
expenditure on season tickets, and season-ticket holders account
for half of the passenger miles travelled on the loss-making
services. As can be seen from the last column of Table 9.1, the
richest 20% of households accounted in 1972 for 57% of the
total expenditure on season-ticket travel. This proportion was
even higher than for rail expenditure as a whole.

   The proponents of subsidisation will reply that the reason why
rail travel is a luxury good is that it is so expensive that only
the affluent can afford it. This argument could be used to justify
the subsidisaton of Rolls Royce cars, caviar or anything else that
happens to be an object of expenditure for those with high
incomes. However, it could be the case that a high proportion
of those who would be attracted to the railways if fares were
brought down would be from the poorer sections of the community, so that *further subsidisation* would have a favourable
effect on the distribution of income. To test this possibility, let
us assume that non-business demand for rail travel would double
if no fares were charged, but that none of this extra demand would
come from the richest 20% of households. In 1972 personal
expenditure on all BR passenger services came to about £215
million, and, of this, the richest 20% accounted for 51% or
£109·65 million. This would be what they would gain if rail transport were provided free, since we have assumed that they would
not make any extra journeys. The benefits to other income groups
would consist of two components. Those already travelling by
rail would gain £105·35 million, while the extra journeys made
by members of these income groups would, if the demand curve

were linear, provide consumers' surplus benefits of £107·5 million. The total gains in consumers' surplus would therefore come to £322·5 million. If so, the richest 20% would enjoy 34% of the welfare benefit, which happens to correspond almost exactly to their proportion of total consumers' expenditure. Hence, even on assumptions which have been heavily loaded against the richest 20%, it turns out that *extra subsidisation* would not make the distribution of income any more equal. Moreover, it seems clear that the *existing subsidies* contribute to inequality.

This might be disputed on the ground that although the share of the benefit from the rail subsidy received by the richest 20% is greater than their share of expenditure, so also is the proportion of tax revenue that they contribute, out of which the subsidy it paid. What this overlooks is that the British tax system is proportional rather than progressive, and that the redistributive effect of the welfare state arises because of the way in which tax revenue is spent. If the taxation to pay the rail subsidy is proportional, while the benefit is regressive, then the overall effect on the distribution of income will be unfavourable. This assumes that the taxation to finance the subsidy does have an equal proportionate effect on different income groups. Although it is impossible to be certain, it seems reasonable to suppose that, if anything, it too is regressive. Chancellors appear to impose the highest possible income taxes that they consider acceptable, and then to raise the rest of the money they require in indirect taxation. Since such taxation tends to be mildly regressive, it can plausibly be argued that if extra taxation is raised to meet the cost of the rail subsidy it will have a regressive impact.

Previous studies of railway closure

Having considered the general case for subsidising BR, and the theoretical foundations on which the cost-benefit analysis of railway services rests, we can now examine the various empirical studies of loss-making lines that have been carried out.

The first cost-benefit study of a rural railway line was Clayton and Rees' report on the Central Wales line,[3] which runs through a remote part of Wales from Craven Arms to Llanelli (90 miles). The service is still operated, though as a through service of five trains per day each way between Shrewsbury and Swansea (121 miles). On the basis of a one-week survey in 1964 of all passengers travelling on the line, Clayton and Rees calculated that the annual social costs of operating the line exceeded the annual social benefits by £23,681. This implied that closure would be justified unless the annual intangible benefits of retention were judged to be worth an amount at least equal to this figure. Clayton and Rees considered that the railway had no role to play in industrial development through the provision of freight facilities, and that, although public transport facilities are essential for the area's tourist trade, they could best be provided by the expansion of bus services. Clayton and Rees suggested that closure of the line might hasten rural depopulation in the area, but they admitted that the precise relationship between lack of transport facilities and the rate of depopulation is unknown.

A much more detailed study of a second rural line in Wales, the Cambrian Coast line from Machynlleth to Pwllheli (57 miles), was undertaken by the special Economic Unit set up within the Ministry of Transport to study the application of cost-benefit analysis to railway closures. On the basis of two one-week surveys of passengers using the line in August and October 1967, the Unit estimated the discounted social benefit of retaining the line over a ten-year period, on the assumption, first, that the line would remain open indefinitely, and then, alternatively, that it would be closed after ten years, thus reducing the need for expenditure on replacement. The net cost of retention for ten years only was estimated at £695,500 by discounting costs and benefits back to 1968 by 8% per annum. The net cost of retention of the line indefinitely was estimated on the same basis at between £748,500 and £927,500, or, if only the Machynlleth–Barmouth section was retained, at £111,100. On the basis of this study, Ministerial consent for closure was given, but the line was reprieved in the summer of 1974.

A third cost-benefit study of a rural rail service was that made by Foot and Starkie of the 26-mile Ashford–Hastings line.[4] Using information from a one-day survey of passengers in 1970, they concluded that the average net cost of retaining the line lay within a range, the average of which, discounted at 10% per annum over ten years, was £189,500. Closure would, they thought, also lead to intangible costs in the form of reduced labour mobility, disruption in the form of the need to change job or house, and increased road congestion, and intangible benefits in the form of reduced road congestion at level crossings and the use of former railway land for alternative purposes. The net intangible benefits of retention did not appear large, so it appeared that closure of the line would be justified. This line was also reprieved in 1974.

The first cost-benefit study of an urban railway closure was the 1963 study by N. Rubra of the North London line from Broad Street to Richmond. BR had estimated that this line lost £95,000 in 1963, and the line was scheduled for closure in the Beeching Report. After considering the way in which the costs of operating the line could be reduced, Rubra attempted to make a rough measure of the social benefits of retaining it. Valuing all the time saved at 5/- per hour, he estimated the annual benefits to rail users in the form of reduced travel time at £441,000, the bus costs avoided at £376,000, and the reduced travel time of other road users at £295,000. Though these quantified benefits were rough estimates, they were very substantially in excess of the financial loss on the line, and it was clear that closure was not socially justifiable.

A second study of an urban line was Else and Howe's study of the Sheffield–Barnsley line in Yorkshire.[5] Using data on ticket sales and passenger flows on the line in May 1966, they estimated the social benefits of retention based on a number of alternative assumptions about the methods of transport that would be used by former rail users after closure. On the basis of their central assumption, they concluded that retention of the line would lead to an annual social loss of £2710. However, they had excluded, as a benefit of retention, the loss of revenue to public transport operators, and their own work suggested that if this had been included, then there would be an annual net benefit of retention of £24,790. On this basis, closure would not be justified.

Neither the Sheffield nor the North London studies collected detailed information from passengers by means of a questionnaire, and both used very rough estimates of the congestion costs which would arise from closure. Two much more detailed cost-benefit appraisals of urban rail services in Manchester have been undertaken recently by Bristow and Rodriguez, and by Foster.[6] Bristow and Rodriguez studied the 25-mile Manchester–Buxton line which, as well as catering for off-peak and weekend leisure trips, carries a substantial commuter flow from the rather isolated town of Buxton through the suburbs of South Manchester into Central Manchester. Postal questionnaires were distributed to all passengers on the line on three days of a survey week in July 1972. The net discounted benefits of retaining the line over the period from 1973 to the end of 1976 were estimated as lying between £1 million and £3 million, though this is an overestimate because of an error which arose in the estimation of the costs of travel by private car.

Foster's study considered two services, the electric Manchester–Glossop line and the diesel-operated Manchester–Marple–New Mills service. This study used a completely different approach to the others. Instead of using information from surveys of existing rail users, data was derived from the South-East Lancashire North-East Cheshire Area Land Use and Transportation Study (SALTS) which had made predictions of transport use by all modes of transport, link by link, for the whole of the Greater Manchester transport network. Using this data, it was estimated that the net discounted benefit of retaining the services over the period from 1973 to 1997 would be £4·5 million at 1971 prices.

All these results are not directly comparable, since they relate to different price levels and use alternative valuations of time savings. Moreover, some of the studies omitted important elements both of cost and benefit and since they appeared more reliable information on BR's revenue from these and other grant-aided services has become available. With the exception of those from the North London line, the studies' figures have therefore been reworked, updated and converted to a common price-level partly to see whether this alters the conclusions on closure, but mainly to try to establish a yardstick for the gross benefit per passenger mile for use in our investigation of the desirability of retaining unprofitable services.

Time savings were valued at the standard DoE rates for leisure and working time at 1971 prices (see p. 190), and all other costs and benefits were converted to 1971 values. Information on 1972 traffic flows was used to allow for the substantial traffic growth since 1964 on the Central Wales line, and for the underestimate of traffic on the Ashford–Hastings line arising from the survey methods used. Recent traffic data were not available for the Cambrian Coast line, where traffic exhibits marked seasonality. If the averages of the 1967, 1970 and 1971 summer weeks and of the 1967 and 1970 winter weeks are taken and converted to annual totals, traffic appears to be 14% higher than it was in the 1967 surveys, and this estimate was used in our revision.

Our revised time-saving figures tend to overestimate the benefits of retaining some of the services because of the way these savings were originally measured. The Central Wales, Sheffield–Barnsley and Ashford–Hastings studies estimated the additional time by bus on the basis of in-vehicle time, and ignored the possibility that walking time might be reduced because bus stops are more closely spaced than railway stations. The Cambrian Coast study appears to have estimated time savings by asking rail users how long their journey would take by bus. This also may lead to overestimation, since people will generally be less aware of times by services they are not using, and may seek to rationalise their choice by overstating the time by the rejected alternative. This method was also employed for the Manchester–Buxton study, where the error was compounded by subtracting in-vehicle time, which was calculated from bus timetables and average car-journey speeds, from estimated journey time. The remaining walking and waiting time, which then included any overestimate of journey time, was valued at a rate double that of in-vehicle time. These problems were avoided in Foster's study because of the different approach used. The SALTS model had predicted travel patterns for 1984 by first estimating traffic flows for the base year of 1966. The model also produced generalised costs of travel along each link of the area's transport network, and these generalised costs were used to determine the least cost method of transport for former rail users in the event of rail closure. The study therefore could allow for differences in access time to public transport, and was not dependent on travellers' possibly inaccurate perceptions of alternative journey times. However, the problem with this approach is that the estimated base year flows may not give a good representation of actual base year flows. Thus, the SALTS predictions for 1966 rail travel greatly overestimate actual rail travel as measured by BR data for 1971. Though the benefits of retention were scaled down to allow for this overestimation, the scaling-down factor may not reflect differences in this overestimation over different sections of line and for different types of journey.

We estimated the loss of revenue to public transport operators following closure, using revenue data from the services in 1971, and information from the studies concerning the expected proportion of former rail users who would no longer travel after closure. The resultant revenue losses were then multiplied by 0·80 to allow for indirect taxation throughout the economy, since this is a transfer payment. The benefits to those who would no longer travel if the rail service were closed had been valued at the same rate as benefits to those who would continue to travel, instead of at half this rate, by the two Welsh studies and by the Ashford–Hastings study. This, and a further error in the calculation of this item by the Cambrian Coast study, was corrected.

Additional road congestion costs, though not likely to be important in rural areas, were not calculated in the Central Wales and Ashford–Hastings studies, while a figure of £50,000 was included in the Cambrian study, though it appears to be little more than a guess. Else and Howe made a rough estimate of additional peak-hour congestion which would be suffered both by existing motorists and by those tranferring from rail to car within the City of Sheffield. A more detailed estimate was made by Bristow and Rodriguez. The main A6 road paralleling the Manchester–Buxton line suffers from serious peak-hour congestion which would be expected to worsen if the rail service were withdrawn. Information on existing traffic flows along this road was available, and the increase in traffic which would follow closure was estimated from the survey of rail users. The increase in congestion costs was then calculated by means of Transport and Road Research Laboratory (TRRL) formulae which relate traffic flows on a road to average generalised cost per mile per vehicle. This method of estimating increased congestion costs will overestimate the cost of rail closure if some of the existing motorists change their route or cease to travel, since this will reduce road congestion costs back towards their original level. Bristow and Rodriguez could point to the fact that the geographical configuration of the road network around the A6 makes diversion to other routes rather difficult. The problem is more serious with Foster's study, where diversion might be easier, and so the possibility that congestion costs have been overestimated is greater.

Some of the studies included, and others excluded, the benefits of retention in the form of reduced accident costs. We estimated these for all studies, using information published by the TRRL and the Railway Inspectorate. The TRRL have published data for 1968 on the frequency of different types of accident on different classes of road. Data are also available on the estimated costs in 1968 of accidents of differing severity.[7] These costs include the costs of damage to vehicles, medical and police costs, the costs of lost output of accident victims, and a *minimum* estimate of the subjective costs of injury and death to victims and their relatives. These figures enabled us to calculate the accident cost per vehicle mile on urban A and rural A roads. Increases in road traffic following rail closure were estimated from traffic flow figures for the services concerned, from information on the likely modal split after closure, and from national vehicle-occupancy rates for buses, for car trips on the journey to work and for leisure car trips. The reduction in rail accident costs was estimated from information on the number of accidents on the railways in 1972. The number of rail accidents on particular services was calculated by assuming that accidents to passengers are related to passenger mileage, that movement accidents to rail staff and trespassers are related to train mileage, that non-movement accidents to staff and other persons are related to the total number of staff, and that accidents at level crossings are related to the number of crossings or, where data on this were not available, to the mileage of route. These accidents were valued by assuming that the cost per casualty, excluding damage costs, of rail accidents is the same as that for roads. It should be noted that the difference in the cost of rail accidents and of road accidents represented a very small proportion of the total benefits of retaining the services under consideration, partly because of the legitimate inclusion of railway staff and trespassers in the railway accident figures, and partly because many former rail users will not transfer to private cars if rail services are withdrawn.

The avoidable costs of operating the rail services considered for closure have usually been provided by BR, though Clayton and Rees argued that substantial economies, many of which were made soon after, could reduce the costs of operating the Central Wales line. Unlike the Ministry of Transport in their study of the Cambrian Coast line, however, Clayton and Rees did not consider the resource costs of labour with zero opportunity costs.

We therefore made an allowance for such costs. A similar calculation had been made by Foot and Starkie for the Ashford–Hastings railway line, but we excluded this on the grounds that there
is a general staff shortage on the Southern Region. We also
excluded Bristow and Rodriguez's estimate for the Manchester–
Buxton line because unemployment is not a serious problem in
the area served by this line.

TABLE 9.2: *Discounted Social Benefits of Retaining the*
Cambrian Coast Line for a Ten-Year Limited Life from
1968 Onwards

	Discounted value at 8% per annum over ten years		
	MoT study	*Revised figures*	
	1968 prices *(£000s)*	*1968 prices* *(£000s)*	*1971 prices* *(£000s)*
Costs of retention:			
Railway avoidable costs	− 1 768	− 1 768	− 2 159
less Labour with zero opportunity costs	+ 534	+ 534	+ 652
Benefits of retention:			
Additional travel time for adults avoided	+ 37	+ 42	+ 51
Additional travel time for children avoided	*a*	+ 1	+ 1
Loss of benefit on forgone trips avoided	+ 38	+ 27	+ 33
Loss of revenue to public transport operators avoided	*a*	+ 74	+ 90
Road costs avoided	+ 50	+ 57	+ 70
Accident costs avoided	*a*	+ 2	+ 2
Additional bus costs avoided	+ 413·5	+ 413·5	+ 505
Net benefit of retention	− 695·5	− 617·5	− 755

a Not included in original study.

For illustration, our revisions of the cost-benefit results of one
of the studies, the Cambrian Coast line, are shown in full in Table
9.2. Excluding the effects of inflation, our revision of the cost-
benefit studies' figures reduces the social costs of retaining the
Central Wales, Cambrian Coast and Ashford–Hastings lines,
largely because of revised estimates of rail traffic flows and the
inclusion of loss of revenue to public transport operators in the
latter two cases. However, these reductions are small in relation

to the overall social losses made by these lines. The social benefits of retaining the Sheffield–Barnsley line are reduced because Else and Howe originally valued time savings at 40% of the wage rate instead of 25%, while the benefits of retaining the Manchester–Buxton line are substantially lower, largely because of the incorrectly high value of vehicle-operating costs used in the original study. Nevertheless, the net benefit of retaining both lines remains positive. The study by Foster of the Manchester–Glossop and Manchester–New Mills lines was made at 1971 prices, and we made no revisions to its conclusions, though the possibility that the road congestion benefits have been overestimated should be borne in mind.

SOCIAL BENEFITS AND RAILWAY OPERATING COSTS

We have now considered cost-benefit studies of seven railway services, three of which can be described as rural and four as urban. With regard to the three rural services, the quantifiable benefits of retention are less than the measurable benefits of closure. In addition, the unquantifiable benefits of retention do not appear to be likely to be sufficiently large to outweigh the net quantifiable benefits of closure. Closure appears less justifiable for the urban services. All four appear to create measurable social benefits sufficient to cover their specific costs of operation, though it should be noted that neither the Sheffield–Barnsley nor the Manchester area studies indicate social benefits sufficient to cover their full costs, which include joint costs allocated according to what is known as the Cooper Brothers formula.

In Table 9.3 the gross social benefits of retaining the services, including that part which is reflected in BR's revenue, have been expressed as a rate per passenger mile. After the figures have been reworked and made as comparable and comprehensive as possible, there is a certain similarity between the benefits per passenger mile from the different services. These benefits, at 1971 prices, all lie between 2·1 and 2·4 pence per passenger mile, except in the case of the Central Wales line where the figure is somewhat lower. It therefore seems that a useful working rule would be that social benefits per mile from grant-aided services

TABLE 9.3: *Social Benefits and Railway Costs per Passenger Mile (1971 prices)*

	Social benefit per passenger mile (pence)	Specific costs[a] per passenger mile (pence)	Total costs[a] per passenger mile (pence)
Central Wales line	1·79	3·05	6·42
Cambrian Coast line	2·20	. .	. .
Ashford–Hastings	2·28	2·39	3·05
Sheffield–Barnsley[b]	2·12	1·25	3·02
Manchester–Buxton	2·18	1·48	2·66
Manchester–Glossop/ Hadfield Manchester–New Mills/Marple	2·37	1·75	3·80

[a] Includes depreciation and replacement provision, but not interest.

[b] The cost figures for this line relate to the Sheffield–Barnsley–Leeds service.

averaged roughly 2·2 pence per passenger mile at 1971 prices. It follows that we can compare social benefits per passenger mile with costs per passenger mile, service by service, to discover the broad overall number of services which could not be justified by cost-benefit analysis. Continuation of passenger services on social benefit grounds will be justified if the social benefits per passenger mile exceed the avoidable costs per passenger mile of retaining the services. From these avoidable costs should be subtracted any costs which represent labour that would otherwise be unemployed, though this factor should only be relevant in the more remote areas of the country.

Data on the costs of each grant-aided service as estimated by the Cooper Brothers formula for grant aid purposes are available for 1971.[8] These costs are divided into four components: specific operating costs, joint facilities and overheads, administration and interest. The provision for replacement and renewal, which includes both historic depreciation and provision for renewal at replacement cost, is also distinguished separately, even though such provision is also included within the specific and joint cost categories. The joint cost category includes the costs of track, signalling, terminals, and other facilities which the grant-aided services share with other passenger and freight services. This category presents the most serious problem because it is difficult to determine what proportion of joint costs would be saved if a particular service or group of services were withdrawn.

However, there are a number of services which do not appear to generate sufficient social benefits to cover even their specific costs of operation. There were in 1971, 34 services aided by the Government which had specific costs above 2·2 pence per passenger mile, despite the allowance which was made for labour with zero opportunity costs. The services had specific costs in 1971 of £4·0 million, and revenue of £1·3 million. Assuming benefits of 2·2 pence per mile, they generated social benefits of £2·8 million. The immediate financial saving from closure would therefore be £2·7 million, and the saving in social cost £1·2 million. The latter figure is a minimum figure because of the way we have estimated social benefits, and because the closure programme should permit some saving in joint and administrative costs, which totalled £2·8 million in 1971.

The 34 services included in this initial closure plan, which we denote as closure programme A, are, in the main, rural branch lines. Their closure would reduce the total route mileage open to passengers by 560 miles. The short length of most of the lines and the fact that they are located in predominantly rural areas means that the bus will be an adequate and much more economic alternative, and that although many journey times will be lengthened, cases of genuine hardship are likely to be rare. Of the four longer services, the Central Wales and Cambrian Coast lines have already been appraised by cost-benefit analysis, and were found to be not worth retaining.

In 1971, 9% of the estimated costs of grant-aided services consisted of administrative costs, and joint facilities and overheads accounted for a further 39%. Though closure of one or two services might not permit any administrative savings, a larger-scale closure programme should allow administrative costs to be reduced *pro rata*. With regard to joint costs, many grant-aided services share track and terminals with other aided services so that closure of a group of such services would permit savings. Further, though joint costs are often shared with freight services, any freight services which would continue after closure would need very much reduced track facilities, with track maintained to low standards and very little, if any, signalling required.

Of those grant-aided services which would remain if closure programme A were implemented, 38 had specific, joint and administrative costs per passenger mile below 2·2 pence and therefore seemed worth retaining on social benefit grounds. A further 20 services with costs above 2·2 pence were services in PTE areas that the Executives believe to have a long-term future and are planning to retain. The remaining services were then examined to discover whether it was likely that closure would enable cost savings of over 2·2 pence per passenger mile to be made. There were a considerable number of cases where this was doubtful because services shared facilities with Inter-City or freight traffics which are unlikely to be withdrawn. However, there were 55 other services where the cost of retention appeared so high that their closure appeared justified, and these we denote as closure programme B.

At 1971 prices the specific costs of these 55 services totalled £9·6 million and their joint and administrative costs totalled £10·5 million. They earned revenue of £7·0 million, and on the basis of the passenger mileage carried they generated social benefits of £14·5 million. If their specific costs only could be saved by withdrawal, the financial gain to BR would be £2·6 million, and the social *loss* £4·9 million. On the other hand, if all joint and administrative costs could be saved, BR would be £13·1 million better off, and there would be a social gain of £5·6 million. In practice, the actual savings will lie within this range but nearer the latter rather than the former figures. If both programmes A and B were implemented, and if only half the joint and administrative costs of operating these services could be saved, then the net financial saving would be £13 million at 1972 purchasing power. Of this, about £2½ million would represent a reduction in capital expenditure on assets needed to replace the services' capital stock.

In all, our two closure lists contain 89 services out of the 192 provincial services aided in 1973. They do, however, account for only 19% of the passenger mileage travelled on provincial grant-aided services and only 2·7% of the total passenger mileage on BR. Programme B would involve the withdrawal of passenger services from 1577 miles of route, and with programme A would reduce BR's total mileage open to passengers from 9002 miles to 6865 miles. The main areas affected by the closures would be East

Anglia, South-West Wales and Central Wales. Some services would be withdrawn from the Highlands of Scotland, but the North Sea oil industry would be likely to save some others whose future has long seemed in jeopardy. We estimate that programme A would lead to an average of one additional death and nine serious injuries per annum, while programme B would lead to a further six deaths and 69 serious injuries. There would probably be a *reduction* in injuries of a less serious type because the proportion of slight relative to serious accidents is higher on the railways than on the roads.

Our conclusions on the desirability of reducing the route network are not very different from those reached by the DoE economists in 1972, which were misreported in the press at that time. The Department considered three closure programmes involving the withdrawal of 44, 73 and 123 services respectively. They considered the benefits from service withdrawals at 1971 prices, but at 1981 real resource costs. The Department did not have a direct estimate of the resource savings from closure of the first group of services, which were estimated to cost £7·3 million for grant aid purposes in 1971, but believed their 1981 social benefits would lie between £2·2 and £3·0 million. The second group of closures would add £8 million to the 1981 resource savings with a loss of social benefits of between £3·7 and £4·8 million, and the third group of closures would add £26 million to 1981 resource savings for an additional social benefit loss of between £11·7 and £17·0 millions. The Department concluded that their rough estimates of the costs and benefits of closure constituted a *prima facie* case for submitting all 123 services to the detailed scrutiny of the closure procedure.

The Department believed that their estimates of the social benefits of retention were, if anything, overestimates, and described them as 'high higher' because they took a generous view of the advantages which the services conferred. Nevertheless, their investigation implied a higher social cost of retention than our own study suggests. This arose largely because the Department's cost figures relate to 1981 and so include the effects of rising real labour costs between 1971 and 1981. In fact, the ratio between social benefits and railway revenue implied in our study is very similar to that implied by use of the DoE's 'high', as opposed to their 'higher', estimate of social benefits.

As we have seen in Chapter 8, some productivity gains will be possible on lightly used services. For example, one-man operation should be possible in some cases, more pay trains can be introduced, and track and signalling facilities can be reduced. The likely savings in manpower from all sources were estimated for each of the services in our two closure programmes, and these savings appeared to be equivalent to a saving of 10·5% of the specific, joint and administrative costs of operating all 89 services in 1971. Although the percentage cost saving was remarkably similar for the two groups, the way in which the economy was achieved was rather different. While the economies are substantial and should certainly be realised if the services are to remain open, they have already been swamped in advance by the 20% rise in the real earnings of railwaymen between 1971 and 1974. As the real costs of operating rail services rise, more and more services are likely to become socially unprofitable.

Because of this, and because we, like the DoE, have tried to overstate rather than understate the benefits of retention, our closure programme is probably on the low side. Moreover, although we have managed to quantify most of those social benefits that appear to be of any importance, we have ignored the problem of income distribution. Unless the grant-aided services which we have included in our closure programme are a complete exception to the rule that it is the richer members of the community who obtain most benefit from the subsidies which rail services receive, this strengthens the case for closure. Nevertheless, our study has necessarily been of the broad brush variety, and detailed investigation would be necessary to determine precisely which of British Rail's loss-making services are socially unprofitable and should therefore be closed.

THE OPTIMAL PRICING OF THE USE OF ROADS

Our discussion of the retention of unprofitable rail services has assumed the continuation of present pricing and taxation policies for the use of roads. However, as we argued earlier, it is these policies, and the consequent divergence between the social and private costs of road use, that create one case for the subsidisation of urban railway lines. By reducing the cost of rail travel and keeping open lines which could not be made profitable, some traffic is kept off the roads, and congestion and other social costs are lower than they might otherwise be. This is a second-best policy, and it is desirable that the problem should be tackled at source through the introduction of road pricing. Even if rail subsidies were effective in achieving the correct balance between road and rail, providing all transport services at prices below costs will distort land-use patterns by giving a stimulus to the over-expansion of the conurbations. In addition, the resource costs of implementing road-pricing schemes may often be considerably less than the resource costs of rail subsidies.

At present, road investments are appraised by cost-benefit analysis. Provided full allowance is made for the external costs created by roads and for the impact of such investments on the distribution of income, then correct use of this technique will ensure that roads will only be constructed if the benefits to society exceed the construction and other costs imposed. This assumes, however, that use of existing road capacity is optimal, and it has long been recognised that the present free-for-all system on urban roads leads to an undesirable level of congestion, and that economic welfare can be increased by reducing traffic flows by means of a system of road pricing. The case for road pricing can best be explained by means of a diagram.

In Figure 9.2 the private marginal cost (*PMC*) curve shows how the cost per trip, including time costs, of travelling by car along a given road link varies with the volume of traffic. At first the cost does not change because if there is only a small flow of traffic, additional vehicles will not impose congestion on existing road users. However, there eventually comes a point (flow *F*) where the addition of a further vehicle to the flow will reduce the speed of other vehicles and hence impose congestion costs on them. Once congestion exists, the addition of a further vehicle to the flow will impose costs on the community in two ways. Firstly, there will be the costs of that vehicle's own trip, as measured by the *PMC* curve, and secondly that vehicle will impose congestion costs on all other vehicles, because their journey times will lengthen and their operating costs will rise. The net increase in cost is termed the social marginal cost, and is shown in the diagram as the *SMC* curve. This is a short-run

The Rail Problem

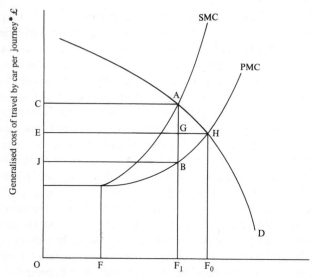

Flow of vehicles per period of time

*Generalised cost includes both money costs and time costs measured in monetary units.

marginal cost curve which excludes the costs of building the road; such costs are irrelevant for determining optimal use of existing capacity. In the absence of road pricing, motorists will continue to travel as long as their valuation of the trip, as measured by the demand curve for travel, exceeds the costs which they themselves incur, as measured by the *PMC* curve. The flow of traffic will therefore be F_0. The optimal flow, however, occurs where the D and *SMC* curves intersect: that is, at flow F_1, since any increase in flow above this point adds more to the community's costs than to its benefits. The optimal flow can be achieved by a tax or charge on road users equal to *AB*. In practice, heavy goods vehicles could be charged a higher rate to reflect the greater congestion they impose, though it might be desirable to exclude buses on the grounds that the congestion per passenger carried is much lower than for cars. It would also be desirable to allow for external costs such as noise and pollution in the estimation of the *SMC* curve.

The benefits of the tax are equal to the reduction in the real resource costs of trips made (area *JEGB*), minus the loss of consumers' surplus for those motorists dissuaded from travelling (area AGH). However, the immediate beneficiary is the Government which gains the tax revenue (area $JCAB$), while those motorists who continue to travel suffer a loss (area $ECAG$).

Our previous discussion has assumed that motorists are fully aware of those costs of motoring which they themselves incur. In practice, account must be taken of the known tendency of motorists to underestimate their operating costs. Surveys of road users, and studies of the perceived costs implied by travellers' choices, have indicated that motorists believe that their running cost is equivalent to what they spend on petrol. The cost of a journey is very much greater because the frequency with which tyres have to be replaced, the amount of maintenance that a car requires, and even the time it lasts partly depend on the distance it travels. Indeed, the total expenditure that is mileage-related is roughly double the cost of fuel. If so, urban traffic flows will be above the level at which demand is equal to PMC, i.e. greater than F_0 on the diagram, and hence even higher road taxes will be necessary to restore traffic flow to its optimum level. Estimates made by Bamford and Wigan of the benefits of introducing marginal social cost pricing on a hypothetical road network have shown that the assumption that motorists *do* accurately perceive costs would lead to a considerable underestimate of the true benefits of introducing road pricing schemes.[9]

Though introduction of a road pricing scheme for urban areas appears to be desirable, many problems remain. The choice of optimal rates of tax will be difficult to determine. Methods for actually collecting the taxes have been discussed and investigated since the Smeed Committee's Report in 1964. Although some form of electronic metering system would be most satisfactory and would be technically feasible, other simpler forms of restraint such as more severe restrictions on parking or access, or a system of licences for city-centre areas could be used as an interim measure.

While it would be desirable to introduce some form of road pricing in urban areas, there does not appear to be a case for its introduction on uncongested roads where additional vehicles do not impose costs on other road users, and the short-run marginal costs of road use are borne by each individual road user. Although each road user may not perceive his own costs correctly, this could be most effectively remedied by an increase in the fuel tax. Once this were done, use of such uncongested roads would be optimal and the additional imposition of road charges would impose welfare losses on those road users who would be dissuaded from travelling by the charge they would have to pay. Benefits would only arise if it were thought to be desirable to attempt to reduce environmental costs through pricing, but, as will be argued in the next chapter, it is difficult to devise appropriate taxes, and externalities can often be reduced much more effectively by other methods.

Though tolls could be levied on motorways, congestion is at present only a problem on stretches of motorway in urban areas that should in any case be included within urban road pricing schemes. Congestion may occur in the future on inter-urban motorways due to traffic growth, but we estimate that congestion on most existing inter-urban motorways is unlikely to be a serious problem before the end of this century. The benefits of introducing congestion pricing on those few stretches of inter-urban motorways where congestion might occur from the mid 1980s will have to be balanced against the administrative costs of collecting the tax (which would be particularly high in Britain because of the large number of access points), and against the benefits and costs of the alternative policy of increasing road capacity.

It should be noted that governments will, in raising taxes from road users, usually have other objectives as well as the maximisation of economic efficiency. In view of the severe constraints on government expenditure, it may well be desirable that total tax revenue raised from different classes of road users should at least equal the costs incurred by the Government in providing and maintaining the road network. This is considered in the next chapter. In addition, since road users are generally the better-off members of society, road taxation can be used as an important source of revenue, with no necessary connection between the costs of the road network and the amount of taxation that is raised. Finally, fuel tax can be used to correct inaccurate perceptions of motoring costs or to reduce expenditure on imported oil when there is a severe balance of payments deficit. Such alternative objectives of road taxation policy may conflict with the efficiency objective, though this might be avoided by a two-part tariff, with a fixed annual sum, and variable taxes related to the short-run costs of using the roads. In a sense, the present system of value added tax and car tax on the purchase of vehicles and an annual excise licence, on the one hand, and a tax on fuel on the other, is of this type, though the relationship between the fixed component and the variable component may not be optimal.

OPTIMAL ROAD PRICING AND RAIL SUBSIDIES

Setting urban road prices equal to short-run marginal costs will inevitably alter the position of urban rail services, because some former road users will now transfer to rail. Consequently revenue from the rail services will increase and, provided costs do not rise as rapidly, the rail deficit should fall. It is now also necessary to reconsider the railways' pricing policies. If prices of road use are set equal to marginal costs, so too should be prices of rail services. In practice, this is extremely difficult because of the problem of identifying the appropriate marginal costs in an industry where output is produced under conditions of indivisibility.

The impact of urban road pricing, and of relating rail prices to marginal costs, on the need for rail subsidies must now be considered. Rail subsidies may still be required if the average costs of providing rail services exceed the demand for rail services at any possible fare, or if spare capacity can only be used up by setting a price below average costs. In the South-East, where the gap between revenue and costs is not large and where demand is inelastic, it would be possible to avoid the need for subsidies by raising rail prices once road prices have been increased, and we have already allowed for a 15% increase in real fares in our forecast of future London and South-East revenue. As we have seen, commuter services are used mainly by the better-off members of society, so that subsidies will have regressive effects on income distribution. Moreover, the payment of subsidies may reduce the incentive for railway management to reduce costs, since the subsidy is related not to the social benefits which the rail services confer, but to the financial loss which results from their operation.

While road pricing in the other conurbations should also lead to some transfer of traffic to rail and hence to an increase in rail revenue, it is unlikely that any changes in rail pricing policy could eliminate the need for rail subsidies. The choice as to whether the subsidised rail services should be retained could then be determined by the application of cost-benefit analysis. While the traffic on rail would be greater than it had been before the introduction of road pricing, and this would increase social benefits, the costs of closure in the form of increased road congestion would be less than before and this would reduce social benefits. It is therefore not possible to conclude whether retention of the rail services would be more or less socially justifiable before or after the introduction of road pricing, though the financial loss should be reduced.

The choice of whether to maintain rail services will rest with the new Metropolitan Counties. As a result of the 1972 Local Government Act, a new system of block grants for most forms of transport expenditure in each area is to take effect from April 1975. Each County Council has to submit to Central Government a Transport Policy and Programme (TPP) setting out its objectives for transport policy, and details of its forecast expenditures over a five-year period. This is in contrast with the previous situation where grants were given at different rates for different types of project, and it will transfer much more responsibility for resource allocation to County Councils responsible for highways, public transport policy and land-use planning. The decision to finance rail operating subsidies and new rail investment in the conurbations will therefore have to be, in a time of strict financial stringency, compared with competing demands from alternative forms of transport.

One policy option which has received increasing attention in recent years is the improvement in the quality of urban bus services by means of the introduction of reserved track facilities. The use of bus-only lanes in existing urban streets has recouped high rates of return both in London and elsewhere. In addition, hypothetical comparisons in Britain and America of the costs and benefits of constructing new rail and express-busway systems have yielded results in favour of the busway systems, even for the densest flows of traffic.[10] Though it is not possible to reach general conclusions from the particular assumptions which have been made by these studies, it is clear that all these alternative public transport systems must be investigated if maximum benefits are to be obtained from the resources available.

CHAPTER 10

The Allocation
of Freight Traffic

In this chapter we consider the question of how far the existing legal and commercial conditions facing firms lead them to use the transport mode which minimises the *social* costs of transport; that is, the mode which minimises the sum of the private costs borne by the consigner *plus* the external costs borne by the rest of society. If one mode creates more external costs than another, then charges that only reflect private costs will lead consigners to choose the mode which minimises their own private costs, even though the alternative mode might lead to lower social costs.

Our discussion of road taxation policies in the previous chapter indicated that prices to road users should reflect short-run marginal costs, with the resultant prices then giving the correct signals for road investment using cost-benefit analysis techniques. With regard to the allocation of freight traffic, it is important that taxes paid by road hauliers should reflect those costs which they impose but do not bear themselves. These costs include the costs of providing and maintaining the road network, plus external costs. As it is impossible to discover whether taxes cover these costs, journey by journey, we will consider whether users of heavy goods vehicles *as a whole* pay sufficient taxation to meet the costs they impose on the community. We first consider the costs which road hauliers impose through the need to provide and maintain the road network; go on to review the various external costs such as accidents, noise, air pollution, congestion and vibration which lorries create; and then attempt to cost these externalities in order to determine whether road hauliers as a whole pay sufficient taxation to cover the total costs they impose. In addition, because of the difficulties of devising a pricing system which is able to levy the appropriate charges, we also discuss regulations, such as those concerning maximum noise and pollution emissions, which might be imposed or amended in order to reduce the social costs of transport. Though measurement may be difficult, the objective of such regulations is to achieve optimum levels of externalities; that is, to ensure that external costs are reduced up to, but not beyond, the point at which the additional benefits from further small reductions in the external costs are equal to the costs of achieving these reductions in the external effects. We next consider the possibilities, costs, and environmental benefits of transferring traffic from road to rail. Finally, we examine whether decisions concerning the allocation of freight traffic are made on the basis of the price paid, or whether, for instance, habit and irrational motives play a part.

ROAD TRACK COSTS

A considerable amount of effort has been devoted to the identification and analysis of the costs of constructing and maintaining the road network. The work on these public road costs, or track costs as they have come to be known, has been concerned with the question of whether the ratio between tax revenue and track costs is equal for different vehicle categories. There does not appear to be any good reason why the ratios for motorists and road hauliers *should* be equal, since, because the demands for road space by these two groups of users are not substitutes, inequality of ratios will not lead to misallocation of resources. As we have seen, what is relevant for the efficient allocation of freight between road and rail is the relationship between road taxation, public road costs, and external costs *for road haulage.*

The estimation and assignment of track costs is fraught with conceptual and statistical difficulties. Such costs and their breakdown among different vehicle classes were first calculated by the Ministry of Transport for 1962 in their submission to the Geddes Committee on Carriers Licensing. Subsequently, a more detailed study of track costs, with the earlier estimates updated to 1965–66, was published by the Ministry in 1968.[1] Their report concluded that all vehicle classes were paying more in excise tax and fuel duty than their share of road track costs; the ratios between revenue and cost being 2·1: 1 for cars, 1·5: 1 for buses and coaches, 3·2: 1 for light vans (that is, goods vehicles under 1½ tons unladen weight) and 1·8: 1 for heavy goods vehicles.

Road track costs include the capital costs of the road network, plus the costs of maintaining, cleaning, lighting, policing and administering that network. The Ministry estimated the capital costs of the road system in two alternative ways. First, it used the current expenditure method, and simply calculated the actual capital expenditure made on roads in the year concerned. Second, the Ministry employed the public enterprise method, which is more complex, and likely to be subject to wide margins of error, since it involves an attempt to calculate what the capital charges for the road system would be, if it were organised like a nationalised industry, by estimating historic costs of investment in the road network.

When the Ministry made its original survey of 1962 track costs, it found that the two methods gave more or less the same result. However, there was a considerable divergence in the results calculated for 1965–66. On the current expenditure basis the capital cost was £215 million, whereas the capital charge as estimated by the public enterprise method was £390 million. Other track costs, which are of a current nature and so are the same whatever the basis used for estimating capital costs, totalled £235 million. This figure includes a sum of £15 million to cover those accident costs, such as hospital expenses, which are borne by the Government.

Since in discussing optimal policy towards the roads it is appropriate to ignore costs which have already been incurred and cannot be avoided, i.e. to treat bygones as bygones, there are strong grounds for not using the public enterprise method. In addition, it is difficult to use this method when allocating road costs among different vehicle categories, as it is not meaningful to allocate the historic costs of constructing roads for types of vehicle which were not in operation when the roads were constructed. Use of the current expenditure method, while far from perfect, does enable a better comparison to be made between the capital costs of the road track, and the costs of the rail track as they are to be treated under the 1974 capital reconstruction. Henceforth, rail track costs will be estimated on a current expenditure basis, with annual track costs equal to actual expenditure on track and signalling, and bygones treated as bygones.

Road track costs can be allocated by attributing that part of the cost which is known to be caused by a particular class of vehicle to that group, and by dividing the remaining costs according to some yardstick which seems reasonable. A proportion of road construction costs is caused exclusively by the need to provide higher clearances and stronger carriageways to cater for heavy vehicles. On the basis of estimates by the Ministry of Transport's road engineers, a figure of 15% was used for all major capital projects, and 20% for minor capital improvements. The remaining capital costs were allocated amongst vehicles on the basis of miles travelled, but each mile by a heavy vehicle was counted as equivalent to two miles by a car, to reflect the fact that heavy vehicles occupy more road space because they are larger and slower.

Heavy vehicles also impose a high proportion of the costs of maintaining and repairing road surfaces. Very extensive tests conducted by the American Association of State Highway Officials (AASHO) indicated that the responsibility of vehicles for damage to the road surface increases in proportion to the 4th power of the increase in laden axle weight. Though these results may not be entirely applicable to British conditions, it is clear that the heaviest vehicles are responsible for all but a very small proportion of surface maintenance costs, and the Ministry of Transport allocated the total cost of maintaining the surfaces of classified roads to this type of vehicle. Surface maintenance costs for unclassified roads (that is, roads purely of local importance) were allocated to all vehicles on the basis of vehicle miles. Other road track costs were not regarded as being exclusively caused by particular types of vehicle, and were consequently allocated on the basis of vehicle miles. The results of the Ministry's calculations are shown in Table 10.1. Revenue from purchase tax on new vehicles was equal to £144 million in 1965–66, but was excluded on the grounds that this tax does not directly affect the use of the road network.

As these results are now almost a decade old, they need to be updated. The cost allocations among vehicle classes were therefore re-estimated for 1972–73. The same method for allocating costs was used as the Ministry had employed in 1968. As can be

TABLE 10.1: *Revenue and Public Road Costs,*
1965–66 and 1972–73 (current prices)

	Tax revenue[a]		1965–66 Public road costs[b]		Balance of revenue over cost
	£m	%	£m	%	£m
Cars	534	(59·5)	253	(58·0)	281
Public service vehicles	36	(4·0)	24	(5·5)	12
Goods vehicles:					
Heavy goods vehicles	223	(24·8)	126	(28·9)	97
Light vans	105	(11·7)	33	(7·6)	72
Total goods vehicles	328	(36·5)	159	(36·5)	169
Total[c]	898	(100·0)	436	(100·0)	462

[a] Fuel tax and excise duty only.

[b] Includes public accident costs.

[c] Excludes two-wheeled motor vehicles.

seen from Table 10.1, there was very little change in the relative
responsibility of different road users for public road costs between
1965–66 and 1972–73. Figures of the revenue derived from different road users cannot be estimated from published information,
but a breakdown for 1971 is available although it makes no
distinction between light vans and other goods vehicles.[2] If it is
assumed that the proportions of the excise and fuel duties contributed by different vehicle classes did not change markedly
between 1971 and 1972–73, we can compare the relationship
between revenue and cost for different vehicle classes in 1965–66
and in 1972–73.

While revenue from cars as a proportion of public road costs
allocated to cars was the same in 1972–73 as in 1965–66, revenue
from goods vehicles as a proportion of public road costs allocated
to goods vehicles dropped sharply, from 2·1 in 1965–66, to 1·4
in 1972–73. The amount by which revenue from all goods
vehicles exceeded the costs they appear to have imposed fell
from £169 million in 1965–66 to £158 million in 1972–73, which
was a decline of 40% in real terms. It is possible to make only a
rough estimate of the contribution of light vans to revenue in

Revenue/ cost ratio	Tax revenue[a]		1972–73 Public road costs[b]		Balance of revenue over cost £m	Revenue/ cost ratio
	£m	%	£m	%		
2·1	1293	(69·8)	610	(60·3)	683	2·1
1·5	36	(1·9)	35	(3·5)	1	1·0
1·8	. .		301	(29·8)	. .	. .
3·2	. .		65	(6·4)	. .	. .
2·1	524	(28·3)	366	(36·2)	158	1·4
2·1	1853	(100·0)	1011	(100·0)	842	1·8

1972–73. This contribution appears to have been about £130–£140 million, implying that heavy goods vehicles contributed about £385–£395 million, and that the balance of revenue over public road costs for these vehicles stood at around £85–£95 million.

Thus we have discovered that road hauliers as a whole continued to cover the public road costs which they imposed in 1972–73. However, if the surplus of tax revenue over public road costs is regarded as a charge for the external costs which road hauliers also impose on the community, then this charge fell substantially between 1965–66 and 1972–73 at a time when the external costs it might be expected to cover were rising. The mileage travelled by heavy goods vehicles rose by 8·9% between 1965 and 1972, and the mileage performed by the larger vehicles more likely to create external costs increased at a much more rapid rate. These external costs must now be examined in detail, beginning with accidents, and going on to noise, congestion, air pollution and vibration.

THE EXTERNAL COSTS OF ROAD HAULAGE

The contribution of heavy lorries to road accidents

In 1972, 7763 people were killed, 91,338 seriously injured and 260,626 slightly injured on Britain's roads.[3] The cost of these accidents to the community, as estimated by the Transport and Road Research Laboratory, was £550 million. The extent to which vehicles are involved in accidents has fallen more or less continuously since the Second World War, so that although the number of motor vehicle miles rose fivefold between 1949 and 1974, the number of road users killed and seriously injured has no more than doubled. In 1972 the involvement rate per mile travelled for heavy commercial vehicles (that is, those over 1½ tons unladen weight) was below that for cars in serious and slight accidents, largely because of the higher proportion of goods vehicle mileage outside built-up areas, but the involvement rate in fatal accidents was double that for cars. Furthermore, it is estimated that very heavy goods vehicles over 4½ tons unladen weight have an involvement rate over twice as high as those in the 1½ to 4½ tons weight range. This high involvement rate of heavy vehicles is primarily due to their size, since the severity of an accident is generally related to the mass of the object which is encountered.

The total contribution of commercial vehicles to accident costs in 1972 can be estimated by considering the effect of the removal of different classes of vehicle. Published figures show the numbers of goods vehicles of different unladen weights involved in fatal, serious and slight accidents in 1972 in built-up and non built-up areas. If we assume that in the absence of a particular type of vehicle, such an accident would not have happened, we can estimate the reduction in accident costs which would then occur. Removal of goods vehicles over 4½ tons unladen weight in 1972 would have led to reductions of 1067 fatal, 3976 serious and 8277 slight injury accidents. The cost of these accidents, using 1972 average costs per fatal, per serious and per slight injury accidents, can be estimated at £33·8 million. The corresponding reductions in accident costs to be achieved by removing cars, commercial vehicles under 1½ tons unladen weight, those between 1½ and 3 tons unladen weight, and those between 3 and 4½ tons unladen weight are, respectively, £340·0 million, £44·4 million, £8·0 million, and £8·4 million. The sum of all these figures for all vehicle classes will exceed total estimated injury accident costs because many accidents involve more than one type of vehicle. However, these estimated costs include only a *minimum* figure for the subjective costs of each type of accident, and they exclude the costs of damage-only accidents.

Not all of these accident costs should be treated as an addition to public road costs. A substantial proportion of them will already be covered by the road haulage industry through insurance payments, while the public costs in the form of medical, funeral and ambulance costs have already been included in our 1972–73 estimate of public road costs. There will, however, be subjective costs which the road haulage industry imposes on other road users and which will not be fully covered by insurance payments. Using the *minimum* figures of the Transport and Road Research Laboratory (TRRL) for subjective costs per fatality, per serious injury and per slight injury, it can be estimated that the *minimum* subjective costs of accidents involving commercial vehicles over 1½ tons unladen weight totalled £15 million in 1972. As with our previous figures, these are the costs which could be *avoided* if this class of vehicle were excluded from the roads, and not the costs actually *caused* by this type of vehicle.

It is, of course, important that these serious accident costs, however they are borne, should be reduced. One method by which accidents involving goods vehicles can be minimised is through government-imposed standards concerning the design and maintenance of vehicles, the qualifications of their drivers, and the maximum hours of driving time permitted. A new licensing system for road haulage came into force in March 1970 and, at the same time, the steady decline in the rate of heavy-goods vehicle involvement in accidents accelerated. It seems quite possible that this improvement was due to the licensing reforms. Despite this, the safety standards of heavy goods vehicles can still be faulted. In 1972, the proportion of accidents where technical defects were judged by the reporting police officers to be a contributory factor was higher for goods vehicles than for cars, and highest for goods vehicles of over 4½ tons. The police con-

sidered that vehicle faults were wholly or partly to blame for
6½% of the accidents in which these large lorries were involved.
This could be partly because relatively fewer accidents occur as
a result of poor driving. Nevertheless, the random roadside checks
that are carried out by the Licensing Authorities' vehicle examiners confirm that a substantial proportion of the lorries on
Britain's roads are faulty. In 1972–73, 4·1% of the 102,662 heavy
goods vehicles they inspected were judged to be unsafe, and a
further 18·4% were defective. Despite this, the amount of the
fine imposed by magistrates for the relatively small number of
successful prosecutions for offences relating to safety is low.
The ultimate deterrent rests in the power of the Licensing
Authorities to revoke the haulier's licence by withdrawing it
completely, to suspend it for a limited period, or to curtail it by
reducing the number of vehicles the holder is permitted to
operate. In the year 1972–73, 178 licences were revoked, 114
suspended and 759 curtailed. This represents a significant increase
over 1971–72 but is low in relation to the total number of
offences, and it seems evident that the Authorities' deterrent
powers should be used more strongly to weed out those operators
who continue to flout the law. In order to achieve this, a substantial increase in the resources available to the Licensing
Authorities and their traffic examiners will be both necessary
and desirable.

There are many other ways in which casualties in road accidents can be reduced. Compulsory wearing of seat belts should
yield substantial gains, since it has been calculated that if all
drivers and front-seat passengers in cars with belts had worn
them in 1972, there would have been 13,000 fewer serious injuries
and deaths. More modest gains should result from continuing
research into the effects of vehicle design, road layout and speed
limits on accident levels, and from consequent changes in legislation. It is also desirable that road users should be made to bear,
through increased insurance premia, the costs of hospital treat-
ment which are at present borne by the Government.

Noise from road traffic

One of the most serious external costs of road transport is noise,
and heavy goods vehicles are the most important contributor

to traffic noise. Road traffic noise is in turn the most serious cause of noise, disturbing more people in Britain than all other sources of noise combined.[4] Generally traffic noise increases with flow up to a certain point, after which the noise level remains fairly constant with further traffic increases. This point is around 1200 vehicles per hour on urban roads and 2500 vehicles per hour on motorways. The faster the speed of the traffic flow, the greater is the noise emitted. At faster speeds, tyre noise becomes as important as engine noise, and the difference between the louder noise emitted by diesel-engined heavy vehicles and the quieter noise from petrol-engined cars is reduced. In general, the greater the proportion of heavy vehicles in the traffic flow, the louder will be the noise.

Noise may be reduced by a number of alternative methods. It may be possible to reroute traffic, though this may create noise elsewhere and increase vehicle operating costs and time costs. New roads may be constructed in cuttings or tunnels. This can substantially reduce noise, but it is very costly. Where it is possible to construct barriers, noise can be cut by a half, though the barriers may be regarded as unsightly. Alternatively, sound-proofing can be installed in houses close to busy roads, or noise can be reduced at source by constructing quieter vehicles. Finally, over a longer period, town planning can be used to ensure that buildings which are not sensitive to noise, such as warehouses or factories, are located close to the noisiest roads. While most of these methods for reducing noise can be accurately costed, they do have different types of effect, which makes a comparison of alternative methods of noise reduction difficult. For example, money spent on reducing vehicle noise at source will reduce noise in areas where it is not a problem, while money spent on double glazing will be of no benefit to pedestrians.

While comparison of methods of noise reduction creates problems, valuation of the costs imposed by noise is even more difficult. A number of alternative methods have been employed, but no convincing estimates have so far emerged. Nevertheless, it seems clear from questionnaires that traffic noise causes considerable disutility. The Wilson Committee on the Problem of Noise suggested maximum acceptable levels of noise inside the house which should not be exceeded for more than 10% of the time.[5] These were expressed in weighted decibels, or dB(A), which is a logarithmic scale where every increase of 10 dB(A) roughly corresponds to a doubling in loudness. The daytime levels that the Committee decided on were 40 dB(A) in country districts, 45 dB(A) in suburban areas, and 50 dB(A) in busy urban areas.

In 1970 it was estimated that out of Britain's urban population of 46 million, 21 million lived in dwellings where the external noise level was above 65 dB(A) for over 10% of the time and 8·5 million lived where it was above 70 dB(A). Prior to the increases in fuel prices, it was thought that increases in traffic (and population) would raise these figures to 29 million and 14 million respectively by 1980. The noise level inside a house will be about 10 dB(A) lower if the windows are open and 15 dB(A) lower if they are shut. It is therefore evident that those unfortunate people who live where noise exceeds 70 dB(A) cannot even reduce the noise to an acceptable level by shutting the windows; and there must be an important minority who live under almost intolerable conditions.

The numbers who are seriously affected by noise could be substantially reduced if traffic noise could be cut by 10 dB(A). If this could be achieved, those exposed to external noise of over 70 dB(A) would be reduced to 0·9 million and those to noise above 65 dB(A) to 4·3 million, even with the expected growth in traffic and population. For this to be attained it would be necessary to reduce the maximum noise from heavy vehicles from the present figure of 89 dB(A), under test conditions, to 80 dB(A). A major research programme is currently being mounted to build prototypes of such quiet vehicles, but the production version will not appear before the 1980s and computer simulations indicate that traffic noise will not be reduced significantly until 50% of the heavy goods fleet has been replaced by such quiet vehicles. A 10 dB(A) reduction in traffic noise is therefore not feasible before the late 1980s. However, the Noise Advisory Council believe that a 5 dB(A) reduction in traffic noise could be achieved by 1980, and this by itself could halve the numbers worst affected by traffic noise, and reduce those exposed to levels above 65 dB(A) by one-third.

In 1974, maximum noise levels, measured under ISO test conditions, for vehicles constructed in the United Kingdom were 84 dB(A) for cars, 77 to 86 dB(A) for motor cycles, and 89 dB(A) for heavy goods vehicles. Before Britain joined the Common

Market it was intended that these maxima should be reduced by about 3 dB(A), and attempts are now being made to amend the EEC directive governing vehicle noise levels. The possibilities of reducing noise from commercial vehicles have been surveyed by Clifford Sharp, who concluded that a level of 86 dB(A) for vehicles under 200 bhp can be reached by encapsulating existing engines, though there will be cooling and maintenance problems.[6] On a variety of assumptions, Sharp has estimated the costs of reducing engine noise from present levels to 86 dB(A) for heavy lorries under 200 bhp, and 89 dB(A) for those few over 200 bhp, as lying within a range between £6·3 million and £18·9 million per annum at 1971–72 prices, with most of the estimates clustered around £11·9 million per annum. A level of 80 dB(A) can, however, only be achieved by a basic redesign of engines. If engine noise were reduced to 80 dB(A), tyre noise would become the main source of lorry noise.

Though TRRL studies have concluded that quietening lorries should bring considerable reductions of noise on roads carrying high traffic flows and many heavy lorries, reductions of noise emitted by cars will be necessary to reduce noise on less heavily trafficked streets with low proportions of heavy vehicles. Quietening of cars will also contribute to the noise reduction on more heavily used streets. It appears that a 5 dB(A) reduction in the noise emitted by cars would be technically feasible and would reduce their noise limit to 80 dB(A).

The question which remains unanswered is whether the benefits from the alternative noise reduction policies will exceed their costs. In view of the considerable concern over the costs imposed on the community by noise, and in view of the large numbers of people who would gain by the reductions in noise which appear to be technically feasible, it would seem that there is a strong case for many of the suggested changes in policy. Where the costs of reducing noise are low, as with traffic management measures such as the prohibiting of heavy lorries from some streets, there will be a clear case for the introduction of such measures. Further, the enormous disruption caused by the construction of new roads in urban areas suggests that great care should be taken in their planning so that environmental costs are minimised, and that those who would suffer from their construction and operation are adequately compensated. Under the 1973 Land Compensation Act, those property owners severely affected by new road schemes may choose to sell their property to the local authority. In addition, compensation is paid to those who do not move if new works will create sound levels over 68 dB(A) one metre in front of their building's facade for over 10% of the time. Compensation may also be paid for temporary removal during construction. There is a strong argument for extending the principle of compensation to those who suffer from noise and other environmental effects from existing roads. Such compensation might cover the costs of installing soundproofing if external noise from existing roads has reached the levels where compensation is now paid for houses where occupiers are expected to suffer noise from newly constructed roads. If compensation were limited to those households who would still suffer from an external noise level of 68 dB(A) for over 10% of the time *after* traffic noise has been reduced by 10 dB(A), we estimate the total costs of soundproofing at around £250 million. This estimate is based on the cost of double glazing for two rooms of each house affected. The finance for this increased compensation might be raised from urban road users in proportion to the noise they create.

Congestion

Lorries cause delays to other road vehicles because of their relatively low speed, their slow acceleration, and their size. One partial solution, investigated by Sharp and Jennings, is to increase minimum power to weight ratios.[7] On the basis of figures provided by the TRRL on delays caused by heavy vehicles, Sharp and Jennings concluded that there would be a net gain from increasing the minimum power/weight ratio from 5 to 6 brake horsepower per ton for vehicles of 32 tons gross laden weight. However, their estimates showed that a further increase to 8 bhp per ton would yield a net loss, and that there would be no net gain or loss from increasing minimum power/weight ratios to 8 bhp per ton for vehicles up to 30 tons gross laden weight.

The TRRL had calculated delays caused by heavy vehicles of three different power/weight ratios by driving three articulated lorries with different power/weight ratios over a 1000-mile representative section of trunk and primary roads used by goods vehicles, and observing their effect on other traffic.[8] The estimation of the total delays caused by all heavy vehicles is difficult, because vehicle statistics are classified by unladen weight ratio. Some figures of the power/weight ratios of models being produced in 1968, classified by unladen weight, have been published by Sharp and Jennings.[9] Assuming that these power/weight ratios can be applied to the 1972 population of goods vehicles in different unladen weight categories, it was possible to make a rough estimate of congestion costs imposed by all goods vehicles over 2 tons unladen weight in 1972. The average delays caused per mile run by different types of vehicle were multiplied by the annual mileages for these vehicles. These delays were then valued at 1972 values of time, with an allowance for increased operating expenditure.

Total delay costs estimated in this way were £37 million for urban roads and £29 million for rural roads. Though the assumptions about the numbers of vehicles of different power/weight ratios on which these costs are based must be suspect, a minimum estimate of congestion costs can be made by assuming that all goods vehicles have a power/weight ratio of 10 bhp per ton or over, since delays imposed do not appear to decline markedly once power/weight ratios rise above 10 bhp per ton. The resultant minimum figures for congestion costs are £34 million in urban areas and £27 million in rural areas, and we can therefore say that delays imposed by heavy goods vehicles over 2 tons unladen weight totalled £34 to £37 million on urban roads and £27 to £29 million on rural roads in 1972.

Air pollution

The Government's Programmes Analysis Unit has estimated the measurable costs of all forms of air pollution in the United Kingdom in 1970 at £405 million, of which some £37 million was accounted for by motor vehicles.[10] These costs, many of which are very rough estimates, include costs of cleaning, deterioration of metals and textiles, loss of agricultural production, and loss of output due to illness. Although diesel-engined vehicles accounted for 25% of the fuel used by motor vehicles, the amount of air pollution which they cause is much less serious than may often be supposed. Though smoke causes the most concern to the public, it is the invisible pollutants, such as carbon monoxide, which can cause serious health risks in high concentrations. While such concentrations rarely occur in urban streets, the oxides of nitrogen and lead compounds may have a long-term effect which is as yet not fully understood. However, the petrol engine is by far the main offender. Diesel engines emit virtually no carbon monoxide, about one-tenth as many hydrocarbons and about a third as much of the oxides of nitrogen as petrol engines, and their fuel is not treated with lead additives. This suggests that diesel engines' share of vehicle pollution costs must be less than their share of fuel consumption. If the Programmes Analysis Unit's estimate is converted to 1972 prices, the maximum figure for the cost of the air pollution that heavy goods vehicles cause is therefore only about £10 million. In contrast, cars must have imposed a cost of well over £30 million.

Nevertheless, diesel engines may emit high levels of smoke and produce an unpleasant smell. Legislation prohibits the emission of avoidable smoke from road vehicles, and if they are properly adjusted diesel lorries should not produce smoke. However, checks carried out by the Department of the Environment's vehicle examiners at locations where smoking is most likely to occur revealed that, on 14 May 1974, 13·4% of the 40,000 heavy goods vehicles observed were emitting excessive smoke. The level of fines for the relatively small number of successful prosecutions remains low, and there is a case for more rigorous enforcement of the law.

Vibration

Traffic-induced vibration causes annoyance to individuals and may under certain circumstances damage buildings. A detailed survey by the TRRL points out that the human body can perceive low levels of vibration which may also cause rattling of doors, windows and crockery and which, besides being unpleasant, may arouse the usually unfounded fear that damage is being caused.[11] However, though individuals may begin to perceive vibrations (measured by peak particle velocity in millimetres per second) as low as 0·15–0·30 mm/s, annoyance probably only occurs for vibrations over 2·5 mm/s; architectural damage (such as cracking of plaster) does not become a risk until vibrations reach 5 mm/s, and minor structural damage may occur with vibrations of 10–15 mm/s. If road surfaces have been constructed in accordance with the Specification for Road and Bridge Works, 1969, vehicles do not normally create vibrations sufficient to cause architectural damage or to be perceived by individuals. It is irregularities in the road surface, caused by wear and tear or by badly restored trenches, which create undesirable vibrations. Where the road surface is in reasonable condition the maximum peak particle velocity lies in the range of 0·1 to 1 mm/s at a distance of three to five metres from the edge of the road. This increases to 2 to 3 mm/s for roads in poor condition with irregularities up to 25 mm, and values might rise to 5 mm/s, the threshold level for architectural damage, for the occasional pothole. It is therefore necessary to ensure that road surfaces are adequately maintained, particularly where the surface has had to be disturbed to lay cables. In addition, there may well be a case for routing traffic away from the more vulnerable ancient buildings whose structures are giving cause for concern.

As heavy vehicles are largely responsible for that part of the deterioration of road surfaces which is due to traffic, it might be reasonable to divide vibration costs between heavy goods and passenger vehicles, and those agencies responsible for disturbing the road surface. Although no attempt has been made to quantify the costs of vibration, a maximum estimate would be the costs of maintaining road surfaces so that there were *no* irregularities creating vibrations of over 2·5 mm/s, the level at which vibration appears to begin to cause annoyance. This is a maximum because the costs of achieving these standards might be greater than the benefits from reducing vibration to this level. In 1972 it was estimated that the costs of maintaining road surfaces in urban areas were around £20 million per annum, and by 1972–73 the figure had probably increased to around £25 million. It is impossible to estimate how much extra expenditure would be necessary to eliminate vibrations over 2·5 mm/s, but we suggest that a 50% increase, of which £10 million might be allocated to heavy vehicles, gives some idea of the maximum costs which such vehicles impose.

The reduction of heavy-vehicle flows in environmentally sensitive areas

We have now considered the main environmental costs of the heavy lorry and discussed the ways in which they might be reduced. It would also be possible to reduce many of these external costs by reducing the flows of heavy vehicles on those roads where, or when, their adverse environmental effects are most severe. In particular, it would be possible to set aside specific routes for heavy lorries, and to ban them from other roads except for access. The Heavy Commercial Vehicles (Controls and Regulations) Act of 1973 gives local authorities the power to specify through routes for commercial vehicles over 3 tons unladen weight and to prohibit or restrict their use on other roads. All local authorities are obliged to survey their area and to formulate written proposals for the routing of lorries by the beginning of 1977 (1978 in Scotland). The local routes they identify will be linked to each other by a national network using motorways and the best of the trunk roads. A consultative document produced by the Department of the Environment in July 1974 outlined the main features of the national network, which will initially apply to vehicles over 24 tons laden weight or 12 metres length. Very little is known about the actual journeys made by heavy lorries, and more research is to be instituted to attempt to discover the additional costs which a national lorry network would impose.

Research is also being undertaken on transhipment depots. If these were located on the edge of towns, there would be a reduction in the movement of heavy goods vehicles in town centres because loads would be transferred from the larger vehicles using the national network into smaller lorries for local delivery. It is, however, far from clear that the environmental impact of a larger number of smaller vehicles will be less than that of fewer but larger vehicles. Surveys of freight distribution in urban areas have shown that while removing flows of vehicles with more than two axles would reduce noise, replacing these vehicles with twice as many smaller vehicles would restore it to its original level. Further, an increase in the number of small vehicles would be likely to produce more road accidents in urban areas. More fruitful may be the reduction in the total number of vehicles in urban streets by the concentration of deliveries to retail stores in as few vehicles as possible. As well as reducing environmental costs, such rationalisation can also lower distribution costs. Some of the largest retailers have set up distribution depots to which individual suppliers deliver in bulk. Deliveries to individual stores from the distribution depot can then also be made in bulk, eliminating the large number of deliveries formerly made to each store by each separate supplier. The number of deliveries to independent retail stores can also be cut down by restricting deliveries to one day per week, and it is possible to further limit their environmental impact by concentrating them in off-peak periods. Some experiments have been made with evening and night-time deliveries, but there may be difficulties if staff have to be employed to receive the goods, and noise will be a problem in residential areas. More successful has been the restriction of deliveries during the morning and evening traffic peaks by means of parking controls.

Revenue from heavy goods vehicles, road track costs and environmental costs

In Table 10.2 we bring together our estimates of heavy goods vehicles' share of public road costs and of their contribution to the Exchequer through fuel tax and excise duty in 1972–73, with our more tentative estimates of the external costs created by the road haulage industry. We have estimated tax revenue at between £385 and £395 million, and public road costs, including public accident costs, at £301 million. We suggested a figure for subjective accident costs of £15 million, and this may be regarded as a minimum figure even though the responsibility for these accidents cannot all be laid on the road haulage industry. We estimated congestion costs caused by goods vehicles over 2 tons unladen weight as lying between £61 million and £66 million in 1972. To this must be added a smaller sum to account for congestion caused by heavy goods vehicles between 1½ and 2 tons unladen weight. We suggested a maximum figure of £10 million for the costs of air pollution caused by diesel vehicles, and a maximum figure of £10 million for the costs of vibration imposed by heavy vehicles. The major external cost, noise, could not be valued but public opinion appears

TABLE 10.2: *Revenue, Public Road Costs and External Costs of Heavy Goods Vehicles, 1972–73 (current prices)*

	(£m)
Tax revenue[a]	385 to 395
Public road costs[b]	301
Surplus	84 to 94
External costs:	
Subjective accident costs	15 (minimum)
Noise	26 (minimum)
Congestion	61 to 66 (minimum)
Air pollution	10 (maximum)
Vibration	10 (maximum)
Tax revenue minus public and external costs	− 28 to − 43 (maximum)

[a] Fuel tax and excise duty only.
[b] Includes public accident costs.

to favour the reduction of maximum noise emissions from heavy vehicles from 89 dB(A) to 86 dB(A) at an estimated annual cost at 1972–73 prices of £13 million. In addition we have suggested compensation for soundproofing houses suffering an external noise level above 68 dB(A), and estimated the total cost of this at £250 million, provided traffic noise is reduced by 10 dB(A). If this cost is spread over a ten-year period, and half is allocated to heavy goods vehicles, we get an overall annual cost of noise emitted by them of £26 million. This may still be a minimum figure because it does not allow for the costs either of reducing heavy vehicle noise below 86 dB(A), or, alternatively, of soundproofing houses whose noise level would remain above 68 dB(A) unless heavy vehicle noise were reduced to 80 dB(A). Finally, we have made no allowance for the costs of visual intrusion imposed by goods vehicles. When public road costs and these estimates of external costs are subtracted from tax revenue, there is no longer a positive surplus of revenue over costs, but an estimated shortfall of between £28 million and £43 million. Since it is likely that we have underestimated noise costs, the actual shortfall will be greater than this.

These results suggest there should be an increase in the taxation levied on heavy goods vehicles. If road pricing is introduced, as suggested in Chapter 9, there would be a reduction in the estimated costs of between £34 million and £37 million imposed through congestion by heavy goods vehicles in urban areas. Changes in government policy already announced, and others discussed in this chapter, should considerably reduce the other environmental costs of road haulage, and thereby reduce the case for increasing taxation on the road haulage industry. Thus, for example, legislation to make goods vehicles quieter would reduce noise costs, while the costs of modifying vehicle design to conform with new specifications would be borne by the industry. Once the effects of these changes in government policy had been estimated, then consideration could be made as to what further increases in road haulage taxation would be desirable to cover the remaining external costs, such as compensation for double glazing, not borne by the industry.

While it is desirable that road hauliers as a whole should cover the costs which they impose, it would be even better if they could be made to bear them on each journey they make. Except for urban congestion costs, this is more difficult to achieve. Taxes on heavy goods vehicles would have to be extremely complex, and be related to axle loads to cover maintenance and vibration costs, to power/weight ratios to cover rural congestion costs, and to the type and capacity of the engine to cover noise costs. It would be difficult to revise the present excise licensing system to achieve this, particularly since vehicles with the same physical characteristics will be used on different types of road, and will travel empty and partly loaded for part of their mileage, thus creating different environmental costs. However, this is a subject where further research is required.

It should be noted that our analysis does not imply that there is a case for reducing the total level of taxation, including revenue from road pricing schemes, on the motorist. The gap between tax revenue and public road costs for the motorist has been estimated at £683 million in 1972–73, and this gap will have increased because of the rapid increase in fuel taxes. Nevertheless congestion costs imposed by cars are believed to be equal to several hundred million pounds, while the subjective costs of accidents involving cars, even excluding those accidents in which heavy goods vehicles were also involved, totalled at least £80 million in 1972. The Programmes Analysis Unit's estimate of air pollution costs implies a figure of at least £30 million attributable to the car. Though the unmeasured costs of noise and visual intrusion might not be sufficient to raise public road and external costs above tax revenue, there would not necessarily be a case for reducing such taxation, because of motorists' inaccurate perceptions of the true cost of using road vehicles, and because governments may legitimately raise general revenue from the car-owning sector of the community.

THE TRANSFER OF TRAFFIC FROM ROAD TO RAIL

Having discussed the relation between the charges levied through taxation on road hauliers and the costs which they impose on the community, we can now consider whether the social costs which road haulage imposes could be reduced by the transfer of traffic from road to rail. In considering the contribution which such a transfer can make, it is necessary to consider the scope for transfer, the costs of the operation and the external benefits which might result.

Conventional rail freight traffic which has to be either collected or delivered by road has consistently been one of the least profitable of railway traffics. While the private costs of using rail for this type of traffic are high, it is by no means self-evident that use of rail produces environmental gains, because local collection and delivery must be made on congested urban roads to and from rail terminals which are often located in inner-city areas. Thus in *Living with the lorry*, Sharp has indicated that for three specimen wagonload flows, between the Leicester and London areas, the balance of environmental advantage lies with road rather than rail for at least two of the flows. Similarly, the use of Freightliners rather than road transport throughout might increase environmental costs if the trunk road haul could be made largely on motorways. A study made in the late 1960s by the Ministry of Transport showed that, on average, rail transport involving collection and delivery, rather than road haulage throughout, would increase lorry mileage on congested streets.

Even if the balance of environmental advantage did lie with Freightliners for many flows, our discussion of the economics of Freightliner operation in Chapter 6 has revealed how limited is the market which Freightliner's internal services can hope to capture. The absence of large flows over sufficient distances to support Freightliner services means that we only expect non-maritime traffic to increase from 3·4 million tons in 1972 to 6·4 million tons in 1981. Since about 2 million tons of this traffic will be transferred by the Post Office and the London Brick Company from existing rail services, and much of the remainder will be due to traffic growth, the actual transfer of traffic from road to rail will be very small. Nor is there any substantial pool of road traffic which could be transferred to Freightliners by changes in government policy. A recent survey revealed that in 1970 only about 10 million tons of traffic in commodity groups suitable for containerisation travelled between conurbations located more than 100 miles apart. As Freightliners are not even competitive for many flows over 200 miles, their environmental advantages would have to be shown to be substantial to justify changes in policy designed to transfer even a part of this 10 million tons of traffic to rail.

If traffic is to be transferred to rail on environmental grounds, then road collection and delivery through urban streets must be avoided. Therefore rail will mainly be suitable for traffic between existing or newly constructed private sidings. While rail is most suitable for trainload movements, there are few bulk flows of goods on the roads which could be carried in full trainloads. British Rail has itself analysed the detailed data from the 1967/8 Road Goods Survey on inter-zonal flows over distances of 50 miles or more, and has discovered that there are few flows of heavy dense commodities which it is not already carrying, and that flows over long distances on roads are usually small consignments of general merchandise. Therefore, if further traffic is to be transferred to rail, it must use wagonload services. In the past, these services have been uncompetitive with road, on grounds of both cost and service quality. Specimen figures quoted in 1967 showed that rates by wagonload rail service for a 10-ton load were 45% above those by road for a haul of 125 miles between private sidings. The relative rail cost can be expected to fall as distance increases, but clearly the break-even distance by rail is very high. In addition, journey times by rail were much longer than those by road. In 1969, 65% of wagons arrived within 48 hours of dispatch, but 7% took longer than a week to arrive. Added to the long average transit time was the problem of wagons which got 'lost' in the system; in Bayliss and Edwards' survey of the demand for freight transport, it was reported that BR had lost 2% of the consignments between 1 and 5 tons which the firms dispatched by rail, although some of these consignments may eventually have turned up.[12] Finally, traffic by conventional wagonload services was particularly susceptible to damage because of shocks received in shunting.

There will, however, be substantial improvements in the quality of BR's wagonload services. The TOPS computerised freight information and movement-control system will provide information on the location of every wagon in the system, and customers will be able to obtain immediate details of the where-abouts of every consignment in transit. The system will also indicate the position of empty wagons so they can be moved quickly in response to users' needs. The use of the TOPS system by itself would not reduce rail transits to the point where they were competitive with those by road. However, in Chapter 7, we argued that replacement of many existing wagons by a new air-braked fleet would be justified. These new wagons will be used on the developing air-braked wagonload network onto which all wagonload traffic which has a long-term future will eventually be transferred. The air-braked services will in many cases offer overnight transits, and so will be competitive with road services in terms of speed over the longer distances. In addition, although wagons will be remarshalled en route, this will not be undertaken in conventional yards by loose shunting, so that damage should be considerably reduced.

It might also be possible to develop high-capacity container services for wagonload traffic if cheaper forms of gantry cranes can be produced. Such cranes were developed by BR for its experiments with automatic wagons, when it was estimated that they would cost £2000 each at 1970–71 prices. These container services might then also be able to share terminal and trunk rail haul facilities with existing Freightliner services. In the longer term, consideration might be given to the construction of local rail container depots located outside the centre of urban areas, so that local delivery by lorry would not be made on congested roads. Finally, if road transhipment depots proved to be feasible, rail facilities might also be provided within such depots.

While these are possible ways in which rail freight services might be developed, it is necessary to estimate their costs. We shall therefore examine the expense of running an air-braked service for wagonload freight under very favourable conditions. Our estimates were based, item by item, on BR's freight train costs during 1973 after allowing for the subsequent rise in the price of diesel fuel. It was assumed that guards and second men are not carried on freight trains; that vans with a capacity of 19 tons are used; that 67% of this capacity is utilised; that vans make two loaded trips per week in service; that trains consist of 20 vans and average 30 mph; that there is no empty running; and that reasonably high throughputs are achieved through private sidings in order to spread siding construction and maintenance costs. A margin of 10% was then added to direct costs to allow for contingencies such as late running. Track, signalling and administrative costs were estimated from an updated 1971 estimate of the share of BR's freight business in these costs, with track and signalling allocated on the basis of ton mileage and administration costs allocated on the basis of tonnage. The cost per ton mile worked out at 3·0 pence for hauls of 50 miles, 1·8 pence for 100 miles, 1·4 pence for 150 miles, and 1·2 pence for 200 miles. These costs include the capital and maintenance costs of locomotives, wagons and sidings, drivers' wage costs, fuel and the costs of terminal shunting and documentation. They do, however, exclude the costs of any remarshalling en route and of trip working to and from private sidings. These two items will depend on the total volume of traffic sent through the wagonload system, but are likely to increase costs to an important degree.

These costs of rail wagonload services which, it must again be stressed, were estimated on a basis very favourable to rail, can be compared with costs per ton mile by road. In 1973, the average cost of operating an articulated van of 10 tons unladen weight with a carrying capacity of 21 tons running 1000 miles per week was estimated at 23·7 pence per mile. If overall costs are increased by 10% to allow for the expected rise in road haulage costs between 1973 and 1981, and a margin of 20% is added for overheads and profit, we arrive at a cost of 2·2 pence per ton mile. This assumes that the same proportion of capacity is filled as on the railways, but in practice load factors are likely to be higher for road transport because of the flexibility in road-vehicle sizes available. Nevertheless, it appears that rail will only be competitive for distances over 75 miles. In practice, the methods we have used have underestimated rail costs and may also have overestimated road costs, so that the break-even distances will in fact be higher, especially if road collection and/or delivery is required for the rail traffic. Our discussion of Freightliners revealed how limited the long-distance market is in Britain. In addition, use of wagonload services between private sidings implies reasonably large consignments to achieve satisfactory load factors in rail wagons, and sufficient numbers of consignments over which the costs of installing and maintaining private sidings can be spread. It therefore appears that any large-scale development of wagonload services between private sidings would require substantial government subsidies in order to make rail charges competitive with those by road.

So far we have considered the possibilities for transferring freight traffic from road to rail, and indicated the costs which might be involved, but we have scarcely considered the environmental benefits which might be gained. Although BR stresses these environmental benefits, it does not appear to have carried out any studies to measure them. However, as part of their Review of Railway Policy, the Department of the Environment investigated the likely environmental impact of the transfer of rail traffic to road in three case studies: of coal from Gedling Colliery in Nottinghamshire, of china clay from Fowey, and of general merchandise from Central Bristol. No details are available, but the Department concluded that while significant congestion would not arise on major roads in these areas, some congestion, noise, visual intension and accidents would occur on minor roads, and these adverse consequences would only be partly alleviated by road improvements.

Following these investigations, a more detailed study was commissioned from consultants. The consultants considered three further case studies, involving the evaluation of the social costs and benefits which would arise in 1976 following the transfer of two existing rail traffics to road, and of one road flow to rail. Most of the rail traffic does not appear to have involved collection or delivery by road, and the study did not consider intra-urban distribution of freight by road from urban railheads. The case studies were chosen to represent situations where a transfer of freight between road and rail would be possible, and where there might be expected to be a noticeable change in local environmental conditions. The rail traffics consisted of 1·9 million tons of coal distributed throughout Great Britain from seven collieries in the Nottingham area, and of 3·6 million tons, mainly of wagonload steel and scrap, forwarded and received by fifty rail terminals in the Sheffield and Rotherham area. The reverse traffic considered was of 387,400 tons of finished steel which currently travels between Sheffield and the West Midlands by road. The first two flows would increase daily lorry movements by 1000 and 2420 respectively, while the switch from road to rail would lead to a reduction of 145. After determining which links in the road network would be affected by the changes in lorry movements, the consultants attempted to measure the external costs and benefits which might be expected to result, in the form of road repairs and maintenance, accidents, congestion, noise, air pollution, vibration and visual intrusion. The last two items proved impossible to value.

The consultants estimated that the transfer from rail to road would lead to external costs of 2·1 pence per vehicle mile at 1972 prices for the Nottingham colliery traffic and of 1·9 pence for the Sheffield area traffic; while it was calculated that the shift from road to rail would produce an external benefit of 1·9 pence per vehicle mile. The external costs and benefits included changes in the costs of providing and maintaining the road network, that is changes in public road costs. Of the net external costs of the two transfers from rail to road, 43% consisted of road repairs and maintenance, 21% of accident costs, 19% of road congestion, 14% of noise costs and 3% of air pollution. The breakdown of the external benefits of the road to rail transfer was similar. Air pollution was valued using the Programmes Analysis Unit's estimates. Changes in noise costs due to changes in road traffic were evaluated using a method which is likely to overstate their true cost, but the small proportion which such costs represent of total external costs means that any overestimation will not have a serious effect on the main conclusion. The noise benefits from reduced rail traffic were not valued, but they were likely to be much less than the noise costs of extra road traffic. For example, in the Nottingham area it was estimated that while 18,000 households would suffer increased noise levels of between 0·1 and 0·6 dB(A) because of increased lorry traffic, only 1600 households would benefit from noise reductions of between 0·2 and 0·8 dB(A) because of reduced rail traffic. In addition, surveys of sensitivity to rail noise found that people living near railways appear to be surprisingly immune to train noise. The study discovered that most of the individual changes in noise were small, as were increases in visual intrusion, pollution and vibration, and that the average changes in noise generated would be less than 1 dB(A) for road and rail traffics. The smallness of the changes in noise levels was to be expected because the elimination of a small proportion of heavy vehicles in the traffic flow will not lead to any significant fall in traffic noise; for example, on a road on which 40% of the traffic flow consists of heavy vehicles, a halving of this proportion to 20% would reduce noise by only 2 dB(A).

Although not all external costs and benefits could be evaluated, it does appear that the most important ones were. On this basis the consultants concluded that a net external cost or benefit of the order of between 1·6 and 2·4 pence per vehicle mile could be tentatively applied to other transfers of wagonload traffic from or to rail. The consultants did not consider the private costs that would be incurred by BR or by road hauliers in carrying the different traffics, and could not therefore add private and external costs in order to find which mode would minimise the overall social costs of transport for each of the three flows studied. However, road taxation would generally be sufficient to cover external costs of the orders estimated by the consultants. In 1972 fuel taxation paid by heavy goods vehicles varied from 1·9 pence per mile for a vehicle of 4 tons unladen weight to 3·2 pence per mile for a vehicle of 10 tons unladen weight. In addition, excise licences would in most cases add rather less than 0·1 pence to the tax cost per mile. This suggests that whether traffic should go by rail or road can be determined by profitability. If an undertaking finds it more profitable to use road rather than to use rail it should be permitted to do so because the marginal external costs which it imposes will be fully reflected in the road taxation that is paid. Furthermore, BR should operate only those freight services that are profitable, or can be made profitable, because any traffic that it relinquishes will cover its full social costs when it passes onto the roads.

We have not specifically considered the effects on fuel use of the transfer of traffic from road to rail. This is because fuel costs, like all other costs, cannot be considered in isolation. If imported fuel is regarded as imposing balance of payment costs, then it is up to the Government to raise taxation on imported fuels to reflect their scarcity value to the economy. Choice of transport method can then be chosen on the basis of these fuel costs plus all other costs. It should be noted, however, that while rail transport is less fuel-intensive than some other methods of transport, its advantages in this respect are often not as great as is sometimes supposed. In 1973 it appears that BR achieved an average of between 120 and 175 ton miles of freight hauled for each gallon of diesel fuel consumed by diesel locomotives. This allows for empty and light running in connection with freight working, but not for fuel used in the collection and delivery of goods by road. The maximum ton mileage per gallon of diesel which could be achieved by road haulage would vary between 120 and 150 ton miles with goods vehicles over $3\frac{1}{2}$ tons unladen weight running fully loaded and with no empty running. These figures indicate that particular transfers to rail might even increase fuel costs, though transfer to rail would be more likely to reduce fuel use, particularly since fuel used by diesel locomotives does not increase in line with increases in the tonnage hauled.

TABLE 10.3: *Seat-miles per Gallon of Oil*

	Miles per gallon	Seating capacity	Seat-miles per gallon
Petrol:			
Private car	20–40	4	80–160
Diesel oil:			
Double-deck bus	7	75	525
BR dmu* 2-car	3·5	118[a]	413
BR dmu 3-car	2·1	219[a]	460
BR dmu 4-car	1·5	292[a]	438
Long-distance road coach	8	57	456
BR 8-coach diesel-hauled train	0·8	436	349
Electricity:			
BR emu* 3-car	1·5[b]	250	375
LT emu 7-car	0·75[b]	840	630[c]

[a] Average for British Rail stock.

[b] Based on a conversion factor of 1 GWH of electricity from 286·8 tons of oil input.

[c] Includes standing passengers

* dmu = diesel multiple unit, emu = electric multiple unit.

For passenger transport, the illustrative figures for seat-miles per gallon in Table 10.3 indicate the clear advantage of public transport over the private car, and also show that public transport by road may often be less fuel-intensive than that by rail. Because of the smaller individual units used on the roads, it should also be possible to obtain higher load factors on buses and coaches than on trains, and thereby obtain lower fuel use per passenger mile as well as per seat-mile. Though rail transport can use electric power, this may involve a lower output of seat-miles per gallon than does diesel rail transport, and although electricity can be generated by fuels other than oil, the high resource cost of peak-hour electricity cannot be ignored.

EFFICIENCY IN MODAL CHOICE

The final question to be answered is whether, given road haulage costs which cover the environmental as well as the other resource costs of transport by road, consignors will choose to send freight by the most efficient mode. This question is difficult to answer since the most efficient mode will not necessarily be the cheapest, because of differences in quality, particularly in speed, freedom from loss and damage, and availability. In practice, price appears to have a relatively small impact on modal choice. The study by Bayliss and Edwards considered the factors influencing choice of mode for freight traffic using data from 13,600 consignments in a General Survey covering two routes and 16,600 consignments in a Commercial Survey covering five specific industries. The study indicated that price did not play a dominant role. Firms were only aware of the price by an alternative mode for between one-quarter and one-third of the total consignments surveyed. In those cases where price was known, over a quarter of consignments in the General Survey were sent by a mode more expensive than the cheapest alternative, and of these one-third were sent by a mode over 25% more expensive than the cheapest available. Thus, where own-account haulage was 25% more expensive than the cheapest alternative, this would increase the probability of carriage by an alternative by only 6%.

Bayliss and Edwards' study does not answer the question of

whether freight transport modal choice is efficient, since it does not indicate whether firms will choose a higher cost mode even when the rejected mode provides as good a quality of service. It is clear, however, that many firms operating their own road goods vehicles have a very poor idea of the costs which their road haulage operations incur. A study by Clifford Sharp of 96 firms in the Birmingham area indicated that only about one-fifth of the firms had detailed costings which would enable them to make an informed choice between different methods of transport. A study by Cook, based on interviews with transport managers of large firms in the Black Country between 1964 and 1966, reached similar conclusions, and revealed that transport departments are often given a low priority by higher management and that there is sometimes inertia in changing to an improved mode from established methods of operation. Cook also discovered a certain amount of apparently irrational hostility towards British Rail.[13]

In practice, it is likely that many firms who do not at present send goods by rail will be unaware of the detailed costs of sending their goods by BR since the great bulk of rail traffic is now carried at negotiated rates which are known only to BR and the consignor of the goods. A firm will therefore not know the costs of rail transport unless it makes a serious and time-consuming approach to the railways. This difficulty is not so serious as it first appears because the nature of rail transport, with its emphasis on heavy bulk flows, means that a high proportion of rail business will come from a few large firms. In 1971 over 50% of BR's freight revenue was obtained from 30 major customers, and 75% from 300 customers. It is the largest firms which are likely to be able to put the greatest effort into determining the costs by road and rail, and so it is those firms whose traffic is most suitable for rail who are in the best position to determine whether they should use BR. Nevertheless, there is still a case for the provision of information to firms, particularly those whose use of rail is at present limited, and some government expenditure on disseminating information to the relatively small number of potential rail users would be justified.

The alternative to better information is direct action by the Government to try to improve the efficiency of modal choice. This was the aim of the system of quantity licensing that was pro-

vided for in the 1968 Transport Act. Goods vehicles above 16
tons gross weight (about 5 tons unladen weight) engaged in hauls
over 100 miles, and under 100 miles for certain bulk commodities,
were to be subject to quantity licensing. Such licences were to
be issued to road hauliers, but would have been open to objection
by BR or the National Freight Corporation on the sole grounds
that rail could be used without detriment to the consignor, the
onus of proof that road would provide the best all-round service
resting with the applicant. While the aim of the quantity licensing
system cannot be criticised, its proposed method of operation
can, since the determination of the optimal mode would inevitably be a matter of judgement on which licensing authorities and
applicants might well disagree. If permission to use road transport were refused, the applicants might have avoided the quantity
licensing regulations by using smaller vehicles or intermediate
transfer depots, which would have reduced economic efficiency.
In fact, the quantity licensing regulations were never invoked,
partly because of a realisation of the likelihood of evasion and
partly because the reappraisal of Freightliner economics meant
that the network was not expanded to the level expected when
quantity licensing was formulated.

Whether some other form of quantity licensing should be
introduced is a moot point. To make a rational judgement it
would be necessary to have far more information than is at
present available about the way in which firms decide between
different modes of transport, and the extent to which they reject
rail although it is the cheapest alternative and provides an
efficient service. This would seem a legitimate subject for government enquiry. Nevertheless, there are a number of immediate
steps that the Government might take. First, as already suggested,
it should collect and disseminate information on the costs of
using the different forms of transport and on the quality of
service they provide. Second, in order to make firms realise how
much their own road-vehicle fleets cost them, once they own a
substantial number of vehicles they should be compelled to
establish one or more road transport subsidiaries with their own
accounts. Third, firms might be required to disclose those flows
of traffic that are potentially suitable for rail movement, and
when new flows are introduced it should be compulsory to notify
BR so that it can tender for the traffic.

CONCLUSIONS

In this chapter we have outlined the serious environmental costs of road haulage, and have discussed policies by which such costs might be reduced. Of these policies, transfer of traffic to rail has a relatively limited role to play. We have suggested that, in total, taxes on road hauliers should be devised to cover the social costs imposed. Our review of the overall position suggests that at present road hauliers as a whole are not covering the costs they impose, and that the relationship between tax revenue, road track costs, and external costs has changed markedly since 1965. Taxes on road haulage should therefore be increased, partly through the introduction of congestion pricing in urban areas, until tax revenues are brought into line with the costs imposed. Although road hauliers do not at present cover the *average* costs that they impose, one study of potential rail to road transfers indicated that the *marginal* public road and external costs which these particular transfers would create *would* be covered by existing road taxes. In such circumstances if decisions on modal choice are made on the basis of profitability, then rail *will* be chosen if it is the mode which minimises social costs. Finally, however, we noted some evidence that irrationality and habit play a part in determining choice of mode, and outlined ways in which government policy might be used to remedy this situation.

CHAPTER 11

Conclusions:
Towards a Self-Financing Railway

In its Interim Rail Strategy the Railways Board concluded that in conventional commercial terms the railways could not be made viable and that additional financial support would be required if, as it proposed, the existing network was preserved and investment was doubled. How much assistance the railways would require was not disclosed but it was evident at the time, and has become even clearer since, that it will be massive. National resources must not be wasted and there are many calls upon the public purse. It has therefore been our object in this book to take a searching look at the two fundamental assumptions on which the Board's case for a large and virtually open-ended subsidy rests: namely, that it is doing all that it can to keep its costs down and that there are overwhelming social and environmental arguments in favour of rail transport.

CONCLUSIONS

We do not believe that either of these assumptions is correct. After examining (in Chapters 2 to 6) how much traffic the railways are likely to carry in 1981 it was found (in Chapter 7) that the programme of capital expenditure proposed by British Rail is unnecessarily large. In the Interim Strategy the Board urged that over the period 1973–81 it should be allowed to invest nearly £200 million a year at 1972 purchasing power, but our investigations suggest that an expenditure of £114 million per annum would be sufficient to enable BR to cater for the business available and to

250

undertake desirable cost-cutting projects. Then (in Chapter 8) it was discovered that the Railways Board will need something like 33,000 fewer workers than it is planning to employ, despite the lower level of investment that has been assumed. Our forecasts for manpower and traffic imply that labour productivity should increase by 4½% per annum over the period 1973–81, which does not seem an impossibly high figure.

The social arguments for supporting the railways (examined in Chapters 9 and 10) turn out to be much weaker than popularly supposed. Rail passenger travel is a very dubious candidate for public expenditure because it is, to a quite exceptional extent, consumed by the affluent and its subsidisation is therefore likely to make the distribution of income less equal. Moreover cost-benefit analysis suggests that it is not worth subsidising many of the present grant-aided services outside urban areas because the losses which they incur are so large that they outweigh the social benefits that they confer. In urban areas it is better to deal with the problem of road congestion by means of road pricing than to subsidise the railways. Subsidisation involves a loss of welfare and is likely to prove ineffective because of the huge amount of public expenditure that would be required to bring about any substantial transfer of traffic from road to rail. Motorists are not very responsive to rail fare reductions and the bulk of the money the Government provides will be absorbed in subsidising existing rail users. A railway freight service capable of attracting any worthwhile quantity of road goods traffic would be very expensive to run, would make a large loss and, because of the need for road collection and delivery, would have little effect on road congestion. Similarly the accidents, noise and pollution which result from road traffic are better tackled by direct measures than by the roundabout method of subsidising the railways. If only a fraction of the money that will be devoted to supporting BR were made available it would be possible to achieve a major reduction in the costs that road users now impose on the community.

Because the subsidisation of BR is such a costly and inefficient way of dealing with the social and environmental costs to which roads give rise, it is to be hoped that the problem is tackled along the lines that have been suggested. There is a further reason why this is desirable and why, even in the absence of a proper policy towards roads, it is undesirable that BR should be

subsidised. It is most unlikely that the Board will make any
serious attempt to operate at the minimum cost level so long as
it is in receipt of a subsidy and not expected to pay its way. As
we have seen (in Chapter 1) the basic reason why the 1968 Transport Act failed was that it was regarded not, as its authors had
intended, as a spur to greater effort but as providing a holiday
from financial discipline. The moral was (correctly) drawn that
if the Government was prepared to subsidise the least-used part
of the system it would be willing to support the rest. Hence there
was little pressure within the Board to make those economies and
changes in operating practice which railway managers privately
concede to be possible.

The demoralisation that inevitably results from deficit finance,
however this be disguised, is the underlying explanation for the
Board's past failure to reduce its labour force as much as had
been planned and for its present unwillingness to plan those
savings in manpower which stare it in the face. It is scarcely to
be expected that those in charge of the railways will embark on
the painful and thankless task of inducing railway workers to
accept changes in manning, and to give up restrictive practices,
if they have reason to believe that the Government will rescue
them from the consequences of their own inaction. Another result
of subsidisation is a lax attitude towards capital expenditure.
Railway management will come to see its purpose as the creation
of a technically perfect and super modern railway system regardless of the amount of investment required. The lack of justification for so much of the capital expenditure proposed in the
Board's Interim Strategy shows that this is already happening.

Therefore the subsidisation of British Rail would be a pointless
policy in practice, even if the theoretical case was far stronger
than it is. For it is useless to give money to the railways in order
that they can compete more effectively with the roads if it is then
absorbed in excessive costs. BR will not be able to capture any
substantial amount of traffic because the subsidy will be devoted
to meeting the escalating expense of carrying existing traffic.
The Railways Board in its Interim Strategy did not hold out any
prospect that freight traffic would increase, and although a substantial passenger growth was expected this was largely because
of Inter-City expansion which, as the railways' own researches
have shown, is mainly due to the generation of new traffic and not

TABLE 11.1: *British Rail Receipts and Expenditure*
(£ million, 1972 purchasing power)

	1963	1968	1969	1970	1971	1972	1973	1974	1981
Revenue:									
Passenger (Table 2.1)	263	245	258	267	281	274	272	255	349a
Parcels, letters and papers (Table 3.2)	105	84	84	82	78	74	71	59	55b
Freight (Table 6.7)	338	242	237	235	201	178	178	160	201
Miscellaneous	13	12	13	13	13	11	11	9	12
	719	582	591	598	573	537	532	483	617
Expenditure (Table 8.10)	..	590	580	585	574	573	570	625	555
Gross profit (+) or loss (−)	..	−8	+11	+13	0	−36	−39	−142	+62
Saving through withdrawal of unprofitable passenger services	−	−	−	−	−	−	−	−	+15
Profit on ancillaries	+9	..	+8	+6	+6	+7	+7	+6	+10
Capital receipts	..	..	+13	+27	+22	+22	..	..	+20
Total internally generated flow of funds before interest	..	..	+32	+46	+28	−7	..	..	+107

a Includes allowance of £9 million for reduced fare evasion (see page 157).
b Includes allowance of £5 million for 10% price rise to keep rail charges in line with road haulage rates.

to the diversion of road traffic. Unless BR is granted a subsidy of astronomic proportions there is therefore no prospect that any significant amount of traffic will be transferred from road to rail, and it is for such a subsidy that the Board is secretly hoping.

REVENUE AND EXPENDITURE IN 1981

Although the arguments against subsidisation are strong, it does not necessarily follow that British Rail can be made viable. Is the Board correct in its assertion that there is no way in which this can be achieved? Our estimates of the railways' potential revenue in 1981 and of its possible expenditure have been brought together in Table 11.1.

There has over the years been a considerable fall in BR's real receipts. Revenue slumped from about £720 million in 1963 (at 1972 purchasing power) to £580 million in 1968, and by 1973 was down to £530 million. However it is estimated that in 1981 the railways will earn over £615 million, which represents an increase of about 15%. This is about £75 million less than BR suggested in its Interim Strategy but as the railways are always over-optimistic this is little comfort and the question arises of whether our estimate is on the high side. Past trends suggest that it may be. However, much of the reduction in revenue between 1963 and 1968 was due to the decline in receipts from coal and the withdrawal of services because of the Beeching plan; and between 1968 and 1973 there would not have been any great reduction in the railways' earnings had it not been for the continued decline of coal. Although some further reduction is to be expected this factor will be far less important in future. It should also be remembered that the railways have been charging less than the market will bear and that the rise in receipts forecast for the period 1973–81 is wholly accounted for by higher prices and reduced fare evasion.

Between 1963 and 1968 there was, as a result of Dr Beeching and the switch from steam to diesel traction, a large reduction in railway expenditure but over the period 1968–73 it only declined from £590 million to £570 million. It is estimated that, even if BR manages to make the very considerable savings in manpower which are possible, its costs will by 1981 be only a little lower at £555 million. This is partly because of higher expenditure on fuel and partly because of the assumed rise of 3½% per annum in the real earnings of railway workers over the period 1972–81.

When the estimates of revenue and expenditure are brought together it appears that BR should have a gross profit of about £60 million in 1981 compared with its 1973 loss of almost £40 million. The saving through the withdrawal of those grossly unprofitable passenger services where the financial loss exceeds the estimated social benefit has been estimated at £15 million in 1981, after allowing for the reduction in BR's costs which should result from the operating economies that have been suggested and also for the rise in real earnings and the cost of fuel. The railways should also be credited with the net receipts from their miscellaneous activities. In 1973 these produced £7 million, but by 1981 the figure should have increased to at least £10 million through the elimination of the £1 million deficit incurred on restaurant cars; as a result of higher dividends from Freightliners; and through an increase in rents from properties in operational use, which have done no more than keep pace with inflation since 1968 despite the large rise in property values. The final element in BR's cash inflow is receipts from the sale of scrap and land. Of late receipts from scrap have been about £5 million per annum, but they ought to be somewhat greater in 1981 as a result of the withdrawal of socially unnecessary passenger services and the consequent sale of old rails and rolling-stock. The railways' own estimate of their revenue from land sales in 1981 suggests that they should obtain about £15 million and it will be conservatively assumed that their total capital receipts will come to £20 million. If so, British Rail should have a total of about £105 million available out of which to finance its investment and meet any interest payments which it may have.

It has been estimated that the railways should invest about £114 million per annum between 1973 and 1981. During the latter year the amount of capital expenditure would probably be slightly below the average level and the closure of the socially unnecessary passenger services would lead to a saving of around £3 million each year. Investment might therefore be around £105 million. Thus in the absence of any interest payments it looks as if BR could eliminate its cash-flow deficit by 1981. This result should obviously be treated with considerable reserve because it rests on a large number of assumptions each of which can be questioned and disputed. Nevertheless our estimates do suggest that it is possible to make British Rail commercially viable without resorting to drastic surgery or the amputation of any but the socially diseased parts of the system. Even if this should turn out to be impossible it seems clear that the railways could be far more nearly self-supporting in 1981 than they are today, and there is no excuse for the monster cash-flow deficit for which BR is heading.

THE SELF-FINANCING RAILWAY

Although it should be possible greatly to improve the railways' financial position by 1981 it would probably be unreasonable to expect BR to pay any interest on its existing capital debt. As a result of the 1974 Railways Act that part of the Board's interest payment which relates to the railways is being reduced to about £28 million. This should now be waived in order that the task of becoming financially self-sufficient should be capable of attainment; to prevent the railways' difficulties being attributed to inherited obligations and past mistakes; and to compensate the Board for the loss of the subsidy in respect of the social services which it is expected to maintain. The general passenger subsidy which was introduced by the 1974 Railways Act should be scaled down year by year, and by 1981 it should be entirely eliminated. British Rail should not receive a subsidy nor a capital grant from the Government and it should not have to borrow, or be permitted to borrow, from the Exchequer. It will be said that BR will have to charge far more for its Inter-City services than they cost to operate in order to meet the losses that it incurs on its remaining social passenger services. However the size of these losses might not be very great.

By 1981 it should be possible to make the services in London and the South-East pay their way. In 1971 those that were grant-aided had a gross profit of £6 million, after taking into account not only their specific operating costs but also the full expenditure on joint facilities and administration that they were allocated. However, it appears that a small loss was incurred during 1973.

Our estimates suggest that over the period 1973–81 something under £25 million of capital expenditure will need to be devoted each year to these services. If to this we add the gross loss during 1973, it appears that the cash-flow deficit is slightly over £25 million a year. This represents about 25% of the revenue that these grant-aided services earned in 1973. There should be no real difficulty in raising prices sufficiently to increase net revenue by this amount. Demand is probably very inelastic and any large-scale transfer from rail to road could be prevented through road pricing or, until this is administratively possible, by making those who drive into central London purchase a supplementary licence.

The gross loss on those provincial grant-aided services which appear to be worth retaining came to something like £24 million during 1973, if they have been allocated· their proper share of overhead and administrative expenditure. Of this roughly £6 million was accounted for by the Merseyside third-rail electric services, by the Glasgow suburban electric services and by those services on Tyneside which are being electrified. These, as we shall see later, should be hived off from BR and run by the PTEs. The loss on the remaining social services was only £18 million in 1973 but this probably overstates the saving which could be achieved if they were withdrawn. Many of them run over Inter-City and heavily used freight routes which would be retained even if the grant-aided services were withdrawn. This would not matter if their share of track and signalling expenses had been estimated on an avoidable cost basis, but it was not. If to allow for this the official figure for expenditure on joint facilities and overheads is arbitrarily divided by two, the loss on the residual social services is reduced to £11 million during 1973. However to this must be added £4 million to cover the amount of capital expenditure that will be necessary each year over the period 1973–81. Hence the withdrawal of all subsidies for its social services would mean that they would have to be cross-subsidised to the extent of about £15 million. However, the PTEs should, as we shall see, continue to assist those of their services that are not being hived off, and anyway £15 million is a very small amount in relation to the railways' turnover and would involve a trivial misallocation of resources, especially as BR has considerable scope for practising price discrimination.

Another possible objection to the proposal that BR should not be permitted to borrow from the Exchequer is that if its own resources turn out to be insufficient, opportunities for profitable rail investment will have to be passed over. This argument would carry force if it could be assumed that in the absence of the prohibition BR would do its best to cut its costs and would not engage in unnecessary investment. But as experience shows, this cannot be taken for granted.

One of the most important reasons for the railways' financial collapse has been the lack of any countervailing force within the organisation to offset the understandable pressure which builds up from the operating departments for investment in the latest and most modern types of equipment. A self-finance obligation would help to ensure that the railways developed more effective internal procedures to appraise such investments, and to eliminate those whose returns would be insufficient to justify their costs. If some special investment opportunity were to arise for which the railways were unable to provide the necessary finance, it would always be open to the Government to pass a special enabling Act, and for the Board to borrow from the market without a Treasury guarantee.

Any difficulties which may arise when the railways have become solvent may however seem of secondary importance when compared with the problem of how the Government can ensure that BR's loss is eliminated. The first step is to permit, and indeed encourage, the railways to put up their prices where this will lead to an improvement in their financial position. This may seem inflationary, but if prices are held down on the railways and in the rest of the public sector they will almost certainly be higher than they would otherwise be in the private sector. If the nationalised industries are unable to finance their investment and meet their interest payments from their own resources, the Government is almost bound to have to raise more through indirect taxation or to borrow more from the private sector. Higher indirect taxation means higher prices, while the private sector will probably have to save more if it is to lend more. Companies will only be able to save more by raising their prices and earning higher profits; and individuals will only save more if they have higher incomes, which means that their employers will have to increase their prices in order that they shall be able to pay more. In each case there has, sooner or later, to be a price increase which can only be avoided if the Government decides to raise direct instead of indirect taxation; if it is prepared to curb its own expenditure and save more; if other countries are prepared to lend us more; or if there is unemployment, in which case higher incomes can be matched by extra production and no price increase is required. None of these qualifications is likely to hold good for very long because unemployed workers will, for instance, be absorbed and foreigners will be unwilling to go on lending indefinitely.

It may therefore be concluded that if prices are held down by the railways and the other nationalised industries they will before long be forced up elsewhere. The present Government has recognised this and is trying to reduce their deficits. It is to be hoped that British Rail will be accorded priority in increasing its prices because it is here that deficit finance is leading to the most blatant waste of resources. However, it will be a number of years before BR is able to increase its prices by the full amount. For much of its freight traffic it will have to wait until the contracts with its customers permit it to make an increase, and it would only damage its earning capacity if it tried to make too large an adjustment too quickly. Similarly, it will take time for the Board to renegotiate working arrangements with the unions and for the Government to establish the special scheme which is necessary to encourage surplus locomotive staff to leave the railways. Again a considerable period will elapse before BR is able to complete the withdrawal of its socially unnecessary passenger services even if the existing closure machinery is overhauled and modified, as it should be. On the other hand some increase in fares and freight charges can be made immediately, and it ought to be possible to make some quick savings in manpower.

What the Government ought to do therefore, after it has consulted the Board and obtained the necessary professional advice, is to lay down targets for the amount by which the deficit at constant prices has to be reduced each year, and for the reduction in working expenses and the saving in manpower that must be achieved. In order to prevent the Board from pleading that economic conditions have been unexpectedly adverse, some formula must be laid down in advance by which the target is reduced if, for instance, coal consumption falls short of what had been expected. If the railways fail to achieve their objectives for cost and manpower reduction, they would not be able to attribute this to any shortfall in traffic because the smaller this is the fewer workers that will be required. This is why it is essential that BR should be set a target for employment and expenditure, as well as for its profit and loss. These objectives should be published, and the duty should be laid on the Minister and the Board of assessing in White Papers and Annual Reports how much progress has been made towards their attainment.

Perhaps this will be a sufficient spur to action, but it would obviously be wrong to depend on this in view of the Board's repeated failure to reach previous targets, albeit of a less precise nature. The Board should therefore be made to understand that the amount it will be allowed to invest will depend on its success in achieving its targets. Moreover, the new Transport Act that will be necessary should arm the Minister with the power to dissolve the Board, and take over the running of the railways. This should be a powerful incentive for progress towards solvency because those at the top of the railways are largely motivated by the desire to preserve their own empire. It is entirely logical and highly desirable that British Rail should lose its status as a public corporation and be subordinated to a government department if it continues to be so dependent on government subventions. While it retains its separate identity, public funds will inevitably be wasted, because it will naturally believe that its purpose in life is to run the biggest and best railway system regardless of what this may cost. Moreover, because the Board has the responsibility for running the system and is the centre of rail expertise, it is in a strong position to get its way, however sceptical civil servants may be about the plans and proposals which it submits.

The abolition of the Railways Board would put an end to the present deplorable situation in which it devotes its best efforts to extracting money from the Government, and is prepared, if need be, to mislead the civil service. This is illustrated by the scheme for eliminating surplus track capacity under the 1968 Transport Act. BR was supposed to identify what it no longer needed, to estimate the eventual saving, and to receive a grant during the interval before it could be removed. According to one of the Board's former officials,

> there was a certain amount of deceit in the composition of the programme. Routes were proposed for closure or singling to

obtain the grants, when there was no intention of carrying out the physical adjustments. The Settle and Carlisle line is a case in point, but there the deceit had a double benefit for BR because potential savings claimed from closing the route played a major part in justifying the electrification of the parallel North-Western mainline.

In addition, the scheme for this electrification was presented in two parts, one of which covered electrification proper, while the other dealt with the associated proposals for track and signalling. What happened was that benefits were counted twice, since it was claimed that the investment in track would permit a better service to be run, but this improvement was also partly responsible for the revenue increase which was attributed to electrification.

Unfortunately, the Minister would be very reluctant to take over the railways, and the Board's knowledge of this would weaken the incentive effect. However, the threat would carry more conviction if the Government had already acted with firmness by divesting the Board of some of its activities and part of its territory. This is highly desirable on its own merits, and will help the railways to become self-supporting, and the Board to preserve its existence.

HIVING OFF: FREIGHT TRAFFICS

The 1968 Transport Act commenced the process of hiving off, by transferring Freightliners and the old freight sundries service to the National Freight Corporation (NFC). Under British Rail the sundries side of the business had been seriously mismanaged. Sundries were identified in the Beeching Report as one of the areas in which large losses were being made, and savings had to be achieved. Examination showed that the return on the investment necessary if the service was to be thoroughly modernised and reorganised was unattractive. It was, therefore, decided to rationalise operations without undertaking any large-scale capital expenditure. When the National Sundries Plan, as it became known, was put into effect it was found that some of the depots were unable to handle the extra work, due to either inadequate facilities or shortage of staff. Another cause of delay was that the Plan was implemented piecemeal, which meant that staff became confused and demoralised due to the constant stream of re-routing instructions as depot after depot was closed. The result was that revenue fell faster than costs, so that the loss on sundries traffic increased, both absolutely and as a proportion of revenue. During 1968 National Carriers Limited (NCL), as the sundries service then became known, had a working loss of £26 million, at 1972 purchasing power, which was half as large as its revenue of £52 million.

By 1973 NCL's loss had been reduced to only about £5½ million, equivalent to no more than 10% of its earnings which, at £53 million, were slightly higher than they had been in 1968. The principal reason for the spectacular fall in the deficit was the 25% cut in working expenses. This was achieved through a 25% economy in staff, by a similar reduction in the size of the vehicle fleet, by the pruning of over a third of NCL's depots, and by a reduction of around three-quarters in the number of wagon movements undertaken by BR on its behalf. Higher efficiency and tighter management were the result of a different ethos and organisation rather than of new men. Management continued to be largely in the hands of former railwaymen but, because of the hiving off of NCL, and its new company status, it was now clear that they were responsible for its success or failure, that their sole responsibility was to make it a success, and that if they failed this would be evident from its accounts.

While the history of freight sundries prior to their transfer was one of uniform failure, the story of Freightliners was one of partial success. British Rail deserves credit for having got the system started, but it was wildly over-optimistic. It was estimated in the Beeching Report that by 1973 liner-trains would be carrying 39 million tons, of which half would be hauled less than 150 miles. However, as we have seen, even for heavy commodities the break-even distance is only a little short of this. That its estimates were unconvincing was pointed out when they were first presented, and should have become clear to BR once it had some operating experience. Nevertheless, it continued to hope that it would receive 40 million tons of traffic and to plan for an extended network that would contain some 50 depots by the end of 1970.[1] This was justified by the traditional railway argument that Freightliners would have a far greater appeal if they provided a comprehensive service, and that subsidiary depots were necessary in order that traffic might be fed onto the principal routes. This ignored the high cost of establishing even a small terminal, and overestimated the amount of traffic they would receive.

When the Freightliner Company was transferred to the NFC, and the financial position was analysed route by route for the first time, it was found that even those services which were fully developed and had good loadings were mostly running at a loss, although this was partly because under BR the rates had been pitched very low. This, together with greater realism about the amount of traffic that would be obtained, produced a more cautious attitude towards the expansion of the system, and led to the withdrawal of four or five hopelessly unprofitable services. As a result, Freightliners managed to break even in 1971 and, after a financial relapse during 1972, earned an operating profit of £1 million in 1973 from the 6½ million tons of traffic that it obtained. BR now estimates that by 1981 Freightliners will be carrying 11 million tons which, as the system already contains three-fifths as many depots as it was planning when it predicted 40 million tons, shows just how unrealistic this estimate was.

The success of National Carriers and Freightliners under the NFC provokes the question of whether there are any other parts of BR that could usefully be hived off. The most obvious candidate is that part of the railways' traffic which originates and/or terminates at rail-owned terminals. Much of this traffic is collected and/or delivered by NCL. Since this local road work is very costly, payments to NCL must already account for a large part of the total cost and this type of traffic must be wildly unprofitable. In 1971 BR had a working loss of £16 million on its freight traffic, and traffic which passes through freight stations has always been one of the least lucrative types.

Much of it should disappear during the next few years. However, in view of BR's reluctance to relinquish any freight, however commercially unattractive, it would be foolish to assume that all the unprofitable part will be eliminated so long as BR remains in charge. As we have seen, the Board is in the process of introducing new air-braked services for the movement of wagonload freight. Part of the traffic which passes over this network will arrive from customers' private sidings by rail, but some will be collected and/or delivered by road. There is a serious risk that BR will charge an uneconomic rate for this traffic. Responsibility for that part of rail freight which will arrive and/or depart by road should therefore be handed over to the National Freight Corporation, which ought wherever possible to take charge of the rail terminal.

It would probably be possible to go further than this and transfer the responsibility for marketing all the new air-braked services from BR to the NFC. These would run to a fixed timetable and NFC, represented by a new subsidiary which might be called Wagonfreight, could contract with BR for the trunk haulage that it requires, as Freightliners does. Arrangements for the collection and delivery of wagons might have to be on a day to day basis, but the requirements for local trains would have to be fairly regular and predictable or the traffic would not be worth carrying. The new air-braked wagons should be owned by Wagonfreight because, if BR is responsible for their acquisition, there is a very real danger that rolling-stock will be purchased to carry freight on which the profit margin is insufficient to meet the capital charges on the new equipment.

Although the risk of over-investment would be reduced it would not be eliminated, because BR could charge such a low price that capital expenditure would appear profitable when it is not. However, it seems unlikely that BR would charge Wagonfreight too little, partly because it would view it with a certain enmity, and partly because it would not know what profit was being earned on any particular service, and would not want to provide Wagonfreight with too large a profit by undercharging. Moreover, if BR is made to keep separate and realistic accounts for freight such undercharging would, if it proceeded very far, lead to an overall loss. The Government should let the Board know that if this continued it would hive off the whole of the railways' freight side. Although the co-ordination of freight and passenger operations, and the optimum use of locomotives, is best achieved within a single organisation, it is by no means impossible to place freight and passenger work under separate managements. This has already happened in the United States where the passenger side has been hived off to Amtrack.

HIVING OFF: PARCELS TRAFFIC

Should the Board be allowed to retain the Rail Express Parcels Service? That part of the traffic which has to be collected and delivered, and it constitutes the great bulk of Rail Express, barely covers its direct costs, if it even does that.[2] The railways' own profitability analysis suggested that at least £8 million of its systems and administrative expenditure was attributable to parcels, mails and other freight by coaching train. If so the working loss on parcels that had to be collected or delivered by road must have been £5 million or more. Rail Express is not the only public-sector parcels service that runs at a loss. The Post Office reported that its deficit in 1973–74 was £23 million after interest, while National Carriers had a working loss of £5½ million during 1973. BRS Parcels and British Express Carriers, which also belong to the NFC, are the only undertakings which are profitable. In 1973 they had a joint working profit of £2½ million, though even this was equivalent to only 7% of their revenue.

The reason for this unhappy state of affairs is that public-sector parcels traffic has declined from 530 million packages in 1965 to 420 million in 1972, and according to the Freight Integration Council, which has made a special study of public-sector parcels, all four undertakings have excess capacity. National Carriers has estimated that its margin is about 20%, and although no figure is available for BRS Parcels it is evident from the way in which productivity has fallen that there must be a large amount of slack. Over the period 1964–72 there was a reduction of 14% in the number of parcels handled per worker, and of 19% in the number carried per vehicle, despite an increase in the average carrying capacity. There even seems to have been a fall in the number of packages sorted per depot, although the system was greatly improved.

Despite the efforts of the Freight Integration Council, of which the Chairmen of BR and NFC are members and to which the Post Office has sent representatives, the public-sector carriers have failed to reach agreement on the rationalisation and reorganisation of their activities. What is now happening is that the concerns are trying to cut their costs, but to maintain their services and preserve or expand their traffic. BRS Parcels appears to be the only one which is not expecting a substantial growth. The Post Office, for instance, takes a very optimistic view not only of its own prospects but also of those of the public sector as a whole; while Rail Express is hoping for a considerable growth in its carryings, as a result of an increase in its share of the sector's total traffic. As this is likely to decline, some or all of the operators will almost inevitably be disappointed. There will there-fore be no solution to the problem of excess capacity, which may well intensify. It has been claimed that the Post Office will utilise only about half of the capacity of its new sorting equipment. Yet so long as excess capacity remains it is very doubtful whether public-sector parcels can be made profitable, especially as the Post Office, which has for years been running its parcels service at a loss, does not really seem to be trying. According to its Chair-man, it is thinking 'of being able to make the service profitable within about ten years'.[3]

The solution to the public-sector parcels problem appears to be to bring all the carriers together under the ownership of the NFC. At present BR has around 300 principal parcels stations from which road collection and delivery are made, but it is planned that over the next few years traffic will be concentrated on 57 main and 40 subsidiary depots. Moreover there will be a reduction in the number of parcels that are transhipped en route, and an increase in the proportion that are carried in special parcels trains. Even at present only about 20% of all traffic is carried on passenger trains, and the Red Star Service accounts for a signifi-cant part of this. Since Rail Express is already, and will to an increasing extent constitute a self-contained network, there would be no real difficulty in hiving it off, although the profitable Red Star service should probably be left with the railways because it is so closely linked to the passenger services. It would also be possible to separate Post Office parcels from the letter service. Parcels are generally handled separately from other mail at all stages from posting to delivery, and sorting is, as we have seen, being concentrated at special mechanised depots.

The objection to hiving off Rail Express and Post Office parcels to the NFC is that the Corporation has failed to co-ordinate the activities of the parcels undertakings which it already owns. The reduction in National Carriers' deficit has been achieved entirely by means of rationalisation and reorganisation within that concern, and little or no progress has been made towards integrating it with BRS Parcels or reducing the extent to which the two undertakings are in competition. A number of options were considered but were all rejected. A merger looked attractive but the NFC was afraid that if this policy was adopted it would encounter fierce opposition from the Transport and General Workers Union to which BRS Parcels drivers belong. Finally, the Corporation decided that BRS Parcels and NCL should cater for different sections of the market, with NCL providing a comprehensive service and BRS Parcels specialising in fast transits between those industrial areas where the volume of traffic would be sufficient for there to be a direct link. So far this policy has not meant very much, for NCL has been busy introducing fast and reliable services between main centres, and has had a price structure which discriminates more heavily than that of BRS Parcels against traffic moving to rural areas and out of the way places. Nevertheless, the Corporation's generally successful record suggests that it will before long tackle the problem of co-ordination with greater vigour, and that Rail Express and the Post Office parcels service can be entrusted to its care.

What economies could then be achieved only a large-scale investigation would reveal. In theory co-ordination should have considerable advantages, as both the Select Committee on Nationalised Industries and the Freight Integration Council have argued. However, if the number of depots is reduced in order to improve the efficiency and reduce the expense of trunk haulage, there will be a tendency for collection and delivery costs to rise because depots will now serve larger areas. Such considerations may help to explain why the Freight Integration Council found that there would be only a modest saving if the Rail Express collection and delivery traffic was transferred to other nationalised parcels operators, and why the Minister, after receiving its report, decided that the benefits were too small to justify the exercise.

But even in the absence of any economies of scale—and it is difficult to believe that they are negligible—it would still be worth bringing the public operators under common ownership because experience suggests that this is the only way in which they can be prevented from trying to solve their difficulties at each other's expense, and can be made to face up to the problem of excess capacity. As Mr Richard Marsh, the Chairman of the Railways Board, told the Select Committee, there is no doubt that

> the three public sector organisations—the Post Office, the NFC and ourselves—are together producing a less than optimum result for the taxpayers, because we are running the same services in competition with each other and we have in some areas what could be held to be duplicated investment, doing the same sort of thing. We have moved to the situation where we are all carrying much wider ranges of parcels and packages than used to be the case ... If there are three parcel carriers each charged with the job of maximising their revenues in the public sector then there is bound to be an overlap ... It is not a question of knocking heads together. There is a problem about irreconcilable remits.[4]

The solution is to transfer the Post Office parcels service and Rail Express, but not Red Star, to the NFC. The railways and the Post Office should however be given a minority stake in its parcels undertakings and appoint directors to their boards. This would help to ensure co-operation between British Rail and those present and prospective NFC parcels companies which make extensive use of rail for trunk haulage work. Where little use is now made of railways, as in the case of BRS Parcels, BR would be in a position to see that its services were given serious consideration. To guard against the danger that the NFC might go on neglecting the co-ordination of its parcels undertakings, the Minister might be given the power to transfer them to a separate State Parcels Corporation if they were not made profitable within, say, five years.

HIVING OFF: PTES

Serious consideration also needs to be given to the possibility of transferring the electric railway systems in Glasgow, Merseyside and Tyneside to the respective Passenger Transport Executives. The PTEs now have to meet the estimated deficit which the grant-aided services incur within their areas, but are in no position to ensure that BR is operating them efficiently. Because BR refuses to disclose the overall cost of providing joint facilities, or the way in which they are allocated, the PTEs suspect that they may be helping to support some of BR's Inter-City services. The Executives appear to have only the haziest notion of what the various cost categories which BR uses are supposed to cover, and they seem to have very little information about the number of men and the amount of rolling-stock to which the financial figures relate. This is partly because the PTEs have not pressed for information. One Executive has not even taken the trouble to find out what the volume of passenger traffic has been since 1969 on the services which it helps to support because it is largely preoccupied with the problems of running its large fleet of buses, and what time it has to spare is devoted to those rail projects to which it is making or will make a financial contribution.

It would be wrong for the PTEs to seek information for its own sake. However, there are a number of topics that they need to take up with BR. In Glasgow and on Merseyside many of the trains have power doors, but BR has made no move towards eliminating guards. The Tyne and Wear PTE is hoping that the trains on its new light rapid-transit system will be single-manned, and is incurring extra capital expenditure in order that this may be possible. However, it has received no guarantee from the railways that this is how they will be operated, and is in no position to seek one. So long as the Tyne-Wear system remains part of BR, its manning practices will be determined through the national labour relations machinery, and although the Executives can, if they are sufficiently determined, bring pressure to bear on the Board's local officials, they will have very little influence at headquarters.

Manning is but one illustration of the likelihood that the PTE railways will, so long as they remain part of the national system, conform to the general BR practice, regardless of whether it is appropriate. Everywhere except Tyneside it has been accepted that the traditional method of operation, which involves heavy rolling-stock and complicated signalling, should continue. The stopping distance for the lightweight Tyneside rail cars will be little more than a third greater than that of a bus travelling at the same speed, whereas for a diesel multiple unit the distance is four times as long. Hence it is only in the central part of Tyneside, where the interval between trains will be very short, that a complex and expensive signalling system will be necessary. Elsewhere cheap two-aspect signalling will be used, whereas if BR had had its way four-aspect signalling would have been installed. It is employed wherever lines are resignalled in the Eastern Region, and had already been introduced on a considerable part of the Tyneside loop line. This was sheer waste of money because there is no need to have a signalling system that permits speeds of up to 125 mph or more where the trains do not exceed 55 mph. But although this idiotic policy is now being avoided, a considerable amount of unnecessary expenditure has nevertheless been incurred outside the central area where it would, for the most part, have been possible to dispense with signalling entirely. In Cologne and other European cities, light rapid-transit systems operate without any general signalling system, although the trains travel as fast as they will on Tyneside. However, the PTE was persuaded that signalling was necessary. If the Tyne railway had been a separate system run by the Executive, the PTE could not have been dismissed as an amateur body without operating experience, and it would have been more evident to the Railway Inspectorate that Tyneside was a special case.

It therefore seems evident that rail lines within the provincial conurbations should wherever possible be transferred to the PTEs. This would not be practicable in Birmingham, Manchester, South Yorkshire and the West Riding because most of the lines are an integral part of the general railway network; and where they are not they are sometimes not worth retaining. However, it would be a simple matter to hive off the Tyneside rapid-transit system which will, when it is complete, be virtually separate from the rest of BR. Nor would there be any great difficulty in handing the Merseyside third-rail electric lines over to the PTE as they are not used by Inter-City services, or to any significant degree by other passenger services from outside. Apart from a few short stretches of route there is no freight traffic. Similarly in Glasgow the electric suburban railway is a largely separate network which, apart from two sections of main line, is scarcely used by passenger trains from outside. Not that it must be imagined that any insuperable problems arise if the trains of one railway administration use lines which are owned by a different undertaking. This was common in Britain until the railway amalgamation of 1923 and there are a number of London Transport lines over which BR trains operate.

The hiving off of the various areas and activities that has been proposed should make it significantly easier for BR to become financially self-supporting by 1981. Those suburban services in Glasgow, Merseyside and Tyneside which could be transferred to the PTEs incurred a gross loss of about £6 million in 1973. Other things being equal, this figure ought to have been reduced by 1981 as a result of further electrification, the introduction of automatic barriers and the removal of guards. But real wages will increase and it is difficult to believe that the deficit will be any lower, even if the available economies are made. Moreover BR will not have to carry out the large amount of capital expenditure which will take place in the three areas. According to our proposals some £125 million should be invested over the period 1973–81 in the Tyneside rapid-transit system, the Merseyside third-rail network and the Glasgow suburban electric services. By 1981 investment should already be tailing off and capital expenditure might only come to about £10 million. Allowing for both investment and the gross loss, BR might be relieved of a cash-flow deficit of something like £20 million.

Though the PTEs should take over the actual operation of their local rail services where this is technically feasible, it is both necessary and desirable that the Executives should also continue their financial support for other local rail services in their areas. No PTE would wish to take over the operation of a line and incur the deficit, if the alternative would be operation by BR, with BR bearing the cost through cross-subsidisation. Local rail services will continue to be supported under Section 20 of the 1968 Act after the end of 1974, though the methods of estimating the contribution to joint costs are under review. It seems desirable that this arrangement should continue, with rail-operating deficits financed by the Metropolitan Counties. Excluding those PTE services we believe could be hived off, and those whose social benefits seem unlikely to justify retention, BR would be relieved of a further £5 million through the Section 20 grants.

In all there would therefore be a considerable deficit to be financed by the PTEs. However, when road pricing is introduced, rail revenue will increase because of the transfer of some former road users to rail, and because it will be possible for the PTEs to raise rail fares. Nevertheless, it is unlikely that the rail deficits would be eliminated. One possibility is to use part of the revenue from road pricing for the support of local public transport services, and this might be accompanied by a reduction in the Central Government contribution through the Transport Supplementary Grants.

When the PTE deficits of £25 million are allowed for, it appears that British Rail and its ancillary activities should by 1981 have a cash-flow surplus of about the same sum instead of just above breaking even. This is, in effect, a contingency allowance and represents the amount by which our estimates could be over-optimistic, without it being necessary to depart from the concept of a self-financing railway system of the shape and size that has been assumed.

PRODUCT DIVISIONS

Although it is probably undesirable to proceed any further with hiving off at this stage, British Rail ought to divide its business up into separate activities, each of which would have its own management and accounts. At present the railways are organised on a functional basis with separate departments in charge of, for instance, the operation of trains, marketing, finance and civil engineering. Large private firms have been switching over to a product-based form of organisation ever since Du Pont and General Motors gave the lead in the early 1920s. They and their successors discovered that a functional set-up was inefficient, and the introduction of product divisions is the organisational innovation that has enabled big business to prosper and grow. This system has, as we have seen, been used with considerable success by the National Freight Corporation, and it ought to be employed by BR.

The railways' administrative structure has grave weaknesses. The marketing men produce estimates of revenue and are responsible for this side of the budget, while the labour relations and operating departments are in charge of employment, and hence of costs. There is nobody who is really responsible for seeing that costs and revenue are in balance, and the two sides can blame each other if anything goes wrong. The corporate planners are able to draw attention to possible dangers but have no authority to see that problems are tackled. The situation is made still worse by the railways' costing system, and the failure to allocate track, signalling and administrative expenditure. As a result it is not readily apparent where money is being lost, especially as analyses of direct costs are a closely guarded secret.

As such a large part of overhead employment is related to the number of direct staff the allocation of administrative costs should not present any great difficulty, and it would certainly be no more formidable than those that are faced and overcome by other large concerns. Track and signalling costs would be a more serious problem but it should be possible to estimate the proportion that is attributable to each of the main categories of traffic. A surprisingly large part of the system is used exclusively, or almost exclusively, by a particular type of train. There is, for instance, very little freight traffic over the bulk of the London and South-Eastern commuter network, which accounts for 15% of the track mileage (and about a third of track and signalling costs). A further 15% of BR's track is used exclusively by freight trains (although the proportion of expenditure would be lower). The allocation of the cost of the remaining line would be more difficult, but slow tracks that are used by freight and/or stopping trains represent 10% of the total mileage, and over a high proportion of the system there is little or no freight traffic. Moreover the bulk of the coal that BR carries is concentrated on a small part of the network where it is the main traffic, and the same is true of the materials and products that are moved for the iron and steel industry. What therefore British Rail could and should do is to identify the principal type of traffic that passes over each section of track, and then assign to it all those costs that are not directly attributable to other types of trains.

In this way it should be possible to work out the proportion of track and signalling costs that should be recovered from the London and South-Eastern passenger services, from Inter-City trains, from other passenger trains, from coal traffic, from steel and from other freight. As BR is already able to estimate the direct costs for each of these categories it could then discover the profitability of the different traffics and establish separate divisions, with their own accounts, which would take over responsibility for the various activities.

The existing common-service departments would not necessarily have to be split up because they could become the agents of the product divisions. The coal traffic division could, for instance, employ the civil engineering department to maintain those sections of the route for which it had been made responsible because it was their sole or principal user. A similar relationship already exists between BR and British Rail Engineering. Although it might ultimately prove desirable to split up departments and to alter the boundaries of some of the divisions, the new activity structure should be introduced with the minimum of administrative upheaval because otherwise managers' attention will be diverted from the pressing problems that the railways face.

MANAGEMENT AND PUBLIC OPINION

If BR is to be made financially self-sufficient there will have to be a marked improvement in its management. It is evident from the failure of the 1968 Transport Act and from the story of the railways' financial collapse (which was told in Chapter 1) that the Board made no real attempt to achieve the targets that it had set itself or to tackle the problems with which it was confronted. Furthermore our examination of the railways' investment programme and manning (in Chapters 7 and 8) showed that British Rail is prodigal and tolerant of inefficiency. These are strong words but they are amply justified by the evidence, and too much public money is at stake for us to take refuge in the normal academic circumlocution.

How can the standard of management be improved? One answer is new men and a different attitude at the top. Although Dr Beeching made serious mistakes, he did show that it is possible, granted sufficient determination, to alter rapidly the course that is being steered, and to challenge and change existing habits of mind. Since his departure old attitudes have slowly reasserted themselves. It has once again come to be believed that railways are a national necessity, that they deserve far more investment, and that their operating costs are of no great importance. This view is mistaken, because the extent to which the railways, or any other industry, are necessary depends on the costs which they impose as well as on the benefits that they confer. Production can only be regarded as socially necessary so long as the benefits, both public and private, are greater than the costs incurred. Moreover, capital and operating expenditure must be reduced to the minimum level for the output in question if society is to derive the maximum advantage. These principles are of course extremely difficult to apply in practice, but they are the right starting point and the proper slogan. So long as the Board continues to believe as an article of faith in what it calls 'the necessary railway', there is little hope that rational policies will be adopted or that the standard of management will improve.

The alterations in operating practice that have been proposed could not be put into effect if the railway unions were to adopt a position of total opposition and intransigence. It is believed inside the Board that this would be the case, and this is the reason given for its failure even to suggest that second men should be eliminated and that guards should be removed from fully-braked freight trains. This is a poor excuse, because the only way of discovering what attitude the unions would adopt is to begin negotiations. Although they may appear to be completely opposed, it must be remembered that they have come to accept changes that were, to begin with, almost unthinkable. The reduction in the railway labour force in the past has been very much greater than that which we are proposing, and such a rundown was accepted as necessary by the unions and achieved with their co-operation. Negotiation is an educative process, and although it is understandable that the leaders of railway unions will oppose staff cuts, the strength of this opposition may be expected to depend on the extent to which the rate of reduction can be absorbed by natural wastage and on whether the Government, as we have suggested, institutes a special scheme to encourage surplus train crews to find other employment. Finally, it will be difficult for railwaymen and their leaders to question honestly the proposition that it is socially undesirable that workers should be employed who, through no fault of their own, do not add to the national output.

Another even more important requirement if a rational policy for the railways is to be adopted is that there should be a change in public opinion. At present, both among public leaders and large sections of the general public, railways are viewed as a necessary public service, and this catch phrase is thought to be

Postscript

Since this book was completed the Board's financial results for 1974 have been published. BR sustained a gross loss of £142 million at 1972 purchasing power, which was just over £100 million more than the deficit of £39 million than it incurred in 1973 (see Table 11.1). It has been officially stated that during 1975 the Board will require £490 million of support at current prices (*Hansard* Written Answers, 30 June 1975, col. 292, 24 July, col. 312). However this is not directly comparable with the previous figures. First, it includes £90 million of pension payments which we have excluded because they are irrelevant to the system's future shape and size since they cannot be avoided. Second, it includes about £105 million of expenditure on track and signalling which was formerly assigned to capital account but under the Railways Act is now treated as a working expense (see page 25). Third, the £490 million of financial support includes rather under £65 million of interest and depreciation. Allowing for these factors it appears that BR will have a gross deficit of around £230 million, which in pounds of 1972 purchasing power is the same loss that it made during 1974.

Although presented in this way the railways' financial collapse appears somewhat less disastrous than its rocketing subsidy might suggest, the question nevertheless arises whether it is still reasonable to suppose that BR can be made self-financing by 1981. If rail investment is, as proposed, restricted to £105 million and capital receipts come to £20 million (see page 255), the present gross loss of around £140 million would have to be converted into a profit of £85 million. The withdrawal of little used passenger services and the transfer of lines to the PTEs should make a significant contribution to eliminating the present deficit since together they had an avoidable loss of about £20 million during 1974. In addition the PTEs contributed £5 million in respect of those services which cannot be hived off and should remain open, and the hived-off services will involve about £10 million of investment (see page 271). Allowing for these savings and this subsidy an overall financial improvement of £190 million is required.

To achieve this will be a formidable, but not an impossible task. Whether it has become more difficult to make BR self-financing depends on why its loss increased so sharply between 1973 and 1974. The rise of £103 million in the gross deficit was explained by a reduction of £48 million in revenue and by an increase of £55 million in expenditure. The growth in expenditure was in turn due to £21 million of extra expenditure on fuel and the £34 million by which the wage and salary bill increased (see Table 8.10). There was scarcely any change in the average number employed but there was an increase of over 7½% in (real) staff expenditure per employee. This is substantially less than the rise of nearly 11% that was assumed in our expenditure forecasts (see page 180). The discrepancy was almost entirely due to the underestimation of the amount by which the general price level had increased during 1974, viz. by 17% instead of 15½%. There is therefore no reason to believe that we have made insufficient allowance for the (real) growth in earnings per employee. Indeed it is quite possible that too large an increase has been assumed for the period 1973–81 and that our estimate for the railways' staff expenditure is on the high side. It also seems likely, again due to the under-estimation of inflation during 1974, that our figure for the railways' fuel bill is over generous. Hence experience during 1974 does not throw any doubt on the realism of our expenditure target for 1981, which, if anything, now appears slightly easier for BR to attain.

The reduction of £48 million in railway revenue between 1973 and 1974 was explained partly by the fall of £17 million in the volume of traffic, but mainly by the decline of £31 million which arose because BR increased its charges considerably less fast than prices in general. While the price of all final goods and services sold on the home market rose by 17½%, rail charges only increased by 10%. Although the relative reduction in charges explains the great bulk of the fall in revenue, this can be put right without too much difficulty, and it is the decline in carryings which suggests that our traffic forecasts for 1981 could be over-optimistic. This decline was largely due to the coal strike in February and March and to the railways' own industrial troubles during the earlier part of the year. In the period from mid May 1974 to mid May 1975, which is the latest 52 weeks for which figures are available at the time of writing, passenger traffic amounted to roughly 20,175 million passenger miles. This is substantially more than the 18,500 million that was carried during 1973 and only a little less than has been forecast for 1981 (see Table 2.1). If anything our passenger projection appears on the low side, although it should be observed that some of the increase in passenger mileage may have been due to the relative reduction in fares, and that most of the extra traffic is of the cheap day return variety, which means that there has not been a corresponding rise in revenue. Over the same period BR carried 187 million tons of freight. This was significantly less than the 193 million tons transported during 1973, but is fractionally higher than the tonnage that has been forecast for 1981 (see Table 6.7). As the period was one of considerable economic difficulty this suggests that our projection is soundly based.

It seems likely that as the recession intensifies there will be a further decline in freight traffic, but it is likely to recover with the economy. Even if a ratchet process is at work and some traffic is lost for good, BR might, paradoxically, be in a better position to become financially self-supporting. This is because a large part of its freight is hopelessly uneconomic. In the financial estimates in the body of this book it was assumed that BR would continue to carry virtually all the freight traffic that is to be had, because although we were well aware that much of it was wildly unprofitable it was impossible to estimate the amount. However, as a result of the Railways Act, further information has now become available. During 1975 BR is likely, in current pounds and on its new accounting basis, to lose £70 million on its freight and parcels traffic (*Hansard* Written Answers, 24 July 1975, col. 312). Of this, capital charges represent £30 million, but the remaining £40 million is an avoidable loss. Moreover this is a minimum figure because no account has been taken of investment in freight rolling-stock which is still treated as part of capital account, and because the amount of overhead expenditure that could be escaped if freight traffic were eliminated has been assessed on a very conservative basis at about £80 million. (Only 16% of administrative, track and signalling costs have been assigned to freight as against the 36% which was attributed in an earlier study made within the Board.)

It is to be hoped and expected that most freight traffic can be made profitable by increasing prices and reducing costs. However the railways carry about 65 million tons of wagon-load and other traffic that makes substantial use of the marshalling yard system and it is estimated that this incurs a loss of about £50 million, excluding capital charges but including avoidable overhead costs. This represents a loss of about £0.75 per ton and it is evident, since this traffic fails even to cover its direct costs, that there is no hope of making the bulk of it economic. Because of the poor quality of service that is provided BR has little scope to raise its prices and cost reduction would require large scale investment in new air-braked wagons. Much of this grossly unprofitable traffic is likely to have dis-appeared by 1981 and BR should abandon what remains.

It seems reasonable to suppose that, of the financial improve-ment of £190 million that BR needs to make between 1974–75 and 1981 if it is to become self-supporting, the elimination of unprofitable freight might contribute £40 million. This differs from the previously mentioned loss of £50 million because of the conversion to 1972 purchasing power which serves to reduce the figure, and because of some reduction in capital expenditure on wagons which serves to increase the sum. It should be noted that not all of the saving of £40 million would be an addition to the railways' possible cash flow surplus of £27 million in 1981 (shown on page 272), because the present deficit should have been reduced somewhat by 1981 partly as a result of the cost cutting measures that have been proposed, and partly due to the loss of traffic that has been allowed for. A further con-tribution towards the financial improvement that BR requires could be made by increasing rail prices. As we have just seen, the railways would have earned something like £30 million of extra revenue in 1974 if they had done no more than increase their charges as fast as the general rise in prices, and, if they had raised them sufficiently to offset the amount by which they fell short of the general inflationary rise in 1973 they would have earned a further £15 million. When the financial benefits from higher charges and the elimination of unprofitable freight are taken into account, it appears that the remaining financial improvement that BR needs to make is only a little over £100 million at 1972 purchasing power.

It should be possible for BR to close this remaining gap partly by means of selective price increases that will raise the railways' real charges above their 1972 levels (see pages 41 and 100), and partly through the reduction in the wage and salary bill as a result of a much needed improvement in productivity (see Chapter 8). A substantial increase in rail prices is now being made, but there is no sign that the manpower situation is being tackled. Indeed the Board saw fit during 1974 to launch a recruiting drive and by the end of the year rail employment was 5600 higher than it had been at the start. In 1974 output per man year was only 2% higher than it had been five years previously. The stagnation in BR's productivity constitutes the principal explanation for its financial collapse, and a drastic improvement is a prime requirement if BR is to be made self-financing. Despite the greatly increased loss in 1974, there is no reason to change our conclusion that BR can be made self-supporting.

Notes

CHAPTER 1: THE FAILURE OF THE 1968 TRANSPORT ACT

[1] Here and henceforth the operating or working profit or loss (or surplus or deficit) refers to the financial result after depreciation but before interest. The financial result before depreciation and interest will be described as the gross profit or loss, while the result after interest and depreciation will be termed the net profit or loss. Unless otherwise stated all financial figures disregard the effect of government grants and subsidies.

[2] Ministry of Transport (henceforth MoT) *Railway policy* Cmnd 3439, HMSO (1967) pp. 16–21, 63

[3] Stewart Joy *The train that ran away* Ian Allan (1973) pp. 92, 93

[4] Sir Henry Johnson 'Railways' *Institute of Transport Journal* (July 1969) p. 188

[5] Derek Fowler 'The Railways Act 1974' *Public Finance and Accountancy* (October 1974) p. 327

[6] British Railways Board *Review of railway policy: Summary of report to the Government* BRB (1973)

CHAPTER 2: THE PROSPECTS FOR PASSENGER TRAFFIC

[1] The price index used to deflate revenue at current prices to revenue at 1972 purchasing power in Table 2.1, and subsequently, is that for all final goods and services sold on the home market. The index is as follows:

1963	61·70
1964	64·00
1965	67.15
1966	69·99
1967	72·12
1968	75·62
1969	79·75
1970	85·27
1971	92·82
1972	100·00
1973	109·44

[2] A. W. Evans 'Inter-city travel and the London–Midland electrification' *Journal of Transport Economics and Policy* (January 1969)

[3] Centre for Transport Studies, University of Leeds *Inter-City modal split in Great Britain; air vs rail* (1971) pp. 104–5

[4] J. G. Smith 'The effects of speed improvements on the volume of traffic as for recent years experienced by British Railways' *Rail International* (November 1972); J. Tyler 'Development of traffic generation/distribution

models in British Rail and their application to forward planning' in *Models of traffic outside towns* Planning and Transport Research and Computation (International) Co. Ltd (1971)

[5] R. Jackson *Inter urban travel demand in Great Britain* University of Manchester thesis (1973) pp. 133–5

[6] S. Jones 'High speed railway running with special reference to the advanced passenger train' *Chartered Institute of Transport Journal* (January 1973)

[7] Department of the Environment *Passenger transport in Great Britain 1971* HMSO (1973) p. 5

CHAPTER 4: IRON AND STEEL

[1] *Department of Employment Gazette* (April 1974) p. 309

[2] Peter A. Thompson 'The transport prospects of British Steel Corporation's development plans' *British Rail Western London Lecture and Debating Society* No. 509 (26 November 1970) p. 2

[3] Department of Trade and Industry *Steel: British Steel Corporation: Ten year development strategy* Cmnd 5226, HMSO (1973) pp. 9, 13

CHAPTER 5: COAL AND OIL

[1] National Coal Board *Plan for coal* NCB (1974)

[2] G. L. Reid, Kevin Allen, D. J. Harris *The nationalised fuel industries* Heinemann Educational Books (1973) pp. 35–43; Department of Energy *Coal industry examination: Interim report June 1974* Department of Energy (1974) p. 11

[3] Department of Energy *op. cit.* p. 10

[4] Organisation for Economic Co-operation and Development *Energy prospects to 1985* OECD (1974) Vol. 1, pp. 7, 8, 50, 95

CHAPTER 6: GENERAL FREIGHT AND THE OVERALL POSITION

[1] *Quarry Managers Journal* (April 1973) p. 119

[2] A. H. Tulpule *Trends in the transport of freight in Britain* Road Research Laboratory (1972)

[3] B. Warner and S. Joy 'The economics of rail container operation in Britain' *Rail International* (April 1971) pp. 345–56

[4] K. M. Johnson and H. C. Garnett *The economics of containerisation* George Allen and Unwin (1971) pp. 98–114

CHAPTER 7: RAILWAY INVESTMENT

[1] *Railway Magazine* (January 1973) p. 43

[2] C. D. Foster and S. Joy 'Railway track costs in Britain' in *Developments in railway traffic engineering* Institute of Civil Engineers (1967) pp. 56, 58

³ C. J. Clemow 'Planning for railway electrification' *Proceedings of the Institute of Electrical Engineers* (April 1972)
⁴ Department of the Environment 'Cost-benefit analysis of Great Northern suburban rail services' in *Second Report from the Expenditure Committee 1972–73 Urban Transport Planning* Vol. III, pp. 514–16

CHAPTER 8: MANPOWER AND EXPENDITURE

¹ *Submission by British Railways Board to Railway Staff National Tribunal: Pay structure review April 1974* p. 78
² International Transport Workers' Federation *Manning of locomotives and trains* (May 1968) pp. 1, 2, 6
³ ibid. p. 14; H. P. Kaper 'One-man train crews in the Netherlands' *Railway Gazette International* (November 1972) pp. 427, 428
⁴ J. Holt 'Locomotive scheduling by computer—"bash peak" ' *Rail International* (October 1973) p. 1056
⁵ A. Paterson 'Railway track and structures' in *Developments in railway traffic engineering* The Institution of Civil Engineers (May 1967) p. 5
⁶ *Submission by British Railways Board to Railway Staff National Tribunal* Appendix 11
⁷ Dorothy Wedderburn *Redundancy and the railwaymen* Cambridge University Press (1965) pp. 69, 75, 165
⁸ Railway Staff National Tribunal *Decision No. 42 Proposals of the British Railways Board for pay restructuring* (July 1974) p. 64; *Submission by British Railways Board to Railway Staff National Tribunal* pp. 3, 4

CHAPTER 9: THE SOCIAL BENEFITS OF RAIL PASSENGER SERVICES

¹ M. E. Beesley 'The value of time spent in travelling; some new evidence' *Economica* (May 1965); D. A. Quarmby 'Choice of travel mode for the journey to work' *Journal of Transport Economics and Policy* (September 1967)
² Ministry of Transport *The Cambrian Coast line* HMSO (1969)
³ G. Clayton and J. H. Rees *The economic problems of rural transport in Wales* Welsh Economic Studies no. 5 (1965)
⁴ D. H. S. Foot and D. N. M. Starkie *Ashford–Hastings railway line* University of Reading Geographical Paper no. 3 (1970)
⁵ P. K. Else and M. Howe 'Cost-benefit analysis and railway services' *Journal of Transport Economics and Policy* (May 1969)
⁶ M. R. Bristow and F. Rodriguez *A cost-benefit study of the Manchester to Buxton railway* University of Manchester Centre for Urban and Regional Research (1973); C. D. Foster *Report on a social cost-benefit study of the Manchester (Piccadilly)—Hadfield/Glossop and Manchester (Piccadilly)—Marple–New Mills suburban railway services* BR, London Midland Region (1974)
⁷ H. D. Johnson and F. Garwood *Notes on road accident statistics* Road Research Laboratory (1971); R. F. F. Dawson *Current costs of road accidents in Great Britain* Road Research Laboratory (1971)
⁸ *Hansard* (20 December 1972)
⁹ T. J. G. Bamford and M. R. Wigan *The effect on transport benefit evalu-*

ation of user misperception of costs Road Research Laboratory (1974)

10 E. Smith 'An economic comparison of urban railways and express bus services' *Journal of Transport Economics and Policy* (January 1973); Department of Transportation *Evaluation of rail rapid transit and express bus services in the urban commuter market* U.S. Government Printing Office, Washington (1973)

CHAPTER 10: THE ALLOCATION OF FREIGHT TRAFFIC

1 Ministry of Transport *Road track costs* HMSO (1968)
2 Department of the Environment *Lorries and the world we live in* HMSO (1973)
3 Department of the Environment *Road accidents in Great Britain 1972* HMSO (1974)
4 Noise Advisory Council *Noise in the next ten years* HMSO (1974)
5 Sir Alan Wilson *Noise; final report of the Committee on the Problem of Noise* Cmnd 2056, HMSO (1963)
6 C. H. Sharp *Living with the lorry; a study of goods vehicles in the environment* Road Haulage Association and Freight Transport Association (1973)
7 C. H. Sharp and A. Jennings 'More powerful engines for lorries? An exercise in cost-benefit analysis' *Journal of Transport Economics and Policy* (May 1972)
8 P. F. Everall *Social benefits from minimum power-weight ratios for goods vehicles* Road Research Laboratory (1969)
9 C. H. Sharp and A. Jennings *The costs and benefits of applying minimum power to weight regulations to goods vehicles* Transport Research Unit, University of Leicester, n.d.
10 Programmes Analysis Unit *An economic and technical appraisal of air pollution in the U.K.* HMSO (1972)
11 A. C. Whiffin and D. R. Leonard *A survey of traffic-induced vibrations* Road Research Laboratory (1971)
12 B. T. Bayliss and S. L. Edwards *Industrial demand for transport* HMSO (1970)
13 C. H. Sharp *The allocation of freight traffic—a survey, Report to the Ministry of Transport,* University of Leicester (1970); W. R. Cook 'Transport decisions of certain firms in the Black Country' *Journal of Transport Economics and Policy* (September 1967)

CHAPTER 11: CONCLUSIONS: TOWARDS A SELF-FINANCING RAILWAY

1 H. C. Sanderson 'The future of railway freight traffic' *Proceedings of the British Railways (Western Region) London Lecture and Debating Society* No. 498 (2 November 1967) p. 12
2 Freight Integration Council *First report* House of Commons Paper 73 (July 1970) p. 7
3 Select Committee on Nationalised Industries *National Freight Corporation* House of Commons Paper 461 (October 1973) Q 822
4 ibid. Q 646, 647

Index